Social Values and Industrial Relations

Warwick Studies in Industrial Relations

General Editors: G.S. Bain and H.A. Clegg

Also in this series

Industrial Relations in Fleet Street
Keith Sisson
Industrial Relations and the Limits of Law
Brian Weekes, Michael Mellish, Linda Dickens, John Lloyd
*Social Stratification and Trade Unionism**
G. S. Bain, David Coates, Valerie Ellis
*Workplace and Union**
Ian Boraston, Hugh Clegg, Malcolm Rimmer
*Piecework Bargaining**
William Brown
*Disputes Procedure in Action**
Richard Hyman
*The Docks after Devlin**
Michael Mellish
*Race and Industrial Conflict**
Malcolm Rimmer

*PUBLISHED BY HEINEMANN EDUCATIONAL BOOKS

Social Values and Industrial Relations

A STUDY OF FAIRNESS AND EQUALITY

Richard Hyman
Senior Lecturer in Industrial Relations,
University of Warwick

and Ian Brough
Lecturer in Industrial Relations,
Galashiels College of Technology

BASIL BLACKWELL · OXFORD

0 631 16640 8 (hardback)
0 631 16610 6 (paperback)

Printed in Great Britain by
Compton Printing Ltd., Aylesbury

Contents

Editors' Foreword

Warwick University's first undergraduates were admitted in 1965. The teaching of industrial relations began a year later, and in 1967 a one-year graduate course leading to an MA in Industrial Relations was introduced. Research in industrial relations also commenced in 1967 with a grant from the Clarkson Trustees, and in 1970 received a major impetus when the Social Science Research Council established its Industrial Relations Research Unit at Warwick.

The series of Warwick Studies in Industrial Relations was launched in 1972 as the main vehicle for the publication of the results of the Unit's projects. It is also intended to disseminate the research carried out by staff teaching industrial relations in the University, and, where it merits publication, the work of graduate students.

The present volume by Richard Hyman and Ian Brough is wide-ranging in scope and theoretical in purpose. Its starting-point is the use made of notions of fairness in industrial relations, and the extent to which such notions conflict with the major inequalities which exist in work-related power, status, and material rewards. The book goes on to examine the central processes of industrial relations and the social and economic environment in which they operate. The argument developed in this study challenges many of the conventional assumptions of both the student and the practitioner of industrial relations, and hence has relevance for those concerned with any aspect of the field.

George Bain
Hugh Clegg

Preface

This study derives from a research proposal formulated in 1970 when the establishment at Warwick of the SSRC Industrial Relations Research Unit was first contemplated. The aim was to investigate the nature, the sources, and the consequences of industrial relations ideologies, in particular as these involve notions of 'fairness'. It was initially envisaged that this would entail a fairly brief preliminary stage of surveying the relevant literature, constructing a reasonably coherent theoretical framework, and identifying areas of central analytical interest which research might be expected to illuminate. On this basis a programme of empirical investigation could be initiated.

It became very rapidly apparent that what was intended as a minor preliminary would in fact represent a substantial task in its own right. Most literature in the fields of industrial relations, industrial sociology and labour economics has at least a marginal bearing on the topic, and a considerable proportion is more centrally relevant. At the same time, very few authors have explicitly related their writings to the theoretical question of the role of values in industrial relations; most of the relevant literature is immediately oriented to quite different issues. Hence it has been a comparatively major enterprise to survey the most prominent themes in the literature, systematising the discrete findings of researchers from a range of disciplines.

Even more demanding has been the formulation of a theoretical interpretation of what has emerged as our main focus of concern: the structure of inequality in work-related rewards and deprivations, and prevailing attitudes towards this inequality. As we make clear in the text, the approaches which are current in economics, sociology and industrial relations (where they consider these issues at all) are far from satisfactory. Our main task has been to outline an alternative.

We make no excessive claims on behalf of the interpretation which we develop. None of our arguments is dramatically original. We do however seek to relate analytical insights which have not previously been integrated. We do not purport to offer an elaborate and sophisticated theory of inequality in industry. We do however believe that the theoretical approach which we outline offers a potentially fruitful basis for further elaboration; and that if sufficiently developed its superiority to the approaches which we criticise may be demonstrated. In its present form our analysis does not, indeed, permit simple empirical validation. But if future research assigns due weight to those issues on which we focus, we do not doubt that our arguments can be shown to be solidly grounded.

A number of colleagues have commented on drafts of this study. Particularly helpful have been the advice and criticism of George Bain, John Eldridge, Bob Fryer and Steve Hill. None, of course, can be held responsible for the final outcome.

Richard Hyman
University of Warwick, Coventry
February 1974

Chapter 1

Introduction: Fairness and Inequality

Relations between managers and workers, and employers and trade unions, are commonly regarded as a notably hard-headed and unsentimental area of social life. Yet the arguments of those involved in industrial relations are shot through with essentially *moral* terminology. In particular, appeals to the idea of *fairness* abound. The concept provides an inescapable frame of reference in judging the exercise of managerial control, the imposition of dismissals and other disciplinary sanctions, the allocation of tasks and benefits among employees. It has entered the terminology of labour law on both sides of the Atlantic, specific acts by employers or trade unionists being defined as 'unfair practices'. Most extensively, however, the idea of fairness is applied in the context of wages: the relationship between work and income, between the pay of one individual or group and another.

It is of course possible to view cynically this use of ethical language; one writer for example has suggested that 'whether or not wage-fixing remains fundamentally a matter of smash and grab, . . . those who are actually engaged in the business like to dress it up as something more respectable' (Wootton 1962 : 100). Yet appeals to the principle of fairness often display all the indications of sincerity; and the commitment of one side or the other to a particular notion of fairness often appears to exert a significant influence on the actual course of industrial relations.

The ideas of fairness which operate in industrial relations form the central focus of this study. What meanings are attached to such notions as 'fair wages' and 'a fair day's work', and in what ways do such normative beliefs affect the actual determination of the level of pay or intensity of work of different groups of employees? One purpose of this study is to survey existing knowledge on such questions.

But our enquiry does not stop at this point. Britain is a highly unequal society: extremes of penury and opulence persist in proportions which have altered little over the years. Precise quantification of inequality is admittedly impossible; in the face of at least vaguely egalitarian social values, many of its dimensions are closely concealed. 'Ancient inequalities have assumed new and more subtle forms; conventional categories are no longer adequate for the task of measuring them' (Titmuss 1962 : 199). Yet the consensus of recent research is that five per cent of the population own well over half the wealth in Britain.[1] Those changes which have occurred in the statistics of wealth distribution during the present century, it is generally agreed, owe far more to rearrangements in property holdings within families (partly for purposes of tax avoidance) than to genuine redistribution between rich and poor.

In industry the dimensions of inequality are no less obtrusive. Official statistics show that in 1973 half the adult employees in Britain earned under £30 for a standard week. Ten per cent of adults in full-time employment received gross weekly earnings below £18, and 25 per cent below £24; at the other extreme, the top 25 per cent had gross earnings of £44 and over and the top 10 per cent £57 and over.[2] Within the upper reaches of the hierarchy, five-figure salaries are common. Poverty and affluence: the extremes are dramatically documented in a recent journalistic survey, which showed the managing director of a trading stamp company receiving a salary of £260,000 while a shop assistant was paid £754.[3] (If *unearned* income — itself a product of the unequal distribution of wealth — were taken into account, the disparities would be revealed as even greater.)

If high incomes are the basis for luxurious styles of living, low pay leads inevitably to the impoverishment of life which each generation of social investigators rediscovers. The low paid, report Coates and Silburn (1973 : 212), 'are herded together into ghettoes, in which they share not only low wages, but a dozen other social deprivations,

1. See in particular Titmuss 1962; Meacher 1972; Atkinson 1972.
2. 'New Earnings Survey, 1973', *Department of Employment Gazette* (Oct. 1973). There are marked variations between the average earnings of men and women, and of manual and non-manual employees: gross weekly earnings of male non-manual employees averaged £48. Within this group, however, the disparity between the highest and lowest paid was most extreme: the top 10 per cent received £74 and over.
3. 'Their Weekly Bread', *Sunday Times Magazine* (1 Oct. 1972).

from slum houses, meagre public services, squalid urban surroundings, at the material level; to the accompanying moral sense that nothing can be done, that they are at the bottom of the pit'.[4] Conversely, the privileges of the high paid are similarly pervasive. Many are obvious, even ostentatious; others more insidious. The most literal of 'life-chances', life-expectancy (and health in general), varies directly with income and occupational status.[5] In education (whether the state or private sector is utilised) the children of the rich enjoy a substantial advantage over those of the poor, and hence benefit in terms of occupational opportunity.[6] Through this, as through other social mechanisms, inequality is perpetuated intergenerationally. The *political* concomitants of economic inequality, though difficult to assess and impossible to quantify, are nonetheless real: ample evidence exists of the disproportionate political influence of those with privileged wealth and incomes (and this in turn helps explain their success in defending such privileges against egalitarian challenge).[7]

Within work itself the distribution of income is by no means the only dimension of inequality. Non-manual (and especially managerial) occupational groups which receive the highest salaries typically also enjoy such advantages as greater security of employment and stability of earnings, more flexible hours of work, longer holidays, and more congenial working conditions than manual occupational groups. The latter are often particularly exposed to industrial injury and disease and to insecurity of earnings and employment, tend to have the longest standard hours of work and are particularly likely to be required to work shifts and (under their terms of employment or in order to maintain acceptable earnings levels) overtime. The highest paid are usually privileged in respect of 'fringe' benefits, which in the most favoured groups can involve an extensive range of advantages; and they often enjoy incremental salary scales and good promotion prospects (hence *lifetime* incomes may involve even greater inequalities than orthodox earnings data indicate.[8] The variations in the status accoutrements

4. For other recent studies of low pay and poverty, see Abel-Smith and Townsend 1965; Edmonds and Radice 1968; Kincaid 1973; Atkinson 1973.
5. See for example the occupational mortality rates cited in Kinnersly 1973:9.
6. For a variety of studies confirming this point, see Halsey *et al.* 1961.
7. See for example Miliband 1969; Urry and Wakeford 1973.
8. The relationship between income and other work-related inequalities is discussed by Wootton 1962; Lupton and Hamilton 1970; Wedderburn 1972; Scitovsky 1973.

of occupations (most notably, perhaps, the requirement that most manual workers should 'clock in' at their employment and lose pay if late) are indicative of major variations of institutionalised *power* within the workplace.

For within a capitalist political economy, employment is at the same time an economic relationship and one of control; and this duality is in turn closely associated with the interdependence of wealth and the ownership of the productive system. Private property extends to the industrial system itself, the ownership of which is even more narrowly concentrated than wealth in general. Through the asymmetry of the employment contract those with the privileges of economic ownership — and their agents and functionaries — have the right to issue orders; those with only their ability to labour to dispose of are constrained to obey.[9] In the complex hierarchy of industrial management there are of course many who are both subordinates and superordinates, recipients and transmitters of orders. Yet these very gradations of authority are reproduced in the income hierarchy. In general it is those occupations with least formal autonomy, in the most subordinate positions, which receive the lowest pay. As the extent of control over subordinates increases, and the closeness of direction from above diminishes, so income normally rises. At the extreme, those whose wealth is itself a sufficient source of income are able to work (if they do at all) in positions altogether free from subordination.

Inequalities of power in turn structure the nature and quality of work experience. The focus of a mass of research in the sociology of work organizations, and current enthusiasm for (usually imprecise) usages of the concept of alienation, alike emphasise the negative accompaniments of work for most routine employees. As Fox puts it (1973b : ii),

> the bulk of rank-and-file members (wage-earners and salary-earners alike) are subjected to principles of extreme division of labour which leave them subordinated to hierarchical control and discipline; excluded from important processes of decision

9. For an elaboration of this point, see Marx 1959; Commons 1932; Selznick 1969; Hyman 1972b. The twin developments of the limited liability company and a salaried managerial stratum have not radically affected the control structure in modern employment; exaggerated conceptions of the 'separation of ownership and control' and the 'managerial revolution' are cogently criticised by Nichols 1969. Nor do the extent and character of 'public ownership' in modern British industry call for serious qualification to our thesis: for to a large degree the nationalised sector functions to service the private sector and is subject to policy norms which parallel those of private capitalism.

making; and confined to work with which few are able to feel any real moral involvement. . . . Most people in such situations experience, in greater or less degree, a sense of being *used* as inferiorly-treated means in the service of ends determined by superiorly-treated management; ends about which they have not been consulted.

Not surprisingly, studies demonstrate clearly that work satisfaction is closely associated with occupational status and thus with the various accompanying material privileges.[10] The contrasting character of the work experience itself — on the one hand the opportunity for creativity and self-expression, on the other the dehumanising and oppressive role as 'factor of production'[11] — is in some respects the most radical inequality of all.[12]

The Problem of Fairness

The reality of this imposing structure of inequality cannot seriously be questioned; but it is remarkable how little attention this structure conventionally receives. In particular, in industrial relations — where, we have seen, the notion of fairness is a familiar part of the vocabulary — these major inequalities are normally taken for granted, as a natural feature of the environment. Yet any definition of fairness, as we shall see in the next chapter, normally involves some reference to *equality* of treatment. The fact that the idea of fairness is so often employed in a manner which fails to question, and indeed often explicitly endorses, prevailing social and economic inequalities is a paradox which deserves close examination. Its explanation involves theoretical issues of central importance for sociology in general and the analysis of ideology in particular.

10. See for example Blauner 1960.
11. In view of the massive production of waste in modern capitalism, the creativity associated with positions of dominance should not be exaggerated; moreover, externally coercive pressures restrict the scope for autonomy. Yet the contrast with subordinate groups is obvious: if the dominant groups are alienated they are nevertheless, as Marx and Engels put it (1975), 'comfortable and confirmed' in their self-alienation.
12. It is significant that the problem of inequality is typically recognised only in its narrowest pecuniary form: whereas it pervades every area of social life. The narrowness of the conventional focus reflects in part the predominance in capitalist society of money as a standard of worth and meaning in social relations, in part the segmentation and scientism of respectable academic endeavour. While the various forms of social and economic inequality run in parallel, they are not always precisely correlated; and their uneven development can constitute an important source of social instability. This point is of relevance for the argument in our concluding chapter.

The next three chapters are devoted to a detailed documentation of the manner in which notions of fairness are conventionally employed in industrial relations; in particular, we consider the processes through which scrutiny of the fundamental inequalities pervading industrial life is normally excluded. In the second part of the book there is a shift from the descriptive to the theoretical. Despite the incompleteness of our knowledge of the ideas of fairness which are held by the parties to industrial relations, the general characterisation of these values is relatively uncontroversial. For the most part, it is widely agreed, notions of fairness underwrite the basic structure of incomes and work obligations while permitting and indeed stimulating criticisms at the margins. Yet interpretations of the significance of these notions vary greatly. Economic orthodoxy, it is argued in Chapter 5, necessarily denies the practical significance of norms of fairness. It is fundamental to the classical tradition that ethical considerations cannot withstand the compelling weight of market forces in the determination of absolute and relative wages. We argue that such a presupposition is unsatisfactory but that those economists who have attempted to modify or abandon this postulate have been unable to construct a satisfactory explanatory framework with the materials of their own discipline.

The influence of beliefs and values, we suggest in Chapter 6, is more adequately illuminated by the institutional and social-psychological approaches current in the study of industrial relations. Yet the weakness of these approaches is their lack of attention to the social *sources* of the particular values which prevail in the contexts of work and collective bargaining. Industrial relations constitute a particularly controversial area of social life in which the currency of normative judgment exchanges freely. If there are general social processes which operate to structure the beliefs and standards current in a society, their influence will extend to the values impinging on industrial relations. The relationship between beliefs and values, social structure and social action provides of course a persistent focus of sociological controversy. The notion of ideology — a frame of reference, a world-picture or *Weltanschauung,* a set of normative and empirical assumptions which are social-structurally generated[13] — is fundamental to the analysis of this relationship.

13. The concept of ideology — like many other important but value-laden concepts in social analysis — has been assigned a variety of meanings. It is often

Chapter 7 examines the notion of ideology and indicates its relevance to the preceding discussion. If, as seems evident, those with power and privilege in a society can exert considerable influence on the way in which that society is perceived and evaluated, it is not surprising that conventional usage of such notions as fairness limits their potentially subversive or disruptive implications. Theories of ideology thus help to explain the virtual unanimity with which, in industrial relations, a capitalist employment structure and an inegalitarian distribution of wealth and income are treated as just or inevitable. The same theoretical framework helps to explain why this dominant framework of assumptions is not deliberately and systematically challenged by the institutions of the labour movement (even though serious but often unintended challenges do indeed occur). Moreover, the concept of ideology can fruitfully be applied to those academic theories which are discussed in earlier chapters. From this perspective, it is possible to explain convincingly why it is that the prevailing notions of fairness are in the main readily compatible with the existing structure of work and wages.[14]

Presented in this form alone, however, an analysis of the role of values in industrial relations would be one-sided and over-deterministic. The final chapter considers the extent to which aspects of the social structure, and the accompanying ideologies, far from enhancing social stability, are in fact actually or potentially disruptive. It is concluded that contradictory social processes are in evidence, and that the relative strength of the pressures towards stability and instability cannot be confidently asserted.

---

employed with derogatory intent, to denote a set of ideas which are mistaken or intended to deceive — 'false' or 'mendacious' consciousness. In the present context, however, the concept is employed neutrally, without necessarily involving any such evaluative overtones. For two contrasting analyses of the meaning of the concept, see Plamenatz 1970; Miller 1973.

14. On a number of occasions in the following chapters we refer forwards to the analysis which is presented in Chapter 7. Arguably it might be preferable to present at the outset the theoretical overview which we believe essential for an adequate comprehension of the findings that are presented below. But on balance we consider it advantageous to present the following material at the relatively simple level of industrial relations analysis, and then to confront broader issues of theoretical interpretation. For those who feel so disposed, it is possible to read Chapter 7 first.

Chapter 2

A Fair Day's Work

The Notion of Fairness

As the Introduction has indicated, this enquiry involves a number of distinct areas of concern and levels of analysis. But before pursuing these further it is necessary to examine more closely the notion of fairness and the meanings which it conventionally holds. The manner in which the realities of inequality are accommodated in everyday usage of the concept will then form the primary focus of the remainder of the book. The confident and extensive use made, in industrial relations, of the idea of fairness is understandable, in view of its strong normative content. Yet its concrete meaning is far from readily apparent. Moral and political philosophers, a major preoccupation of whom is to analyse the usage of the value-laden terminology of ethical and social controversy, have paid surprisingly limited attention to the concept.

This may reflect the extent to which fairness represents a secondary or derivative concept. Issues of fairness normally arise in the context of the distribution of benefits (or obligations) among, or of an exchange between, two or more persons or groups. A rough but generally accepted definition is that in an exchange there should be reasonable reciprocity or balance between the parties concerned; while when benefits or deprivations are distributed, 'equals are to be treated equally, at least in similar situations' (Bird 1967 : 132). Yet as several writers have argued, the notion of fairness implies only a *prima facie* right to equality of rewards or deprivations: unequal treatment must be capable of justification in terms of some relevant differences in the situation of the individuals or groups concerned.

Fairness is thus a principle that applies to the treatment of individuals; but as defined above it merely characterises the *formal* aspects of such treatment. To state that an exchange should involve reciprocity, or that unequal treatment should reflect relevant situational differences, is not to specify by what criteria reciprocity is to be assessed, what are to count as relevant differences, or how much inequality of treatment is justified by a particular difference. 'The statement that equals should be treated equally and unequals unequally throws no light on what is to be done to or for equals and unequals' (Ginsberg 1965 : 7). It is useful to refer here to Rawls's (1955) notion of 'two concepts of rules'. To assess the fairness of a specific action or situation is to determine whether it meets certain general criteria or principles; but to evaluate those criteria or principles involves a quite distinct *level* of judgment. At this level the rules which underlie the social structure itself may require scrutiny. This points to a common distinction, between fairness and justice. As Rawls argues (1972 : 7),

> The primary subject of justice is the basic structure of society, or more exactly, the way in which the major social institutions distribute fundamental rights and duties and determine the division of advantages from social co-operation . . . The justice of a social scheme depends essentially on how fundamental rights and duties are assigned and on the economic opportunities and social conditions in the various sectors of society.

It is only in a context in which the justice of the prevailing definitions of 'fundamental rights and duties' can be taken for granted that meaningful discussion of the fairness of individual situations is possible.

There have been times when the moral climate of a society has indeed involved the virtually unquestioned endorsement of its principles of political and economic organisation. In many pre-capitalist societies, appeal could credibly be made to absolute standards of economic morality: hence the discourses of medieval theologians which prescribed a structure of wages which was labelled not merely 'fair' but 'just'.[1] Even after the industrial revolution, the same presupposition of authoritative normative principles could be met — as with the Sheffield steel-master who in 1836 argued:

> While the foreman gets his 30/- or 40/- the striker whose labour is more severe only receives his 20/- or 30/-; while he that has served apprenticeship obtains his 20/- to 30/-, the learner and the mere labourer gets his 10/- to 18/-. In all these cases the God of nature has established a just and equitable Law which man has no right to disturb. When he ventures to do so, it is always certain that he sooner or later meets with a corrêsponding punishment (quoted in MacIntyre 1967: 147).

1. For discussions, see Ryan 1916; Fogarty 1961; Healy 1966.

Yet once market forces are extensively involved in wage determination, the outcome cannot convincingly be attributed to divine intent, and controversy becomes accepted as legitimate.

In the absence of consensus on the fundamental principles of social morality, as MacIntyre argues, the use of ethical concepts may be at worst tendentious and at best confusing. Nowhere, as Lockwood points out (1955 : 341), 'is the lack of consensus more apparent than with regard to the notion of "fair wages" '. It follows that the notion has prescriptive rather than descriptive content; and, as Lockwood argues, it is typically employed for one of three distinct purposes. One may be defined as conservative: those wages are considered fair which 'maintain a group's position within the hierarchy and the hierarchy's position within the wider society'. A second is reformative: the notion of fairness is 'associated with wages policy proposals and certain rational criteria, which imply change in the wages structure'. The third is opportunistic: because of the ideological utility of the concept of fairness, it is used to accord legitimacy to wage proposals whose derivation reflects quite different motivations (Lockwood 1955 : 342-4).[2]

Whether the concept of fair wages is employed for conservative, reformative or opportunistic purposes, it is customarily related to one of two main criteria. The first may be termed *internal:* the assessment of the pay of an individual or group by reference to the contribution made or capacities required in respect of such factors as effort, qualification and aptitude. The second may be termed *external:* assessment of pay by comparison with the incomes of other individuals or groups. This analytical distinction cannot be rigidly applied in practice. The use of internal criteria requires at least tacit reference to the pay of other workers whose ratio of pay to

2. It is interesting to compare Lockwood's analysis with the argument of G. D. H. Cole almost half a century earlier (1913: 303): 'The whole intrusion of the conception of "equity" into the determination of wages gives rise to very difficult problems. There is a clear and admitted case in equity for the abolition of sweating, and therefore in sweated trades no great difficulty arises; but as soon as any attempt is made to apply the principle of equity to the whole of industry we are absolutely without a common standard. Advocates of the "right to the whole product of labour" jostle advocates of the "minimum of civilised life" theory; partisans of equal payment come into conflict with "rent of ability" economists; "to each according to his needs" is a formula irreconcilable with its rival "to each according to his services". That some labour is robbed every one will admit; but any attempt to regulate wages as a whole raises the pertinent and searching question whether *all* labour is robbed. It stands, in fact, at the parting of the ways of revolution and reform.'

qualification or contribution may be compared with that of the individual or group in question. The use of external criteria is scarcely possible without some reference, again often implicit, to the actual job content of the groups compared. Formal mechanisms of job evaluation necessarily make explicit use of both types of criteria. Yet arguments about fairness often do give primary attention to one type of criterion as against the other. Reynolds and Shister (1949 : ch. 2), in a study of workers' job attitudes, reported that 'mention of wages fell into two distinct categories'. One type of response focused on the adequacy of wages as a reflection of the nature of the job and the requirements of an acceptable standard of living; such 'comments indicated no comparison with other jobs in the plant or with similar jobs elsewhere'. By contrast, the main concern of other workers was whether they were 'being paid fairly, as compared with workers in other jobs or in other plants'. The contrasting emphases of these two perspectives are encapsulated in the familiar maxims of 'a fair day's pay for a fair day's work' and 'fair comparisons'.

This distinction parallels that between fairness in *exchange* and fairness in *distribution*: in the first case the focus is on the relationship between employer and employee, the fairness or otherwise of their mutual 'wage-effort bargain'; in the second it is on the distribution of income (and other employment-related advantages and disadvantages) among employees in the same or different firms, occupations or industries. Each aspect is examined separately in the following two chapters. Chapter 4 then carries the analysis a stage further by considering how the 'raw' or 'spontaneous' beliefs and values of managers and employees are 'processed' by the various institutions of collective bargaining, and by the intervention of governments and their agencies in such a manner that an inegalitarian structure of work rewards and obligations is insulated from radical attack.

'A Fair Day's Pay for a Fair Day's Work'

'A fair day's wages for a fair day's work' was described by Engels in 1881 as 'the old, time-honoured watchword' of British industrial relations;[3] and today the maxim is as popular as ever. Nor is this surprising. The traditional formula captures the very essence of the

3. 'A Fair Day's Wages for a Fair Day's Work', *Labour Standard* (7 May 1881).

notion of fairness: two halves of an exchange, something given and something received, which though not identical in character possess conventionally accepted terms of trade. The motto, as a *trade union* device, also indicates a concern with the relationship between wages and effort[4] which has been extensively documented.

The Webbs, in their classic *Industrial Democracy,* identified the standardisation of this relationship as the fundamental objective of trade union action. 'Among Trade Union Regulations there is one which stands out as practically universal, namely, the insistence on payment according to some definite standard, uniform in application' (1897 : 279). The principle of the 'Standard Rate', they argued, was applied flexibly. In many industries it took the form of a piecework price list: wages and workloads were both variable, but the relationship between the two was fixed. Elsewhere, as in engineering, unions strongly resisted payment by results: for the nature of the work would necessitate the setting of job prices by individual bargaining, thus preventing *collective* control of conditions. Yet such unions, while insisting on a standard time rate of wages, accepted that their members would provide 'a normal average of work': they objected alike to levels of effort which by normal standards were excessive or inadequate. In this analysis the Webbs followed the earlier argument of Schloss. 'Speaking generally,' he claimed (1892 : 13-16), 'there exists underlying the method of time-wage, no less than that of piece-wage, a more or less definite quantitative basis. . . . In industrial parlance, "Sixpenny-worth of work" is the same thing, whether the worker be on time-wage or on piece-wage.' This commonly accepted ratio of pay to effort was termed by Schloss the 'standard of remuneration.'

In contemporary industrial relations, the same relationship is identified under the term 'effort bargain'. According to Behrend (1957 : 505), 'every employment contract (whatever the method of wage payment) consists of two elements: (1) an agreement on the wage rate (either per unit of time or per unit of output), i.e. a wage-rate bargain; and (2) an agreement on the work to be done, i.e. an effort bargain.' This effort bargain is in most industrial situations implicit and imprecise, resting on largely intuitive norms of a 'fair

4. The concept of effort can be applied with a variety of meanings, some of which involve complex psychological and physiological definitions. Here, as in common discourse, it is used in a broad sense; it is intended to cover all aspects of work performance and not simply physical exertion.

day's work'. Lupton's description (1963 :2) is typical of a range of sociological studies. Within the social world of the workshop, those who were thought to work too fast earned the label 'teararse'; while others whose evasion of work seemed to exceed the bounds of propriety became known as 'scroungers'. Both types became liable to ridicule or ostracism by fellow workers. The observance by most workers of specific levels of 'reasonable' effort is in line with the finding of an American study: 'there is in most factories a standard of a "fair and honest day's work" to which both management and labor adhere' (Collins *et al.* 1946 : 2).

The Problem of Subjectivity

Inherent in the discussion so far is the assumption that any reference to the notion of a fair day's work involves more than an 'objective' statement of fact; it incorporates a value-judgment which is itself likely to reflect a more general set of normative beliefs. However uncontroversial the *abstract* logic of the principle of 'a fair day's pay for a fair day's work', any attempt to give the maxim concrete meaning will necessarily employ subjective standards of value. By virtue of their subjectivity, such standards will be actually or potentially the subject of legitimate controversy.

This argument, it is true, has often been contested. Many practitioners and propagandists of work study have insisted (particularly in the pioneering days of their craft: e.g. Gracie 1949) that their techniques permit a scientific and objective assessment of a fair day's pay. Yet the objections to this claim appear overwhelming. Proponents of the scientific character of work study focus their attention on the rigour of the various *techniques* of work measurement; they neglect the *non*-technical judgments which underlie any application of these techniques. Hence it is possible to gloss over the initial methodological decision *which* aspects of work to measure. However, 'there is no scientifically obtainable answer to the question "What aspects of behaviour should be rewarded?", for this answer can only be provided by reference to a belief system which contains ethical components' (Turner 1971 : 96). Thus work measurement is preceded by a value-judgment of crucial importance; and it is followed by another, the decision on a formula to convert measured work into a specific rate of pay. Even the intervening technical task of measurement is questionably scientific in character; for the key practical job of effort rating necessarily involves subjective judgment on the part of the practitioner, and this has frequently been shown to be reflected in substantial variations and inconsistencies in the standards applied (Marriott 1957; Brown 1963; Klein 1964; Shimmin 1968). Thus central to work study is an 'extraordinary mixture of measurement and intuition' (Baldamus 1957 : 193). To prove acceptable and hence effective, the practice of work study must be rooted in already existent norms of effort; its main function is to standardise and systematise such often imprecise normative assumptions. Baldamus (1961 : 45-6) has emphasized this point: the central task of the work study practitioner is

> to discover the prevailing notions of the 'right' level of effort '*required*' in a particular situation. The success, indeed the very possibility of systematic time-study, including the more sophisticated methods of work measurement, rest entirely on the existence of such preconceptions. . . . Though precision and consistency in the form of technical terms and measuring appliances are indispensable, and even important, they have the function, not of eliminating the intrusion of effort conceptions, *but, on the contrary*, of detecting and making them all the more amenable to consistent guesswork. The true purpose of time-study, in other words, is to guess as consistently as possible the purely subjective element of effort standards, and subsequently to adjust rates of pay in accordance with them.

Thus subjective standards underlie work study. That this is on occasion denied reflects the fact that such standards, in their most general and abstract form at least, are extensively accepted and largely taken for granted. Yet how much consensus in fact exists on the detailed content of a 'fair day's work' in concrete situations? Research into the nature of prevailing standards is limited; and precise analysis is in any case inhibited by the very imprecision typical of such norms. But the evidence suggests there can exist considerable variation in the rigour of the standards accepted in different situations and by different parties in a single situation. Typically there exists 'a cleavage in social ethics' (Collins *et al.* 1946), workers' normative assumptions prescribing a lesser intensity of effort than desired by management. To some extent this reflects the more general problematic of managerial legitimacy. In so far as workers do not normally question the overall structure of control in industry and society, they assent to the abstract notion of 'management's right to manage.' Yet concrete and specific instances of the exercise of managerial prerogatives may provoke conflict and resistance. As Simon has argued (1957 : 108), general agreement on the abstract issue of managerial authority has not normally entailed agreement: this represents 'a question on which employers and employees seldom saw eye to eye, with the result that the motive of legitimacy could create only the narrower authority that the employee thought he owed the employer, not the broader authority that the employer thought was owed to him'.[5]

This 'cleavage in social ethics' has been variously analysed and interpreted. For the Hawthorne researchers (Roethlisberger and Dickson 1939), what was involved was a conflict between the 'logics of cost and efficiency' which motivated management, and the 'logic of sentiments' embraced by workers. Such a formulation tends to devalue the rationality of workers' actions in what is in essence a situation of conflicting rationalities. 'What may be restriction to management may be a "fair day's work" to a worker' (Bell 1962: 248). Since labour is for the employer a cost of production, it is in his interests to minimize unit labour costs and hence to maximize the ratio of the worker's contribution to his wages; and management is charged with the pursuit of this objective. Employees, by contrast, have a reverse interest: wages and salaries represent an income; effort (at least above the point at which physical or mental fatigue is involved) a cost. Workers' commitment to norms of performance which in certain respects conflict with those of management thus reflects an immediate and material conflict of interest; in addition it may provide a focus for social cohesion which is in itself a source of satisfaction and is also the precondition of effective collective influence over terms and conditions of employment.[6]

Yet if the existence of divergent standards of work performance has been extensively documented, the *limits* to this divergence are equally evident. Employees do in general endorse some notion of managerial legitimacy, and are thus predisposed to obey instructions designed to further the managerially defined objectives of the

5. One example of this practical opposition of normative standards is provided by Perrow (1972: 178), who documents the comments of the chairman of the board of General Motors. 'In an appropriately timed Christmas message to employees in 1969, he attacked those workers who "reject responsibility" and who "fail to respect essential disciplines and authority". Two months later he went further in a widely reported speech. "Management and the public have lately been short-changed. We have a right to more than we have been receiving." Tools and technology mean nothing, he said, if the worker is absent from his job. "We must receive a fair day's work for which we pay the fair day's wage." ' For a more general discussion of this issue, see Fox 1971; Hyman 1972b.
6. For an important discussion of the normative basis of shop-floor cohesion, see Sykes 1960 and 1967.

employing organisation. As Baldamus has suggested (1961 : 81-2), the fact that workers are conditioned to assume 'that they are under some moral obligation to accept a certain degree of deprivation connected with employment' provides a crucial social support for an economic system based on wage-labour. This predisposition can in turn be related to more general social processes through which beliefs and values are inculcated.

The Study of Performance Norms

This is however to anticipate an analysis which is to be developed in a later chapter. To remain at the level of the actual norms of performance adopted by workers within their employment: these, it would seem, are the outcome of a partial conflict between this generalised socialisation in obedience and those elements of working-class sub-culture (both outside and inside the workplace) which diverge from the specific expectations of management. Thus three factors would appear to exert a crucial influence on employee norms: the content and efficacy of 'primary socialisation'; the exposure to divergent values; and the rigour of managerial expectations and discipline.

The importance of exposure to the dominant values has been emphasised by Kerr and Siegel (1954) in their classic analysis of the inter-industry propensity to strike: groups like miners or dockers who, occupationally and residentially, form an 'isolated mass' segregated from the influence of the wider society are most likely to engage in industrial conflict which the prevailing values deprecate. By contrast, occupational groups which are more integrated into the broader community have more inhibitions about militancy. The significance of exposure to the counter-socialising influence of distinctive working-class sub-culture is stressed in the same study; the separate communities of the isolated mass 'have their own codes, myths, heroes and social standards' (p.191). The effect of these same factors on performance standards has been demonstrated in accounts of 'rate-busters' who adhere to managerial rather than work-group norms of 'a fair day's work'. Dalton's pioneering study (1948) showed that their backgrounds differed significantly from those of other workers: they were more strongly socialised into the dominant values of capitalist rationality and individual achievement, and had not been exposed to the countervailing socialisation of urban working-class sub-culture.[7] The third factor in the situation which must also be considered is the extent to which managerial demands on workers' performance strain their commitment to managerial legitimacy and encourage the adoption of divergent standards. Gouldner's case study (1954a and b) provides a good example of this point: the traditional 'indulgency pattern' of factory management — the absence of strict discipline or driving supervision — encouraged a collaborative attitude on the part of the labour force; this was destroyed when managerial policy and practice (under the constraint of changed economic conditions) shifted abruptly. In Gouldner's interpretation, workers had originally accepted relatively low wages in their factory as compensated by managerial leniency and a moderate pressure of work; but once these compensatory factors were removed, they reacted *both* by demanding higher wages *and* by reducing their spontaneous co-operation with managerial requirements. (This points to a factor of great relevance to our concluding discussion: in a changing structural context, traditional worker norms can acquire an unintended disruptive potential.)

Such findings are in line with theories developed in recent sociological analyses of the general role of normative values and beliefs in underpinning the social and economic structure of capitalism. Several sociologists — whose arguments are considered in detail in Chapter 7 — have emphasised the widespread endorsement of moral values which underwrite the legitimacy of the social order; but they add that such values are in general so abstract and flexible as to permit 'deviant' behaviour by those who assent to them. In the specific case of work obligations the same is true: 'however powerful, their content is too diffuse to control behaviour effectively in any concrete situation'. Such notions of obligation *support* the institution of capitalist employment but do not 'control the specific activities within the institution' (Baldamus 1961 : 83, 89). Thus those who share the same generalised assumptions in respect of employee obligations may adopt conflicting definitions of a fair relationship between pay and effort. In any work situation, employees may potentially acquire a consciousness of what Baldamus terms 'wage disparity' — a lack of congruence between

7. For other analyses of the importance of worker background for attitudes and behaviour, see Turner and Lawrence 1966; Goldthorpe *et al.* 1968.

pay and effort. When this occurs, and management's demands appear 'unfair' in relation to the level of pay, it is natural that workers should formulate and assert their *own* standards of 'a fair day's work'.

This possibility gives rise, however, to a problem of considerable theoretical importance. Where work groups possess their own standards of performance, do these typically contain a minimum as well as a maximum level of effort? And while workers may be expected to resent and resist what Baldamus terms 'negative wage disparity' (a situation in which they consider they are underpaid and/or overworked), do they typically accept with equanimity the *reverse* situation (in Baldamus's terms, 'positive disparity'), where pay is *above* the level which by their own standards is fair in relation to their contribution?

Jaques (1967 : 155) asserts in colourful language the dire consequences of a situation in which a worker is paid above the level which he considers fair. 'Compulsive elements begin to enter into his attitude,' Jaques insists. 'He may often have some anxiety. . . . He experiences feelings of guilt [which] may be warded off by a devil-take-the-hindmost attitude. He may express resistance to change. . . . Greed and avarice may be stimulated, with a resulting anti-social grasping for further relative gain regardless of the consequences for the common good.' A similar assumption, though more cautiously presented, is inherent in the 'equity theory' developed by American social psychologists.[8] They argue that an employee who considers his pay to be high in relation to his contribution will experience 'cognitive dissonance and that this will in turn create tension. 'Inequity results for Person not only when he is, so to speak, relatively underpaid, but also when he is relatively overpaid. . . . The presence of inequity in Person creates tension for him [and] will motiviate him to eliminate or reduce it.' In consequence it is predicted that an employee who feels overpaid 'may try to reduce the dissonance . . . by working harder' or else 'may cognitively distort his inputs and outputs' (Adams 1963 and 1965). Some experimental studies have been presented as validating this hypothesis.

8. Equity theory postulates that an employee will assess the fairness of his pay (or 'outcome') in relation to his effort or qualifications ('input'); and that this assessment is made by comparing his own input/outcome ratio with that of other individuals. Hence this approach assumes that both internal and external criteria are salient in any appraisal of the fairness of pay.

It is, however, difficult to accept that there exists a general tendency for employees to avoid 'positive disparity'. While Jaques's arguments appear to derive more from intuition than from evidence,[9] the empirical findings of the equity theorists are themselves of questionable applicability to many employment situations, and are in any case not wholly consistent.[10] Indeed, industrial sociology possesses a considerable literature documenting situations in which workers accept, welcome or even deliberately create what might be termed an 'overfair' ratio of pay to effort. Since Taylor's emphasis on the social and economic significance of 'systematic soldiering', the phenomenon of work-group production norms (commonly labelled 'restriction of output') has been repeatedly analysed; while many writers have described the enthusiasm with which pieceworkers negotiate and defend 'loose' job times or prices — at times relishing the opportunity to engage in 'conspicuous loafing' *as well as* achieving acceptable earnings.[11] In any event, it is important to note that the very lack of an objective standard of effort renders the definition of 'working hard' open to considerable subjective re-interpretation; and by this means 'cognitive dissonance' is readily avoidable. (Those in high-paid social positions, of course, find little difficulty in ingeniously justifying their privileges.)

Performance Norms and Orientations to Work

The questions of 'restriction of output' and 'positive disparity' may be fruitfully related to the broader issue of orientations to work. One

9. For an incisive critique of Jaques's theories, see Fox 1966b.
10. For reviews of empirical applications of equity theory, see Opsahl and Dunnette 1966; Weick 1966; Pritchard 1969. Most experimental studies have employed students. Yet the prospective occupational status of students is higher than that of the average employee; and, as Baldamus (1961: 86-7) has indicated, 'moral obligations towards work . . . become increasingly powerful as one goes up the scale of occupational status.' Moreover, such experimental subjects possess neither the background counter-socialisation nor the immediate social support of work-group norms defining employee obligations less stringently. And even allowing for these limitations, such studies are less than conclusive in demonstrating a desire to avoid feelings of overpayment (Pritchard 1969).
11. For representative studies, see, for America, Taylor 1911; Mathewson 1931; Roethlisberger and Dickson 1939; Roy 1952, 1953 and 1954. Significant British studies include Marriott 1957; Hickson 1961; Lupton 1963; Klein 1964; Lerner *et al.* 1969.

common argument is that there has occurred, historically, a transition from 'traditionalism' to 'instrumentalism'. Traditionalism — the persistence of pre-capitalist orientations to work — has been graphically described in Weber's classic study (1930 : 59-60). In the period of emergent capitalism, Weber argues, attempts to stimulate greater worker effort by increasing piece-rates often proved counter-productive: effort and output actually declined. The worker's aspirations were fixed by his customary standard of life; far from seeking to maximise output and hence piecework earnings, he worked merely enough to ensure the traditionally acceptable level of earnings. Weber concludes that man is not 'by nature' acquisitive: quite the contrary. Hence 'wherever modern capitalism has begun its work of increasing the productivity of human labour, it has encountered the immensely stubborn resistance of this leading trait of pre-capitalistic labour.'[12]

While Weber's example relates to pieceworkers, analogous behaviour has been described in the case of those paid by time. Here, traditionalism was associated with fairly precise notions of 'the just wage' and 'a fair day's work'. Such, at least, was typically the case where employees were sufficiently socialised into the prevailing notions of worker obligation.[13] According to Hobsbawm (1964:348),

12. While such 'traditionalism' has been widely documented — it was, for example, a common problem for colonial administrators and for pioneer industrialists in colonial situations — it could be argued that Weber over-generalises in his categorisation of pre-capitalist orientations to work. It is obviously correct to castigate the notion that man is 'by nature' acquisitive; nevertheless, the drive to acquire and accumulate is not unique to the 'spirit of capitalism'. Other structural and/or cultural contexts can induce acquisitiveness — which has, for example, often been regarded as characteristic of the peasantry. In contemporary British industry there is evidence that certain groups of Asian immigrants — though lacking prior industrial experience — exhibit a markedly 'instrumental' orientation to work. (More recent sociological theories of 'instrumental' orientations to work are considered in the next chapter.)
13. Where the worker had not been exposed to the necessary processes of social indoctrination, according to Mill (1852: 110-11), the consequences for the employer were baneful: 'As soon as any idea of equality enters the mind of an uneducated English working man, his head is turned by it. When he ceases to be servile, he becomes insolent. The moral qualities of the labourers are fully as important to the efficiency and worth of their labour, as the intellectual. Independently of the effects of intemperance upon their bodily and mental faculties, and of flighty, unsteady habits upon the energy and continuity of their work (points so easily understood as not to require being insisted upon), it is well worthy of meditation, how much of the aggregate effects of their labour depends on their trustworthiness. All the labour now expended in watching that they fulfil their engagement, or in verifying that they have

'the worker's labour effort, or standard of output per unit of time, was . . . determined by custom. . . . The criteria for a fair day's work . . . depended partly on physiological considerations . . . on technical ones . . . on social . . . on moral ones . . . on economic ones . . . on historic ones and doubtless on others. They were enforced by powerful collective pressure.'[14]

'Strictly traditional behaviour', according to Weber (1947 : 116), 'lies very close to the borderline of what can justifiably be called meaningfully oriented action and indeed often on the other side.' The social ethic which was necessitated by the dynamism of industrial capitalism was, by contrast, essentially calculative. The worker had to transcend the limitations of traditional norms of work and wages; 'he had to be made ambitious and "respectable" ' if he was to respond to the employer's deterrents and incentives (Pollard 1965 : 195-6). He had to cultivate 'a strict economy which calculates the possibility of high earnings, and a cool self-control and frugality which enormously increase performance' (Weber 1930 : 63).

The paradoxical consequences of the inculcation of calculative and utilitarian attitudes to work have often been noted. 'The first generation of factory workers were taught by their masters the importance of time; the second generation formed their short-time committees in the ten-hour movement; the third generation struck for overtime or time-and-a-half' (Thompson 1967 : 86). Similarly, capitalist ethics might appear to invite the worker to apply *in his own interests* the principle of buying in the cheapest and selling in the dearest market, to seek the maximum earnings for the minimum effort.[15] Taken to its logical conclusion such an orientation would imply the principle of 'an unfair day's work for an unfair day's pay'. Thus Leiserson (1931 : 168) suggested that the prevalence of 'restriction of output' could be interpreted as a natural outcome of 'the attempt to teach employees principles of "sound" economics

fulfilled it, is so much withdrawn from the real business of production, to be devoted to a subsidiary function rendered needful not by the necessity of things, but by the dishonesty of men. Nor are the greatest outward precautions more than very imperfectly efficacious, where, as is now almost invariably the case with hired labourers, the slightest relaxation of vigilance is an opportunity eagerly seized for eluding performance of their contract.'

14. Historical conceptions of a 'fair day's work' are also discussed by Phelps Brown 1959: 289-90, who emphasises their imprecise character.
15. For an argument that workers in the nineteenth century did begin to learn and apply these 'rules of the game', see Hobsbawm 1964: 350-51.

and successful business management': workers learned only too well that the widespread restrictive practices of their employers had a coherent rationale.

Such arguments were indeed employed at the turn of the century by those who advocated organised restriction or 'ca' canny' as an explicit employee tactic.

> There is no ground for doubting that the real relation of the employer to the workman is simply this — to secure the largest amount of the best kind of work for the smallest wages; and, undesirable as this relation may be to the workman, there is no escape from it. . . . The employer insists upon fixing the amount he will give for an hour's labour without the slightest consideration for the labourer; there is, surely, therefore, nothing wrong in the labourer, on the other hand, fixing the amount and the quality of the labour he will give in an hour for the price fixed by the employer. If employers of labour or purchasers of goods refuse to pay for the genuine article, they must be content with shoddy and veneer. This is their own orthodox doctrine which they urge us to study.[16]

The notion of 'shoddy and veneer', taken even further, could imply not simply passive restriction but active sabotage, and early theorists of syndicalism did indeed endorse the latter as a natural extension of the former.[17] While sabotage is probably still widespread in contemporary industry, it scarcely ever occurs as an element in an articulated bargaining strategy.[18] And while the go-slow is a common (and perhaps increasingly popular) form of industrial conflict, it is probable that the normal incidence of 'restriction of output' is far less calculative in origin. The same is true of the literal application of bureaucratic rules in a manner which impedes work performance. The deliberate exploitation of the 'dysfunctional' potential of bureaucratic rules can occur explicitly in the work-to-rule, but far more commonly represents what Merton (1968 : 249-60) has termed 'ritualism' — the compulsive application of organisational norms without concern for the ends they are designed to serve. Merton's own interpretation — that 'over-performance' stems from a distortion of personality encouraged by bureaucratic structures — fails to bring out the rationale of 'ritualism' as a medium of *power* (albeit limited in scope) for subordinates who are otherwise weak and vulnerable. As Gouldner discovered (1954a : 174-5), 'the rules served as a specification of a *minimum* level of acceptable performance. . . . The worker . . . now knew just how little he could do

16. National Union of Dock Labourers, *Report of Executive* (1891), quoted in Webb and Webb 1897: 307. Compare Hobsbawm 1964: 365.
17. See for example Cole 1913: 95ff.; Veblen 1963: ch. 1; Roy 1969: xxix-xxxi.
18. See the discussion by Taylor and Walton 1971.

and still remain secure.' The same point has been generalised by Crozier (1964 : 55, 185).

> Rules and routines . . . may have a protective value. They ensure that no one can interfere in the internal affairs of the immediately inferior category. They give, therefore, a certain kind of independence. . . . Subordinates will bargain with their own conformity and use it as a tool with which to bind management. This is just another aspect of the fight for control. Subordinates tacitly agree to play the management game, but they try to turn it to their own advantage and to prevent management from interfering with their independence.

Bendix makes the implications brutally clear (1963 : 445): 'there is no more effective means of organisational sabotage than a letter-perfect compliance with all the rules and a consistent refusal of the employees to use their own judgment'.

Applied consistently, then, such practices on the part of employees would cause economic chaos. As the Webbs noted (1897 : 658), 'the hiring of a workman, unlike a contract for the purchase of a commodity, necessarily leaves many conditions not precisely determined, still less expressed in any definite form'. Part of the explanation of this indeterminacy, as Behrend suggests (1961 : 103-4),[19] is that the exact degree of effort required cannot be accurately predicted. The employer cannot foresee precisely what tasks will require performance, how these shall be assigned among the labour force, and what intensity of work these will necessitate. Hence 'while an ordinary sales contract can be quite specific with regard to the price to be paid and the quantity and commodity to be sold, the employment contract can only give a vague outline of the contractual obligations for which a price is paid.' Similarly, bureaucratic controls, however elaborate, cannot eliminate the necessity for individual discretion and initiative. 'It is a matter of logic and not experience that it is impossible for a rule to determine the conditions under which it is implemented. . . . Compliance with a rule therefore is not removed from the area of disputable judgement' (Albrow 1968 : 157).

The Indeterminacy of Work Obligations

Some writers[20] have insisted that the employee *does* incur a specific commitment in terms of his acceptance of a position of

19. See also Baldamus 1961: 91.
20. For instance, Commons 1932: 284; Simon 1945: 115-16.

subordination within the employing organisation: 'what he sells when he sells his labour is his *willingness* to use his faculties to a purpose that has been pointed out to him. He sells his promise to obey commands.' Yet such a 'promise' is neither unambiguous nor unconditional; and its interpretation is thus a source of potential conflict.

> *Which* commands has the worker promised to obey? Are these commands limited to the *production* of goods and services only? Under the terms of the contract, may an employer legitimately issue a command unnecessary for production? *Who* decides this anyhow, worker or employer? (Gouldner 1954b: 162-3).

Lockwood (1964 : 246) has pointed to a similar source of conflict with the argument that 'whereas the legitimacy of authority tends to take the form of general principles, acts of authority are always specific'. Hence the conclusion is inescapable that work obligations are in practice indeterminate.

For the Webbs, this indeterminacy was a source of grave disadvantage for the worker. 'The employer protects himself by providing supervision and by requiring obedience to his foremen, if not also by elaborate systems of fines and deductions. Whenever there is any dispute as to the speed of work, or the quality of output, the foreman's decision is absolute. . . . The isolated workman . . . is, under an unregulated industrial system, absolutely in the hands of the employer for the period of his engagement' (1897 : 658-9). Such situations of absolute managerial discretion are by no means extinct. Yet in a context of relatively full employment, and of extensive trade union membership, the indeterminacy of work obligations is no longer so evident an advantage to the employer. On the contrary, the growth of collective organisation at the place of employment (which may operate informally even in the absence of trade unionism) permits the situation to be exploited to the benefit of employees. Hence the achievement of a 'co-operative' interpretation of work obligations has come to represent a crucial problem of contemporary management (witnessed in part by the rapid expansion of research and teaching in industrial sociology and organisational psychology).

The basic requirement of managerial control, in Etzioni's well-known analysis (1961 and 1964), is to ensure the 'compliance of lower participants'. Etzioni sets out a threefold classification of 'coercive', 'utilitarian' and 'normative' bases of control, and argues that 'normative power tends to generate more commitment than utilitarian, and utilitarian more than coercive'. The importance of this point is accentuated by the factors discussed above: what is at issue is not simply the passive compliance or obedience of employees but the positive application of discretion and initiative towards managerially approved ends. Reliance on overtly coercive forms of control is almost inevitably corrosive of such positive commitment:[21] yet the contradictions inherent in purely utilitarian forms of control are also plain from the previous discussion. In the language of the 'job enrichment' school, material inducements alone may satisfy the employee but will not motivate him.[22] Or as Westergaard (1970 : 120) has argued from a very different perspective, where the only attachment of the employee to his work is his pay packet, then 'his commitment clearly is a brittle one'. For the sake of his wages he may accept a position of subordination to managerial authority, and agree to perform boring and routine tasks; but any dissatisfaction with the level or security of his earnings corrodes his sense of work obligation. 'The "cash nexus" may snap just because it is *only* a cash nexus — because it is single-stranded; and if it does snap, there is nothing else to bind the worker to acceptance of his situation.'

Thus the 'problem of order' which has so exercised sociologists in their general analyses of society is an issue of parallel importance at the level of the workplace. The arguments of modern industrial sociologists were anticipated by Durkheim's statement (1933 : 211) of the paradox that 'everything in the contract is not contractual'. If, as Durkheim insisted, an area of common normative understandings and assumptions is the prerequisite of stable contractual relations at the societal level, the same is true within the confines of industrial relations. In the early years of industrialism, Mill (1852 : 111) called attention to 'the immense increase in the produce of all kinds of labour, if the labourers honestly performed what they undertake. . . . Conjoint action is possible just in proportion as human beings can rely on each other.' The economic and technological developments since the time Mill wrote have immensely accentuated the importance of such 'reliability'. 'As the delegation of authority and technical specialization have become more important for the successful functioning of modern enterprises, management has had

21. Perhaps for this reason, slavery and analogous forms of forced labour have typically been utilised only on types of work in which worker discretion is minimal. Bendix (1963: 204) cites a study of inmates of Nazi concentration camps, forced to perform wartime factory work, who 'sabotaged the production effort by consistently asking for detailed instructions on what to do next'.
22. For a recent survey and appraisal, see Daniel and McIntosh 1972.

either to rely upon, or to make sure of, the good faith of its employees' (Bendix 1963 : 10). Thus, once more, the relevance of essentially moral considerations is evident.

The very fact that contemporary economic organisations function at all is an indication that workers' orientations to their employment are not merely instrumental but contain important value-attachments. To answer the question raised earlier: it would appear that employee norms of performance *do* in most (even if not all) cases prescribe a minimum as well as a maximum level of effort. 'What evidence we have suggests that workers do not habitually operate at the minimum effort level and that this is not merely due to fear of dismissal' (Behrend 1961:106). Baldamus (1957:195-6) refers to cases (by no means unique, though probably far from typical) where pieceworkers have accepted reductions in job prices which they consider excessively 'loose'. And Crozier notes, on the basis of his study of French workers (1964 : 169), 'the general agreement of all groups about what constitutes a reasonable degree of efficiency'. Management could successfully mobilise the pressure of other employee groups against any section whose performance was below the generally agreed standards.

Discussion of the sources of such moral attitudes often refers to custom and habit. Hobsbawm, as has been seen, suggests that historically 'the worker's labour effort . . . was . . . determined by custom rather than market calculation'; Behrend (1961 : 113) has pointed to the continuing importance of such considerations, suggesting that 'it is plausible that habitual standards of effort or habitual output norms often come to be considered as "fair" standards'; Gouldner (1954b : 164) has suggested that the compatible expectations of management and employees in respect of work performance 'derive . . . from shared *traditional* beliefs and values'.

Tradition, as the earlier reference to Weber made clear, provides a basis for action which is only marginally 'rational', in the sense of stemming from a process of explicit calculation. Hence the significance of the fact that employee controls of output are commonly applied in a far from calculative manner.[23] The same, it would appear, is normally true of industrial sabotage. And where either *is* applied in a highly purposive manner, it is normally directed to a highly specific and limited objective: 'goldbricking' in

23. See the useful discussion of motives for 'restriction of output' in Hickson 1961.

order to achieve an increased piecework price (Roy 1952); 'utilitarian' sabotage designed to facilitate an awkward work process (Taylor and Walton 1971). As an element in a more systematic industrial strategy, such methods are (in Britain at least) extremely rare. The notion that subordinate employees are under a moral obligation to apply themselves with diligence and dedication to the service of their employers — an obligation interpreted far less onerously in the case of more exalted occupational groups — is pervasive in its influence. The Webbs (1897 : 308-9) described the impact of such beliefs within the working class movement, in a passage which reveals their own unquestioning acceptance of a moral standpoint so valuable for employers:

> Systematic loitering will destroy the character and efficiency of even the most resolute worker. In adulterating the product, you adulterate the man. To the unskilled labourers of a great city, already demoralised by irregularity of employment and reduced below the average in capacity for persistent work, the doctrine of 'go canny' may easily bring about the final ruin of personal character. It was an instinctive appreciation of this truth which led the responsible Trade Union officials unhesitatingly to denounce the new departure of the Liverpool dock labourers. It remains, so far as we know, a unique instance in Trade Union annals.[24]

In similar fashion, Hobsbawm (1964:351) has noted that 'the tendency to slack undermined the workers' self-respect even if it improved his market position; and self-respect is a much more fundamental thing than the historically evanescent categories of the free market economy'.[25]

Evidently, then, there is a certain ambivalence in the manner in which workers apply standards of work performance which conflict with managerial expectations. Rarely do they demonstrate an

24. They added that the dock labourers' proposals, quoted above, originated from officials who 'did not belong to the ranks of the workmen'. Despite the Webbs' comments, output restriction was not condemned without qualification; for example Cummings (1905: 54) considered it a natural response to rate-cutting. In the 1850s 'ca-canny, as the go-easy policy is called, was to some extent in existence. . . . Though not defensible to-day with our accredited price lists, it was to some extent defensible then, for prices were arbitrarily fixed by employers. . . . Fair dealing would have prevented the restriction of output and have made it in the interests of workers to obtain the best possible results.'
25. Possibly to meet this spontaneous resistance to the *blatant* performance of an 'unfair day's work', certain theorists of syndicalism and related movements suggested a strategy of 'constructive' sabotage: production workers should apply standards of high craftsmanship rather than 'scamping' their work as instructed by management; shop assistants should inform customers if goods were shoddy or adulterated. In this way, it was suggested, employees would attack their employers' profitability while enhancing their self-respect as workers.

avowedly and unambiguously oppositional intent: a determination to obstruct and undermine managerial objectives. Rather, a notion of work obligation typically exists, but is interpreted in a manner which reflects the divergent interests of employers and workers. (As suggested earlier, there are a number of situational factors which help determine how forcefully this obligation is experienced, and how significant are the qualifications and limitations deriving from consciousness of divergent interests.)

This analytical perspective is helpful in interpreting the concept of 'restrictive practices' of which 'restriction of output' represents only one component. In everyday discourse it is assumed that the use of this concept raises few problems. The Donovan Commission's secretariat (1967:47) defined a 'restrictive labour practice' as 'an arrangement under which labour is not used efficiently and which is not justifiable on social grounds'. While reflecting recognition that a 'restrictive practice, cannot be simply and objectively identified, this formula fails to indicate that the notion of 'efficiency' is itself highly value-laden, and that the social justifiability of a practice can vary radically according to the standpoint of the critic. The 'device of the common rule', a fundamental principle of trade unionism, infringes the autonomy of employer and individualistically inclined worker alike. 'Every rule or regulation which has been introduced into industry to provide workers with some protection restricts management's freedom of action' (Flanders 1964:323).[26] For this reason, every form of protection which unions have attempted to achieve has in its time been denounced as socially unjustified. By the same token *some* social justification can normally be offered even for practices which are subject to almost universal denunciation.[27] The fact that 'restrictive practices' are a reflection of the conflicting interests of employers and employees and are therefore open to conflicting evaluations, that they have both positive and negative aspects, has been well captured in Zweig's characterisation (1951 : 181-9).

26. Daniel (1970:6) has taken this argument even further: 'Any type of organisation is a set of restrictive practices in so far as it allocates certain defined tasks and responsibilities to certain individuals and groups of individuals and not to others.'
27. See for example Cliff 1970. The only exception, presumably, would be where practices have a purely traditional and hence, for their present practitioners, 'non-rational' basis.

A restrictive practice is a many-dimensional phenomenon. It is like a sphinx with many faces, one face directed towards the past, and others directed towards many interests of different orders. There is an element of equity and of law and order in them, a human element and an element of social interest.

Conclusion

The notion of a 'fair day's work' is extensively employed in industrial situations. Its normal usage, if the literature is any guide, is however virtually confined to the performance of subordinate (and in particular manual) occupational groups; rarely is it thought necessary to insist that those in more privileged positions should provide 'a fair day's work for a fair day's pay'. One explanation might be that members of exalted occupations are so manifestly conscientious that such moralising is in their case superfluous. Another explanation seems more plausible : that the notion serves primarily to contain and sublimate a potential conflict between those in managerial and those in subordinate positions. Its use is to sustain a sense of work obligation among those whose work offers little or no intrinsic motivation to high performance, and to denounce those who fail to meet managerial expectations. This is to imply that the concept is to an important extent ideological; and its significance can thus be adequately understood only within the framework of the more general analysis which is developed in Chapter 7.

What also emerges from the preceding discussion is that while some sense of obligation to perform a 'fair day's work' is accepted by most employees, the actual content of their standards of work performance may diverge from those of management. Moreover, even complete normative agreement would not preclude the generation of conflict over effort levels through pressures inherent in the structure of the work situation itself. Such conflicts are however rarely overt and fundamental. They are contained, not merely because of the prevalence of normative standards of performance, but also because of the existence of specific mechanisms of accommodation which serve to mediate the opposing actions and objectives of employers and employees. The nature of these mechanisms will be examined after *external* criteria of fairness — the notion of fair comparisons — have been considered.

Chapter 3

Fairness and Pay Comparisons

External Criteria: 'Fair Comparisons' and the Problem of Subjectivity

In the introductory chapter the analytical distinction was made between internal and external criteria of 'fair pay'; and it was suggested that while the two criteria are logically interdependent, in practice they are commonly applied separately. Their relative importance is a matter of some controversy. Baldamus (1961:9-10) has argued (in terms which appear to involve an unquestioned acceptance of the models of classical economics) that differential payment in respect of 'occupational costs' (skill, training, experience etc.) is wholly uncontroversial; he regards internal criteria alone as a focus for contention. 'Everything that points to a "harmony" of interests appears to be connected with the self-regulating mechanism of occupational costs and rewards within the institution of occupation. And the causes of recurrent disorganization stem from an unbalanced and variable distribution of effort and effort rewards in the context of employment.' Jaques, however, draws diametrically opposed conclusions. While ignoring the effort bargain, he insists (1958:313) that 'all industrial disputes about payments are differentials disputes. They arise over the question of how much one group is getting compared with others.' Both approaches might be considered unacceptably simplistic. At the same time, the fact that comparisons can be regarded by one author as a source of stability and by another as a source of conflict suggests that this process may itself contain inherent contradictions.

External criteria of the fairness of wages, like internal criteria, are essentially subjective, and subjective attitudes reveal considerable variations. Those who argue otherwise must adopt one of two positions: either that some objective system of job evaluation is genuinely possible; or that a system, while not objective, reflects beliefs and assumptions which represent a consensual viewpoint.

The 'strong' argument for the objectivity of job evaluation cannot withstand serious scrutiny. As Wootton has indicated (1962:146-7), there are two points at which the subjective and contingent character of any evaluation exercise is particularly obtrusive. The first is the assignment of weights to the various factors into which each job is analysed (and indeed also the initial selection of these factors from the multiplicity of characteristics which might in principle be evaluated). 'This is obviously bound to be arbitrary: effort, skill, responsibility and environment are mutually inconvertible.' The second is the translation of a particular 'job profile', directly or through some scheme of grading, into a specific 'rate for the job'.

The most fundamental normative assumption of any process of job evaluation — so fundamental that its 'objectivity' is commonly taken for granted — is the premise that employees should necessarily receive differential incomes related to the characteristics of their jobs. For some, this is an unassailable moral norm: 'economic equality, however produced or maintained, is antagonistic . . . to the morality proper to man' (Batten 1923:59); 'there is a conception of each man reaping the just rewards of his own labour which is deep-seated in the mind' (Jaques 1967:175). Just as the punishment should fit the crime, it is argued, so the pay should fit the job. To this essentially retributive principle may be added a utilitarian one: differential rewards ensure a supply of labour to those occupations of greatest social value. This latter is a proposition which, as is argued later, is conventionally but not always plausibly asserted by most of those social scientists who consider the question of inequality. Yet even if it were true — as indeed it is not — that the relative social utility of each occupation could be objectively determined, it would be impossible to demonstrate objectively in consequence that the relationship between their incomes should be of any given order, or that the absolute income for any occupation should be a specific sum. Finally, it is logically quite possible to deny that job differences should be assigned any relevance in the determination of pay, and assert that some quite different principle should apply. The maxim 'from each according to his ability, to each according to his needs', for example, implies a radically different structure of incomes; yet its acceptance or rejection is essentially a question of subjective judgment.

It follows, then, that 'job evaluation is not by any means an objective — let alone a scientific — method of determining appropriate wage relativities' (Turner and Zoeteweij 1966:123). Yet this does not exclude the 'weak' argument, noted above, that job evaluation taps analytically an implicit consensus underlying everyday judgments about pay; that it standardises and systematises what are generally considered to be fair relationships between job content and income. This, it is argued in an important unpublished study (Walker 1965:55-6), 'is what job evaluation practitioners claim, quite explicitly and specifically'.

At first sight the notion of an implicit consensus possesses obvious plausibility. Those involved in industrial relations commonly speak and act as though there exist generally agreed principles bearing upon the relationship between the pay of different occupations. The concept of 'fair comparisons' is extensively employed and has indeed long received some degree of endorsement in British government policy (a factor which receives more attention in the next chapter). It is a commonplace that pay comparisons exert a pervasive influence in collective bargaining.

> As there is no absolute criterion for deciding whether wages are fair, workpeople tend to judge fairness by comparing their wages with those of other workpeople. If workpeople in one occupation in a factory or industry secure an increase in wages, those in other occupations usually demand increases which will restore their relative wages. Similarly, wage increases in some industries lead to pressure for corresponding increases in other industries (Richardson 1954: 291).

If judgments of the relative worth of different occupations were altogether arbitrary and idiosyncratic, they would scarcely possess substance enough to support such widespread dependence by wage-fixers on the language of fair comparisons.

Yet in reality the hypothesis of normative consensus receives only weak support from conventional usage of the notion of fair comparisons. The quotation cited is indeed revealing: members of an occupational or industrial group typically appeal to the principle in order to justify a claim for an increase comparable to that received by some other group, and hence restore the *customary* relationship between their incomes. The notion is not, in most cases, the basis for an explicit criticism or justification of existing relativities, but an argument for the maintenance of these relativities which takes for granted their moral propriety. By contrast, the professed objective of job evaluation is precisely to subject customary pay relationships to critical scrutiny. Wootton (1962:162) has offered a famous comment on the restricted rationale of everyday reliance on the principle of fair comparisons. The problem, she writes, is that everyone accepts automatically 'that every wage bargain must be "fair" or "reasonable" '; yet few are willing or able to offer substantive criteria of what is fair or reasonable. 'That is where conservatism comes to the rescue. Change — always, everywhere, in everything — requires justification: the strength of conservatism is that it is held to justify itself. It is not therefore surprising that the maintenance of standards, absolute or comparative, should be woven as warp and woof into the texture of wage discussions. . . .'[1]

The implication of this argument is obvious. As soon as the focus of enquiry shifts from *movements* in the incomes of different groups to their actual *level,* the normative agreement assumed by many job evaluation practitioners appears far less substantial. Indeed, conceptions of fair comparisons are at once revealed as highly ambivalent. Clegg has emphasised this fact in his argument (1961:211-12) that 'the general public holds contradictory notions of fairness'.

> The method of fair comparison on a national basis provides comfortable incomes for porters and policemen in some rural districts, and leaves them still the poor relations in some industrial areas. On the other hand fair comparison on a local basis would entail paying the Coventry porter more than the station-master in Cornwall, and the constable in Oxford more than the inspector in Dorset. In the absence of dependable evidence I would suggest that it would be commonly thought to be 'fair' in modern Britain for the Steel Company of Wales or Fords to pay more to the driver of a five-ton truck than does, say, the Westmorland County Council. I do not see how this can be reconciled with the proposition that it is fair to pay the rate for the job to postmen in Dagenham, in Swansea and in Keswick.

Yet cogent arguments can be framed both for the notion of 'the rate for the job' on a national basis, and for the notion that wages should match local variations in the cost of living. In effect, such contradictory arguments are typically appraised through *different frames of reference:* hence the contradiction is not explicitly confronted and *both* arguments can be endorsed.[2] In the same manner, different frames of reference may be utilised in applying the principle of comparability to levels and to movements in pay. This

1. The normally conservative application of the principle of fair comparisons helps explain how the notion of fairness can be accommodated to the facts of inequality. This is a vitally important point, to which we return later.
2. For a discussion of the notion of frames of reference in social psychology, see Sherif 1948. An interesting application of the concept to perceptions of incomes is developed by Behrend 1964 and 1973.

may explain, for example, why the TUC has on more than one occasion called both for special treatment for the lowest paid and for the preservation of established differentials. Wootton (1962:110) quotes Stafford Cripps who, as Chancellor of the Exchequer, remarked that 'there are still some cases of low earnings which are very difficult to correct without upsetting the relative wage levels that have been established within each industry for the different grades and classes of workpeople employed in it. This is an immensely difficult problem to solve.' Wootton comments: 'It certainly is: indeed, to raise the lowest level without upsetting differentials is a mathematical impossibility.' Only where different frames of reference are applied, and the contradiction is therefore not explicitly articulated, can it be argued both that the pay level of one group should be raised relative to that of another, and that the increase given to the group should be generalised on grounds of comparability.

A very similar explanation may account for the fact that attitudes towards equal pay for women 'have sometimes tended to be equivocal' (Office of Manpower Economics 1972:29). The notion of 'equal pay for work of equal value' may well be endorsed by many employees, when considered through the traditional trade unionist frame of reference of 'the rate for the job'. Yet as Mill noted (1852:400), unequal treatment of women in terms of pay is widespread and persistent, though not universal; and 'the only explanation that can be given is custom; grounded either in a prejudice, or in the present constitution of society, which, making almost every woman, socially speaking, an appendage of some man, enables men to take systematically the lion's share of whatever belongs to both.' Thus the same employees, applying a different frame of reference, may endorse the conventional norms of inequality.[3] As Wootton argues (1962:153), 'the case for equal pay as between the sexes is now, "in principle" generally accepted'; but the neglect of this principle in practice can be easily rationalised by the use of other perspectives.

One plausible consideration which is relevant here is that comparisons may be more salient upwards than downwards. Clegg (1961:212-13) has called attention to the fact that comparability criteria are used as an argument for levelling up rather than down;

3. For data on attitudes towards sex differentials derived from a survey in the Irish Republic, see Behrend *et al.* 1970a.

and he comments that 'it is an unsatisfactory kind of justice which is fair in only one direction'. Yet it is probably a generally accepted view that wage decreases are 'unfair', especially in a period of stable or rising prices; hence levelling up is alone regarded as an equitable means of redressing 'unfair' relativities. This point is particularly important given, in Wootton's terms (1961:146),

> the apparent irrationality, as judged by *any* standard, of our present wage and salary structure. One may search in vain for the rational compound of skill, responsibility, effort and working conditions of a system which would explain why the ward sister in a general hospital should be paid (at the top of her scale) about one-sixth of the salary of the Dean of Westminster; why the male probation officer should start at about one quarter of the top transatlantic airpilot's rate, and at his maximum just pass the starting-rate of the university lecturer in Greek; or why the sub-officer in the fire brigade should end a little above where the graduate school teacher began, and the police constable after six years' experience get for his full-time employment about five-sixths of the salary of a part-time governor of the BBC.

It follows that virtually every group of employees should be able, without too much ingenuity, to discover another group by comparison with which they are arguably under-paid. Hence it is not surprising that survey evidence suggests that a majority of employees both agree that there exist low-paid groups who deserve exceptional treatment, and are unwilling to accept restraint on their own wage increases to allow these groups to improve their relative position.[4] For they are likely to consider *themselves* underpaid in the context of some different comparison, and for this reason would find restraint unacceptable.

4. *ibid.* It is interesting, however, that this survey showed that willingness to accept restraint increased with respondents' income: a majority (55.1 per cent) of men earning over £30 a week were willing to accept such restraint — possibly because they had less scope for considering themselves under-paid by comparison with some other group. Yet paradoxically, when asked: 'what do you think would be a fair amount for the next general all-round pay increase?' the higher paid ('well over half' of those earning over £30) were particularly likely to mention a percentage rather than an absolute amount. Again, only inconsistent frames of reference can explain why the same group was most ready to accept restraint in the interests of the lower paid and most concerned to maintain percentage differentials. Another significant example of conflicting frames of reference is described by Wedderburn and Crompton (1972: 106), in the context of skilled workers in the chemical industry. 'Despite the fact that the tradesmen compared their own value favourably with that of white collar workers they also expressed a genuine egalitarianism which might well have existed somewhat uncomfortably side by side with their self-conception of their own importance. For it was the tradesmen who thought that significant groups of the general workers were underpaid. In reply to the question "Are there any groups of workers here who you think get paid too little for what they do?" a quarter said "tradesmen", but another quarter named process workers,

From this there follows a general point of great significance. If the conception of fair comparisons held by any individual or group is likely to contain facets which are internally contradictory, then the opportunity exists for selective emphasis whenever a group's own interests are at stake. The predictable tendency, in other words, is to interpret fairness in the most favourable manner; hence groups which are differently situated may well stress different aspects when they utilise the notion of fairness. This is a further argument against the suggestion that job evaluation rests on implicit consensual norms; an argument which, moreover, has obvious empirical support. For as Walker puts it (1965:56), 'In view of the bitterness with which disputes over differentials within the same organisation are sometimes conducted, it is not easy to suppose that underlying these hotly disputed differentials there is a set of general principles acceptable to both groups of workers and to the management of the organisation as well.' It is questionable, for example, whether there exists general support for the value-judgment inherent in many job evaluation schemes that skill and responsibility are 'worth' some three times as much as effort and working conditions — so that the requirement of a modicum of initiative may be thought to justify higher remuneration than exposure to serious danger to life and limb.

The notion of consensual cultural norms is in any case contradicted by the practice of job evaluation exponents themselves. Schemes covering all categories of employees within the same company are, apparently, unknown; not only are senior managers typically excluded, but different schemes invariably apply to manual and non-manual grades. Moreover, while there is considerable consistency in the choice of factors and weights in different schemes — almost certainly reflecting in part the fact that previous schemes are used as models for later variants — important

19 per cent tradesmen's mates, and 32 per cent the general labourers i.e. the lowest paid of the unskilled workers. General workers, however, answered this question almost exclusively as an extension to their own personal grievances about pay. They were also less likely to say that any groups were paid too much for what they did, whereas 70 per cent of the tradesmen thought that the white collar and supervisory grades were overpaid.' Similarly, the coexistence of relatively abstract professions of egalitarianism with pressure for higher material recognition of the role of their own occupational group has been a notable characteristic of some leading British white-collar trade unions in recent years.

variations do occur.[5] Thus white-collar schemes tend to assign particular weight to responsibility and mental skills, while manual schemes often give relatively greater weight to physical dexterity and effort.

One interpretation, cogently argued by Walker, is that 'cultural patterns of evaluative salience' are likely to differ situationally. The elements of a job which a clerk considers particularly deserving of reward are unlikely to be precisely those which have greatest significance for the manual worker. And even among manual workers, different elements may 'stand out' according to the nature of the work: steel process workers may emphasise responsibility; instrument workers, skill; foundry workers, physical effort and conditions. In so far as this is correct, it seems improbable that a single scheme for evaluation will be endorsed as fair by employees whose 'job value reference groups' are different. Empirical evidence exists to support such a view. Thus in the dispute over introduction of job evaluation at the Cowley works of Pressed Steel Fisher in 1968, different occupational groups were clearly applying different criteria in assessing relative worth. The patternmakers stressed their 'high level of skill and . . . need of a knowledge of foundry, machine shop and design requirements'; those who demanded a single grade for craftsmen emphasised the apprenticeship training common to all such groups; while for non-craft employees it was argued that considerations other than formal skill were relevant (Scamp 1968). Very similar differences arose during the introduction of job evaluation at the Longbridge factory of British Leyland in 1968-70. Here, too, certain skilled groups — most notably toolroom workers — laid particular emphasis during negotiations on factors particularly relevant to their own occupations (Ogden 1971). From a completely different context, it is worth noting one of Gouldner's findings from his study of gypsum miners (1954a:120-23). The worker who fixed the pit props was highly valued by the miners for he provided them 'not only with physical safety, but with psychological security as well'. Yet the management, applying the frame of reference of surface factory work, 'considered him entitled only to the comparatively low wages of an unskilled worker'.[6]

5. Thus in some schemes effort is more highly rated than responsibility. For examples drawn from international experience, see NBPI 1968; Thomason 1968.
6. It should be added that if variations exist in cultural patterns of evaluative salience, the same is true of patterns of situational *power*. Strongly organised

Such evidence is necessarily discounted by those who assert the possibility of a rational, equitable and comprehensive restructuring of incomes. Some writers (e.g. Paterson 1972; Wigham 1972) have called for a national system of job evaluation. Another well-known scheme is that propagated by Jaques (who, however, rejects conventional job evaluation).[7] His basic premise is that 'there exist shared social norms of what constitutes a fair or equitable payment for any given level of work, these norms being intuitively known by each individual' (1967:21). Specifically, 'felt-fair pay' correlates with the responsibility inherent in each job, as measured by its 'time-span of discretion' (i.e. the length of time during which the employee is required to use his own initiative, without control or supervision by a superior). Jaques makes it clear that, on this basis, extreme inequalities of income can be justified.

Since a variety of appraisals of Jaques's theories have been cited, it is unnecessary to subject them to a detailed critique in this context. As Fox (1966b:16) has pointed out, Jaques's basic thesis that there exists a consensus that the worth of a job should be asessed *solely* by the criterion of the responsibility attached 'is a simple mis-statement'. Most trade unionists would insist that a variety of other job-related factors be taken into account: working conditions, effort, tools used, training required and so on. Many craft unions, moreover, would insist that their members are entitled to the fully skilled rate of pay simply by virtue of their apprenticeship training — even though they may be employed on work of low skill and responsibility.

It is significant that empirical evidence offered in support of their hypothesis by Jaques and his supporters derives primarily from studies of managerial and other white-collar occupations.[8] Here the

---

and/or strategically located worker groups who are not mystified by the 'scientific' pretensions of job evaluation practitioners can often influence the application of an evaluation scheme in a direction favourable to their specific interests.

7. See Jaques 1956, 1958, 1967 and 1969; other expositions of his approach include Richardson 1971 and W. B. D. Brown 1973. For critical reviews see Fox 1966b; Goodman 1967; Kelly 1968; Gordon 1969; Milkovitch and Campbell 1972.

8. It is perhaps relevant that within the Glacier Company, where Jaques's original research and consultancy took place, proposals to base pay on his principles were rejected by the manual workers. Jaques himself (1969) has recently presented data derived from manual workers which are intended to support his theory but in fact undermine it: they show that employees whose level of

previous comments on job evaluation criteria are clearly relevant: Walker's concept of job value reference groups can be related to the analysis provided by Marris (1966:93). Within managerial circles, he argues, 'in Western countries, "responsibility" seems to be the key ideolog. In these countries the law in question may be stated as a wisespread belief in a one-for-one relationship between income and responsibility, an essentially aristocratic convention of possibly feudal origins.' It is predictable that the convention should receive general assent among managerial employees and those most exposed to their cultural hegemony, thus *partial* support for Jaques's theory is only to be expected. By the same token, occupational groups for whom other aspects of work are particularly salient and receive particular emphasis within a distinctive occupational culture may be expected to reject this same aristocratic convention. Jaques's claim to have provided a *general* theory of norms in relation to fair pay must therefore be discounted.

The Choice of Pay Comparisons

So far in this chapter the burden of our argument has been negative: the pay comparisons which are extensively utilised in industrial relations do not reflect the application of generally agreed analytical principles. On the contrary, the process of comparison in many respects is characterised by inconsistency and arbitrariness. In specific industrial relations situations, the introduction of job evaluation may systematise and 'rationalise' previous processes of comparison; but the fact that a specific frame of reference for judging pay can be deliberately imposed in certain contexts does not contradict our general argument.[9] Moreover, as we have indicated, the acceptability of a formal evaluation scheme depends largely on the limits within which it is applied; the broader and more varied the range of occupations covered, the more likely that differences in 'patterns of evaluative salience' will form an overt focus of

---

responsibility was calculated as the same gave estimates of fair pay for their own work which varied between approximately £750 and £1,400 a year. According to Jaques's own theory, such statements of 'felt-fair pay' should have been equal.

9. The use of job evaluation as a means of structuring and manipulating pay comparisons is considered further in the following chapter.

contention. Hence a comprehensive systematisation of pay comparisons is a chimera. In general the types of pay comparison deemed relevant by employees, managers and union negotiators reflect, and will continue to reflect, a complex of diffuse and inchoate influences.

This is not to suggest that systematic *analysis* of the choice of pay comparisons is impossible: on the contrary. A number of studies have provided important insights into this choice, usually from within the perspectives of reference group theory. At this point we must provide a brief account of the nature of this theoretical perspective — which (as we argue in a later chapter) is of interpretative value but only within relatively narrow limits. To begin with a simple definition: the notion of reference group is employed in sociology and social psychology to denote the source of a frame of reference which structures an individual's attitudes or actions. It can be applied to a collectivity of which the individual himself is or is not a member (membership or non-membership group) or, by extension, to another individual or even an abstract idea.[10]

An analytical distinction of key importance is that between normative and comparative reference groups. A normative reference group constitutes the source of an individual's standards of behaviour or, more broadly, his perspectives on and attitudes towards social action and social relations. A comparative reference group 'is almost tautologically, that with which one compares oneself on some given dimension' (Kelley 1952).[11]

The concept of comparative reference group is closely related to that of relative deprivation; and both have obvious and immediate relevance to the question of pay comparisons. Initially applied to an analysis of the attitudes of American servicemen in the Second

10. In his original formulation of the concept, Hyman (1942: 15) differentiated between 'reference groups' and 'reference individuals'. This distinction is no longer commonly made; hence, as Merton (1968: 338) has remarked, 'the now-established term "reference group" is something of a misnomer. For the term is applied not only to groups, but to individuals and to social categories as well.' For a discussion of the various usages of the concept, see Pollis 1968; Bott's distinction (1957: 165-8) between 'direct' and 'constructed' reference groups is also relevant. Much of the classic literature on the subject is compiled in Hyman and Singer 1968. Runciman 1966 provides a useful introductory survey of reference group theory as it relates to the concerns of the present study; but his approach reveals many of the inadequacies criticised in a later chapter.
11. For an elaboration of this analytical distinction of types of reference group, see Turner 1956.

World War (Stouffer *et al.* 1949), the concept of relative deprivation can, as Merton and Rossi comment (Merton 1968:289), be 'generalized and related to a larger body of theory. Relative deprivation can provisionally be regarded as a special concept in reference group theory'. The central insight of this approach is that people's sense of deprivation (or, conversely, of welfare) is not a simple function of their objective situation but depends also on the frame of reference through which that situation is assessed; and, more specifically, that 'self-appraisals depend on people's comparison of their own situation with that of other people perceived as being comparable to themselves' (Merton 1968:40). A clear demonstration of this point can be provided by an example from *The American Soldier*: men in the Air Corps, where promotion rates were particularly high, were considerably *more* critical of their promotion prospects than were men in the Military Police, where promotion rates were very low. The apparent explanation was that in the first case, men compared themselves with former colleagues who *had* been promoted and thus felt discontented; while in the second, comparisons were with their fellows who had not been promoted. The authors comment that 'without reference to a theory that such opinions represent a relationship between their expectations and their achievements relative to others in the same boat with them, such a finding would be paradoxical indeed' (Stouffer *et al.* 1949:251).

Yet such an analysis raises further problems. As Merton and Rossi argue (Merton 1968:292), any attempt to generalise this hypothesis opens further questions for enquiry. If there is a natural tendency to compare one's situation with that of others 'in the same boat', what causes this predisposition? Who, in any case, is perceived as being 'in the same boat', and what determines this perception? Merton and Rossi point to the analogous idiomatic expression, 'keeping up with the Joneses'. 'Who', they ask, 'are the specific Joneses, in various social structures, with whom people try to keep up? their close associates? people in immediately higher social or income strata with whom they have contact? When are the Joneses people whom one never meets, but whom one hears about (through public media of communication, for example?' Such questions are clearly relevant to the specific problem of pay comparisons. Part of the answer, the writers suggest, is that the choice of a comparative reference group is related to those aspects of the individual's own attributes (or by extension those of his occupational group) which are most significant for him. 'Some similarity in status between the individual and the reference group must be perceived or imagined, in order for the comparison to occur at all' (Merton 1968:296). Thus men in the Air Corps may have thought themselves as qualified as their many former colleagues who achieved promotion, while those in the Military Police were more conscious of their similarities with non-promoted fellows.

It follows that the experience of relative deprivation involves two elements: those of an individual's own attributes which are salient for him (as Runciman [1966] terms it, his membership reference group), and which form the basis of comparison; and the relative advantages and disadvantages of his own situation and that of the comparative reference group. Thus a worker who considers himself as deserving as a higher-paid individual or group in terms of some important characteristic (for example skill, experience, social utility) will feel relatively deprived. On the other hand, if the comparison group is not higher-paid, or if its attributes are thought to *justify* the the differential in pay, this will not occur.

Implicitly or explicitly, the categories of reference group and relative deprivation structure most empirical studies of attitudes to pay relativities. And the conclusion of such studies is overwhelmingly that the choice of reference group is normally unambitious, and relative deprivation accordingly limited. The standard of life desired by the ordinary worker, and hence his criterion of a fair wage, is 'generally of an extremely modest character', wrote Snowden in 1912 (p. 1). Half a century later Runciman's study (1966) reaches the same conclusion. Summarising American literature, he writes (p. 28) that 'even in a society where the ideology of egalitarianism is most powerful, those at the bottom modify their ambitions in accordance with the facts of their situation. . . . Their reference groups will not be those implied by a literal adoption of the belief that there is a place at the top for everyone. Even where equality is an article of faith, the facts of inequality tend to restrict those feelings of relative deprivation which they might be thought to stimulate. The "normal" situation, where inequality is not seen to be markedly diminishing, is for reference groups to be close to home.'

From his own survey data Runciman develops a parallel interpretation. In a national sample survey (conducted in 1962) respondents were asked: 'Do you think there are other sorts of people doing noticeably better at the moment than you and your family?' Only 60 per cent gave an affirmative answer. Lower-paid respondents and non-manual workers were marginally more inclined to give affirmative answers than the higher-paid and manual workers; in particular, manual workers earning over £10 a week were most likely to respond negatively. Those answering positively were asked: 'What sort of people do you think are doing noticeably better?' Many responses were not occupationally specific; but of those that were, manual respondents were most likely to cite other manual groups, while non-manual respondents referred to other non-manuals. Among both manual and non-manual respondents, those who compared themselves with manual groups were more likely to resent their own relative inferiority than those citing non-manual comparisons. From these and other data Runciman draws the general conclusion (pp. 217-18) that 'the reference groups of the less well placed are limited in scope, unspecifically defined, and mildly expressed. . . . The main conclusion to have emerged is the restricted and even illogical choice of comparative reference groups, particular in the manual stratum, on matters of economic class.'[12]

The finding that manual workers tend to compare their earnings with those of other manual workers (or, if they choose white-collar comparisons, that these are typically lower-paid clerical occupations), whereas non-manual workers are more likely to invoke comparisons with higher-paid salaried employees, suggests that the existing hierarchy of incomes is generally regarded as normal and natural. To give two extreme examples of how an uncritical acceptance of extreme inequalities may lead to the choice of totally unrelated reference groups at different occupational levels: within the lowest-paid and most menial occupations, a salient point of comparison is often the level of payment to those in receipt of social security benefit.[13] Within the highest managerial strata, by contrast,

12. The methodological adequacy of Runciman's study is open to criticism. As Westergaard (1970) argues, he tends to exaggerate the significance of marginal variations in the responses of different groups; more seriously, there is no adequate exploration of the *meanings* of these responses. (For example, 'respondents may assume, erroneously, that they are *expected* to relate their replies to their own limited experience'.) Nevertheless Runciman's data do support his general conclusion, quoted above.

13. This is one of the findings of a survey of trade union representatives of manual employees in local government, conducted by graduate students of industrial relations at the University of Warwick in April 1972.

salary horizons 'are very greatly affected by the presence in our society of large unearned incomes, which set standards of consumption to which the occupants of superior posts in industry and other occupations very naturally aspire' (Cole 1957:96). Thus at either extreme of the employment hierarchy the comparison group may be chosen from outside the employment sector altogether.

Further information on the degree to which the overall structure of rewards is unquestioned is provided by the surveys conducted by Behrend and her associates. In Britain (1967:ch. 6), little evidence was found that major income inequalities possessed great salience for respondents or provoked serious discontent. In reply to the question 'who do you think most deserve an early pay-increase?', the most frequently named *specific occupational group* were doctors — on average one of the highest-paid occupations in the country. Asked 'who do you think least deserve a pay-increase?', only 11.7 per cent mentioned high-income groups or 'the rich'.[14] Whereas a relatively high proportion of respondents (23.6 per cent) believed that lower-paid workers in general deserved an early pay increase, specific knowledge as to *which* occupations were low-paid appeared to be very limited.[15]

More detailed information is provided by the survey conducted in the Irish Republic (Behrend *et al.* 1970a and b).[16] Respondents were asked to specify the amount of pay which they thought should be paid to, respectively, skilled manual, lower-grade clerical, semi-skilled and unskilled workers; and to men in eleven named professional, lower white-collar, and manual occupations. The replies showed a considerable degree of consistency in the ranking of broad occupational strata. Thus 76 per cent believed that a factory manager should earn more than a school teacher, and over 90 per

14. It is true that 22.3 per cent mentioned MPs, government ministers or politicians in general, but presumably this primarily reflected popular cynicism towards politicians. While 10 per cent mentioned car workers (who earn more than most other manual groups but far less than many non-manual occupations), only 7.7 per cent mentioned company directors and managers (who are among the highest paid of all).
15. Behrend later commented (1973: 7) that 'many people have stereotyped images of certain occupations in terms of considering them overpaid or underpaid, and have also very inaccurate ideas of what people in these occupations are actually paid'.
16. In some respects the respondents differed significantly from those in the British study. For example, their specification of occupations deserving an early pay increase were more heavily oriented towards the lower paid; and they appeared better able to specify which occupations *were* low-paid.

cent that he should earn more than any other named occupation; while over 60 per cent ranked the school teacher above the other manual or lower non-manual jobs.

Sources of Conflict

Studies such as Behrend's point naturally to the conclusion that, for most people, the broad hierarchy of incomes within British society is unproblematic.[17] Yet such acceptance of the overall structure of incomes does not preclude conflict over the relative worth of specific occupations *within* it. Behrend's Irish survey revealed (1970b:11) that there was considerable dissension over the position of the clerical workers. Only just over half the respondents (51 per cent) held the view that skilled workers should get more pay than clerical workers; 36 per cent of the sample considered that they should get the same amount and a minority of 8 per cent held that they should get more than skilled workers. There appeared also some doubt as to how semi-skilled workers should stand in relation to clerical workers. . . .' Perhaps significantly, clerical workers themselves (social grade C1) were most likely to elevate their own worth. Such disagreements were accentuated when individual occupations were ranked. In many cases the survey 'reveals evidence of lack of consensus. . . . In particular there are twelve comparisons where the most frequent answers represented the views of less than half the sample' (p. 24). Again, respondents' own occupational position appeared to

17. Though it is possible that respondents may have *interpreted* the questions as taking for granted the existing hierarchy, and hence used their assumptions of the pay prevailing in the various occupations as their frame of reference in determining their answers. Behrend's findings may be contrasted with those of North *et al.* (1973). In a sample survey of adults in Great Britain, 46 per cent stated that 'the present share-out of wages among British jobs in Britain is unfair', while 22 per cent considered it very unfair; only 19 per cent considered it fair or very fair. This need not however imply a criticism of the overall earnings structure; since the question referred explicitly to 'the share-out of wages', respondents may have considered merely the relationship of different *manual* occupations. Asked to rank twelve manual occupations in order of worth, respondents gave answers which contrasted markedly with these occupations' actual relative hourly and weekly earnings (the report does not indicate how much consensus occurred in these rankings). In part this finding may be viewed as a more extreme example of one aspect of the survey by Behrend: that there was far less consensus on rankings among manual occupations than there was in ranking manual workers in broad categories within the overall occupational hierarchy. This point is taken up immediately below.

influence their views on fair pay. 'Firstly, as regards the level of the figures in the hierarchy for fair pay there was a tendency for men in the high social grades to think of higher figures as fair. Secondly, as regards *relative* position in the pay hierarchy there was a tendency to give somewhat higher figures for their own or kindred groups or to give lower figures for non-kindred groups' (p.19).

It is interesting to compare such findings with the literature on occupational prestige. Parkin's discussion of this topic (1971:42-3) is particularly useful in revealing the affinities with attitudes to income.

> Certain criteria become institutionalised as 'relevant' for ranking purposes, while other criteria are excluded or defined as 'irrelevant'. Once a given set of rank criteria has been successfully legitimized throughout society, then the main lines of the status order will have been laid down. Obviously, the number of logically possible rank criteria is quite large, so that many different ways of socially grading the same positions are feasible. If, for example, occupational prestige were allocated on the basis of the physical effort, or danger or dirtiness of the tasks performed, it would result in a quite different status order from that in which technical expertise, skill, or responsibility were held to be the relevant rank criteria. In our type of society, rank criteria of the latter kind are accorded much greater legitimacy and institutional backing than are criteria of the former kind; hence professional occupations are assigned a high position in the prestige order while labouring occupations are assigned a low place. This means that it is not necessary for members of society to have a detailed knowledge of different occupations in order to be able to place them mentally in the prestige hierarchy. All that is necessary is that they should have some rough idea of whether or not any given occupation is endowed with the 'relevant' rank attributes.

Again, surveys of prestige ranking commonly report a tendency for respondents to elevate their own occupation within the hierarchy; and often reveal far less consistency in relating occupations roughly similar in nature (especially when there is little general knowledge of their precise job content) than occupations of distinctive social type.

A further point to emerge from the survey by Behrend and her associates is that where the relative ranking of different occupations is agreed, the appropriate differential between them may still be a focus of dispute. Thus the Irish respondents named, as fair pay for the eleven occupations, figures which involved significantly smaller differentials than those prevailing. The median pay proposed for an agricultural labourer was £15.10 (compared with rates then prevailing of £11.60-£12.00), and for a factory manager £34.50. Perhaps significantly, professional respondents (social grade AB) were most likely to name 'realistic' salaries for professional occupations, and hence specified the largest differentials; at the same time, however, their proposals for the lowest-paid occupations were no lower than those of the remaining respondents.

This point can be related to Behrend's findings on attitudes to low pay, already mentioned. Both British and Irish respondents were more likely to nominate the low-paid than any other category of workers as specially deserving a pay increase. They also defined as 'low pay' figures which were significantly above basic rates of pay in a number of occupations; while conceptions of low pay tend to increase with the cost of living. Thus in 1966, the median figure cited by British respondents was £11; this rose to £14 in 1969 and £16 in 1971 (Behrend 1971). The median figures named by respondents in different socio-economic groups were virtually identical.

All this is to suggest that attitudes to pay relativities may be a source of (possibly intense) conflict even in the absence of any *general* questioning of the highly inegalitarian structure of incomes. It is also important to note that comparative reference groups may be less restricted in assessing *movements* in pay than in assessing *levels*. As Behrend's studies indicate, critical comments are often made in respect of increases obtained by politicians and senior civil servants, by workers who would not judge the *level* of their own wages against the salaries of such groups. Clegg (1971:9) refers to the same phenomenon when he states that 'it is embarrassing for the administrators of an incomes policy to have to defend pay increases of twenty to thirty per cent to groups who appear to the great majority of wage-earners to be extremely well off.' Conceivably, the discontent thus provoked might stimulate more explicit and critical attention to the rational of major income inequalities, and encourage relatively sharp and volatile shifts in attitudes and aspirations.

Group Processes and Pay Comparisons

Without pursuing further, at this point, such possibilities (which receive more attention in the concluding chapter), we need merely emphasise that acceptance of the broad income hierarchy still allows considerable scope for the choice of specific pay comparisons. Hence it is necessary to raise such questions as : what determines this choice? how consistent are frames of reference at this level? what factors encourage or inhibit changes in horizons? To answer these it is necessary to transcend the methodology of the social survey, with its essentially *individualistic* focus, and to consider the influence of *group* processes on the choice of pay comparisons.

Often the resort to a specific type of pay comparison may constitute one of the normative assumptions of a particular occupational group.[18] In an engineering factory, for example, it may be taken for granted among skilled grinders that they deserve the same pay as fitters and higher earnings than capstan operators; and any new recruit to their group will be subject to strong though no doubt diffuse pressure to apply the same frame of reference to his earnings. In such a context, for a grinder to suggest that fitting is more highly skilled or that capstan work is equally deserving would be to assail the moral values of his fellows. Thus the notions of comparative and normative reference groups may be interrelated: if workers in the same shop or office constitute an individual's normative reference group (at least where work-related standards are concerned), and if group norms encapsulate pay comparisons, his comparative reference group would appear to be pre-determined. Moreover, the more firmly the individual is integrated within the occupational group, the more unproblematic the given pay comparison will appear — until the group's own standards alter. Fellow-members of the occupation outside as well as inside the place of employment may also constitute a normative reference group: this is perhaps particularly likely where an occupational group possesses — or is attempting to assert — skilled or professional status. In such circumstances, comparability with other craftsmen or professionals will represent a natural normative orientation.[19] This point may be related to Walker's concept, noted earlier, of 'job value reference groups', and his argument that workers tend to perceive as particularly worthy of reward those factors — skill, effort or responsibility — which characterise their own occupation. Empirical support for this argument comes from the Irish survey of Behrend *et*

18. If it is an oversimplification to exaggerate the coherence and consistency of individual perspectives on pay, it is *a fortiori* dangerous to assume that group attitudes are homogeneous. In addition to more random individual variations, such factors as social background and trade union involvement are likely to shape perceptions of pay and occupation. This is an essential qualification to the discussion which follows.
19. As suggested below, in this context it may be of critical importance whether an occupational group possesses the *power* — through its own strategic or organisational strength or through privileged access to the institutions of material and ideological domination within the society — to impose extensively a particular conception of its own worth.

al. (1970b:31): in evaluating pay, manual workers tended to refer to 'hard or unpleasant features connected with the work situation'; whereas non-manual workers were more likely to mention 'responsibility, education or training'. In a more localised setting, Brown *et al.* (1972:33-4) report similar factors as influencing perceptions of the occupational hierarchy in shipbuilding. In naming occupations with the highest status, there was virtual consensus in ranking crafts above non-skilled jobs. But 'the Boilermakers chose metal trades almost exclusively, especially welders . . .; the outfitting workers mentioned outfitting trades, especially electricians, more frequently.'

While the notion of the occupation as a normative reference group helps explain the choice of pay comparisons by the individual worker, the perspectives of the group itself still require explanation. In many cases, a certain situational logic may be involved. This is to say, the context may predispose a group towards the choice of a specific reference group. It cannot *determine* this choice, for any context is open to a range of different interpretations and evaluations. Pope (1942:60) cites the example of cotton-mill workers in North Carolina, whose earnings were far below those prevailing in New England. 'Apologists for wage rates in the county have compared them with agricultural income and wage levels in neighboring mills'; whereas striking employees were conscious of the broader national comparisons. This example might suggest that what is perceived as the logic of the situation can vary with the *interests* of the group concerned. It can also vary with its general *orientations*: if Carolina millworkers are in general satisfied, or at least acquiescent, they may be most conscious of those aspects of their situation which imply restricted comparisons; if militant, or at least dissatisfied, they may perceive their situation in a manner which accentuates relative deprivation. This raises an important issue: is relative deprivation a cause or consequence of dissatisfaction with pay? Does the choice of a particular reference group precede or follow the desire for the relevant level of income? Both Runciman (1966:16) and Parkin (1971:62) have raised this question; the most plausible answer would seem to be that the casual relationship is rarely unidirectional. In most situations, particularly where *changes* occur in reference groups and satisfaction with pay, the two processes would appear to be mutually reinforcing.

If the situation of a group in no way uniquely determines the pay comparisons chosen, it nevertheless sets a framework for this choice. Perhaps the most important factor suggested by studies of pay comparison is that proximity increases the probability that a group will be spontaneously adopted for purposes of comparison; there is a tendency, in other words, for familiarity to breed pay comparisons. Other things being equal, those with whom an occupational group has the closest and most frequent relations are most likely to provide a frame of reference for judging the wage-work bargain. 'Equity among various tasks on a single job is of the most immediate and direct concern to the employees on the job' (Livernash 1954:341). A study of newspaper printing (Sisson 1975) has shown that pay comparisons were most pressing between occupational groups who, because of the technology of production, worked close together and at a similar pace. In coalmining, the work of Scott *et al.* (1963) similarly indicates how the structure of work can generate spontaneous comparisons. Haulage workers complained that pay did not reflect the differential requirements of 'hard' and 'soft' haulage jobs; more importantly, they resented the far higher earnings of face-workers, with whom they came into regular contact. (In addition, most haulage men were either aspiring or else former face-workers.) By contrast, maintenance workers who were not in such immediate contact with the higher-paid face-workers were less likely to make this comparison and were therefore more satisfied with their pay. Under-officials, for whom a major grievance was the lack of additional pay for overtime worked, were clearly conscious that the ordinary workmen under their charge *did* receive such payment. More generally, of course, comparisons by foremen with their subordinates are often noted: a feeling that workers' earnings from overtime or piecework have eroded their 'proper' differentials is likely to generate spontaneous discontent. Piecework, it is also commonly reported, tends to provoke a sense of grievance among shop-floor employees where apparent anomalies and inequities occur. This was the general conclusion, documented with what would seem to be rather selective examples, of the NBPI in its report on Payment by Results Systems.[20] Specific examples are provided by a number of studies: for example in the docks (Liverpool

20. Report No. 65, Cmnd. 3627 (May 1968). The NBPI took no account of studies of *collective* work-group controls of the operation of payment by results systems designed to prevent the occurrence of inequitable earnings differentials within or between groups. Where such controls are successfully applied, it would appear that employee dissatisfaction with the payment system is far less

University 1954; Mellish 1972; and Wilson 1972) and in engineering (W. A. Brown 1973). Again, proximity would appear to encourage consciousness of earnings differences between workers on similar jobs — or of the erosion of traditional differentials between occupations; whereas more distant inequities are more likely to be ignored.

This is to suggest that internal plant comparisons are more likely to occur spontaneously than external ones. In a study by Rimmer, for example (1972:16), 'reference groups were limited: men would relate their earnings to others in the same shop, but rarely to earnings in other foundries. . . . The extreme fragmentation of the technical processes and of the piecework payment system meant that large inter-foundry disparities were not uncommon, and heavy earnings fluctuations, due to variable overtime and production stoppages, complicated comparisons. Thus core-makers in one foundry could be earning nearly twice as much as core-makers elsewhere.' This quotation indicates that there exist a variety of situational factors which may inhibit external comparisons. Yet clearly, such comparisons *are* made in industry — particularly since most workers do have experience of a number of different employers, and have social contacts with employees of other firms. 'Spontaneously and frequently, men measure the plant by comparing it with others in which they have once worked,' Gouldner (1954a:46) has reported. Yet whether such spontaneous individual comparisons help shape the *collective* aspirations of a work group is more doubtful.

One factor which may exert critical influence is the structure of collective bargaining institutions and procedures. This is of such importance that it is considered separately in the following chapter. Another factor which is in some ways related may be discussed here: occupational status and the structure of the occupational career. There is important evidence, even if limited in quantity, that the pay comparisons of an occupational group may well be structured by such factors. The most obvious contrast here is between workers whose occupational expertise is largely tied to the individual employer, and those whose skills are far more extensively transferable. Organisational sociologists have emphasised a similar distinction in the contrast between 'cosmopolitans' and 'locals':

---

common. See for example Sykes 1960; Lupton 1963; Cunnison 1966; Lerner *et al.* 1969.

'those low on loyalty to the employing organisation, high on commitment to specialised role skills, and likely to use an outer reference group orientation'; and 'those high on loyalty to the employing organisation, low on commitment to specialised role skills, and likely to use an inner reference group orientation' (Gouldner 1957:290). Even more clearly relevant is the distinction in labour economics between internal and external labour markets. In the former, labour is recruited to specific occupations from existing employees lower in the firm's occupational hierarchy (possibly after undergoing any necessary additional training): in the latter, recruitment is from suitably qualified workers outside the firm (Kerr 1959; Robinson 1970; Mackay *et al.* 1971).

In the United States, where the internal labour market is of particular importance (with the principle of promotion by seniority often formally agreed as the basis for recruitment to all but the lowest-level manual occupations), it is natural that the plant itself should set the framework of pay horizons. This provides the context for Sayles's description and analysis of intra-plant comparisons (1958:103-4).

High activity is associated with a somewhat ambiguous prestige position. Work groups in the upper middle ranges of skill and earnings have met some of the criteria which justifies in their eyes, if not in management's view, pay and working conditions 'almost' comparable to those enjoyed by the recognised top skilled personnel. . . . These middle-range workers expect to be much better off than those they see as being *below* them in importance, and almost as well off as those they recognize as being *above* them in job skills. They utilize the same reference groups to establish their skill level, seizing upon one criterion, such as the fineness of the tolerances for the work they are doing, and excluding others which do not support their case. We have referred to special interest groups because these groups have particular economic goals: securing better work standards, greater protection in the case of technological change, higher hourly rates, more overtime, looser incentive standards, and so on. Each of the goals has a *comparative* aspect: better than, greater than, higher than, looser than, more than the conditions or status of some other group. The plant grapevine carries general impressions as to how hard various groups work for approximately what general order of income — although the accuracy of these impressions leaves much to be desired. Actually we know very little about how these comparisons are made, and need to know much more before generalizing on how a group decides it is being paid equitably or inequitably.

The economist has stressed interplant comparisons as the dynamic force in the labor market. We would suggest that with the impact of seniority, retirement, job guarantees, and the protections of unionization, the internal (to the firm) labor market becomes an equally important determinant of worker behavior. An interesting example of the effect of 'other work groups' was furnished by a steelworker official. He observed that foundries are often hot spots, highly aggressive in seeking fulfillment of their demands *when they are part of larger manufacturing organizations.* However, when the plant is entirely devoted to the foundry operation, they are relatively weak and inactive. We might speculate that in these more diversified plants the position of the foundry is ambiguous. Earnings are high to compensate for the difficult working conditions, the work is heavy, and more recently there has been a serious shortage of applicants for this kind of work; but the reputation of the foundry is very low among other employees, who tend to look down on foundry workers because of the hot, dirty, heavy work they perform.

By contrast, a *craft* structure (far more important in Britain than in the United States) presupposes the transferability of skills from one employer to another. Here there is a natural tendency (reinforced by a 'vertical' structure of union organisation) for comparisons to be made with fellow-craftsmen in other firms. Hence in the nineteenth century, British craft unions pioneered the principle of the standard 'district rate'; and the maintenance of the economic and technical preconditions for the inter-firm mobility of fellow craftsmen has remained, as Flanders (1964) has stressed, an essential *moral* component of the craft culture.[21]

One example of the way in which such contrasts in occupational career patterns can structure worker orientations is provided by the British steel industry. The system applied to production workers closely parallels that in American industry: recruitment to each grade above the lowest is by promotion, strictly according to seniority, from the grade below. This procedure does not, however, apply to maintenance craftsmen, who are therefore mobile between firms and other industries. In consequence, the production worker's horizons are very much confined to his firm: it provides him with 'a pattern of aspiration and promotion for his working life'; whereas the craftsman's perspectives are far less constrained (Scott *et al.* 1956). The specific implications of the craftsman/process worker distinction for attitudes to pay has been demonstrated by Wedderburn and Crompton (1972). Craftsmen were particularly likely to compare their earnings with external groups, in particular tradesmen working for contractors; and 'the almost daily contact they had with the contractors' men, in pubs for instance, contributed to their feelings of dissatisfaction with their own pay' (p.37).[22] They

21. It is an interesting question whether labourers, and other workers near the bottom of the occupational hierarchy, may parallel craftsmen in resorting to external pay comparisons. Such workers typically display the greatest job mobility of any group; and lacking *any* generally recognised skill, they lack salient non-transferable skills. In the past, this has provided the basis for movements for a district-wide minimum wage (see for example Hobsbawm 1964: ch. 10; Hyman 1971a). However, there are few workers who in reality are wholly unskilled; and it is normally easy for labourers, but difficult for craftsmen, to make upward pay comparisons within the workplace. This point is considered further below.
22. Where contractors are employed in a factory or site, their rates of pay provide

'were less committed to the Company and expressed a willingness to move if "something better turned up" and many were looking for or had looked for other jobs' (p. 142). Wedderburn and Crompton summarise the contrast between the two groups with the argument that the attitudes of skilled tradesmen to their work situation could be understood 'only by reference to their craft training, to their craft ethos and their sense of independence of any single employer'. Hence 'in explaining the attitudes and behaviour of the tradesmen it appeared to be at least as important to look outside the immediate work situations as at factors within it. . . . For the general worker, however, the evidence pointed to factors in the immediate work situation having a considerable impact upon certain attitudes and behaviour.'

Another important difference between craft-conscious and other groups of workers, and the unions which represent them, has been analysed by Turner (1952, 1957b, 1962). He argues that 'open' unions containing lower-skilled workers have tended to take the lead in movements for general pay increases; whereas 'closed' craft-oriented unions have been preoccupied with the maintenance of traditional differentials. In part, this difference may reflect the situational logic of a group of manual workers who are normally at the top of the manual pay hierarchy.[23] Other manual workers can select the higher earnings of those above them as a target for their own aspirations. But craftsmen would normally have to turn to *staff* employees to find a higher-paid comparison group within the firm; and such a comparison, as the previous discussion had emphasised, is conventionally excluded from the horizons of manual workers. Hence it is not surprising that craftsmen tend to evaluate their pay by external comparisons and by defending their differentials *above* other groups of workers. (In addition, of course, their relationship to the pay of different crafts may be of special significance.)

A related question is the *meaning* of pay for different occupational groups. As Katz (1954:95-6) has indicated, this cannot be assumed to be a constant. Money is not so much an end in itself

---

a natural focus of comparison for maintenance and construction workers. Thus the CIR (1972: 25) considered variations in terms and conditions among contractors at the Alcan site in Northumberland to be a major source of grievance and conflict.

23. If they are not — as is the case, for example, with maintenance craftsmen in steel or with some time-rated craftsmen in engineering piecework factories — then their discontent is likely to be intense.

as a means to the satisfaction of other wants and desires; and the more extensive the operation of market relationships, the more varied the potential uses of workers' earnings. Thus 'we do not know what workers are dissatisified with when they find their earnings unsatisfactory. . . . To understand the basis of wage dissatisfaction and industrial conflict would entail a thorough study of the worker's total life space.' A man may be concerned primarily to obtain material security for himself and his family; or he may wish to improve his immediate standard of living; or he may seek those consumer goods which represent 'the symbols of prosperity demanded by group standards'; or he may simply take it for granted that his income should increase steadily over time.[24]

Another possible motive has received particular emphasis from writers in the 'human relations' tradition: pay can have important symbolic significance. One worker has written (Sutcliffe 1969:295) that in demanding more money, workers are in part 'seeking those things that make them human — a certain dignity, a measure of equality, and above all their self-respect. In our culture, a man's pay is a status symbol as well as a means of existence, so "not getting the rate for the job" is a blow to a man's pride as well as his pocket.' Similarly, a study of coalminers (Dennis *et al.* 1957:65) has emphasised that 'a man's status as a strong and skilled worker, and as a man worth his pay, is conveyed by what shows on the pay-note'. Whyte (1955:218-25) has argued that in most workplaces there exists an informally recognised hierarchy of social status and prestige, reflecting such factors as the relative skill or experience required in different occupations and their importance in the work process. Earnings are expected to reflect and symbolise this prestige hierarchy; hence any imbalance between the social and economic status of a group is likely to generate discontent and conflict. Sayles's research (1958:153) has indicated a similar inter-

24. Conversely, as Patchen (1961) suggests, future prospects may be taken into account when appraising present pay. Hence favourable promotion opportunities, or the expectation of progression along an incremental scale, may colour attitudes to existing relativities. This may be particularly true in white-collar employment hierarchies (e.g. university teaching or the civil service), where promotion aspirations may induce junior staff to regard with equanimity the far higher salaries of their superiors. While similar opportunities for advancement are rare indeed in manual employment, Turner (1952) has suggested that the promotion structures in steel production, coalmining and cotton spinning help explain the unusually large pay differentials in these industries.

relationship of occupational prestige and attitudes to pay. This is obviously a relevant consideration in explaining the preoccupation with differentials often displayed by higher-skilled workers: the lower-skilled workers, being normally the poorest, might be expected to be particularly concerned with the *material* question whether their pay is adequate for a tolerable standard of living; whereas the higher-skilled, being less acutely subject to problems of simple subsistence, might be expected to give more attention to the *symbolic* aspect of wages.[25]

It would be wrong to assert a simple dichotomy between comparative or symbolic and material meanings of pay. Comparisons are implicit in any definition of a minimum 'living wage', and notions of tolerable subsistence will vary between different social strata (witness the recent discovery, in certain Sunday newspapers, of the phenomenon of 'middle class poverty'). This, indeed, is a basic proposition of reference group theory. Moreover, in a society in which massive resources are devoted to the advertising of consumer goods, there are strong pressures to induce a constant upward revision of the norms of an acceptable standard of living.

Changes in the cost of living may also affect perceptions of pay, a primary concern with symbolic or status implications giving place to greater awareness of standard-of-living considerations. Such changes have formed the focus of research by Behrend, who comments (1964:92) that

> the frame of reference for judging the fairness of a particular wage-rate may be a reference group or reference person but it could also be something quite different such as the cost of living, one's past experience of incomes or one's present knowledge of incomes in the labour market. What complicates the problem is that one may apply different frames of reference at different points of time and in different situations; and that one may apply several frames of reference simultaneously.

25. Maslow's (1943) theory of a 'hierarchy of needs' has often been applied by social psychologists to argue that pay loses its salience for the employee once subsistence needs can be adequately satisfied. The above analysis implies, on the contrary, that pay may remain salient but its *meaning* for the worker may alter. For this reason, the concept of 'instrumentalism', defined primarily in terms of preoccupation with monetary rewards (e.g. Goldthorpe *et al.* 1968; Ingham 1970), may be an inadequate category for the analysis of workers' orientations since it does not distinguish between the material and symbolic aspects of monetary rewards. One author associated with this perspective (Lockwood 1960) has argued, correctly, that it is 'sociology gone mad' to assume that a worker's desire for material rewards 'is necessarily a desire for the "status symbols" of the middle class'. Yet, equally, it would be wrong to discount the possible strength of status considerations within the manual working class.

Thus a major criterion in a worker's appraisal of his pay may be whether money income has risen in proportion to the cost of living. This is apparent, for example, in the study of Reynolds and Shister (1949:23): the most often cited single factor in comments on a fairness of wages was the 'cost of maintaining an adequate standard of living'. Similarly, Behrend *et al.* (1970b:29) have reported, on the basis of their Irish survey, that 'the most frequent specific statement made for considering that certain people were underpaid was "the cost of living" '.

Two propositions might plausibly be adduced in this context. The first is that such considerations are particularly likely to be made explicit in periods of rapid price inflation. The second, suggested by Behrend (1964:92-3) is that 'inflation represents a fluid, dynamic situation where reference points are shifting through time; prices and incomes are rising, blurring and eventually invalidating the original reference points. The shifting of the reference points makes it difficult to obtain a clear picture of one's financial situation.' The fluidity of the situation could be reflected in the simultaneous use of conflicting frames of reference. Thus, 'many individuals seem to use past prices as an essential frame of reference for judging current prices' — even though their *incomes* may have risen faster than prices. Hence in some circumstances, employees may experience inequity on the basis of comparison over time even though their incomes have in fact increased, since they fail to relate accurately their perceptions of changes in their costs and income.[26] Behrend's research (1964 and 1966) suggests that perceptions of price movements are typically imprecise. Knowledge of past — or indeed present — prices of specific commodities or services is limited; and a generalised awareness of an inflationary process apparently creates a readiness to assume that *any* specific price is rising: 'the expectation of upward movements of prices in time of inflation becomes a frame

26. Behrend reports (1973: 22-4) that 59 per cent of respondents to a survey in 1966 considered that their income had not kept pace with rising prices; amongst the lowest occupational categories the proportion was considerably higher. While precise calculation is impossible, it seems unlikely that so high a proportion in reality suffered a decline in real incomes; thus Turner and Wilkinson (in Jackson *et al.* 1972) calculate that there was on the average a small increase in the real net incomes in this period — although the rate of increase was slowing considerably. In their Irish survey in 1969 Behrend *et al.* (1970b: 31) found that over half the respondents thought their standard of living had improved; only 16.8 per cent considered that there had been a deterioration — though again, this view was more common among the lowest occupational categories.

of reference for prices' (1964:99). The tendency to believe, erroneously, that certain commodities have risen in price may generate a cognitive exaggeration of the rate of inflation which feeds back upon the perception of pay: hence Behrend's finding (1966:281) that 'a tendency to make high price judgments was associated with discontent with present income'.[27]

Leaving aside the implications of inconsistent frames of reference or inaccurate perceptions of wage or price movements, it should be noted that no simple relationship need exist between the trend of real income and satisfaction with pay. Such a relationship is apparently assumed by Behrend when she writes that 'with incomes, comparison with past and lower earnings should in theory provide a favourable picture' (1964:103). Yet a significant improvement in real income over time may be part of an individual's *expectations*; in which case any increase which fails to meet these expectations may be unfavourably regarded. Moreover, the elements of reference group theory already considered are relevant here. An increase which does not equal (or is thought not to equal) that achieved by another salient individual or group may be considered inequitable. Or if a pre-existing differential which is considered unfair is reduced but not eliminated, this may still be considered unfair.

A further problem arises at this point. While it is perhaps a commonplace that the higher paid are particularly concerned with differentials, there is far less agreement on *how* differentials — and movements in differentials — are perceived. If it is the *proportionate* relationship between incomes which is salient, then a general flat-rate increase would be perceived as narrowing differentials, and a percentage increase as maintaining them. If on the other hand it is the *absolute* amount which is salient, then a percentage increase would be perceived as widening differentials and a flat-rate increase as maintaining them. Assuming that the prevailing differentials are uncontroversial, which perspective is applied will determine whether a given wage increase is perceived as fair or unfair. Empirical evidence on this question is somewhat inconclusive. Reynolds and Shister (1949:29-30) found a fairly even division of worker attitudes: 54 per cent of respondents to a fixed-choice question favoured flat-rate increases, 42 per cent favoured percentages, while 4 per cent were undecided. It is interesting that the responses revealed no

27. This process can of course be affected also by inaccurate perceptions of past and/or present income and hence of the movement of pay.

significant difference between higher- and lower-paid employees. The absence of any clear-cut worker tendency towards one or other perception of differentials is also suggested by a survey of white-collar employees, by Hinrichs (1969). Asked to state salary increases which they would consider large, small, and average for themselves, higher-paid respondents specified figures which were higher in absolute terms but smaller proportionally than lower-paid.[28]

There are other studies which suggest that self-interest may be more directly reflected in the choice of perspective. Turner (1952, 1957b) has argued that the structure of trade union organization and collective bargaining tends to determine the type of wage increases negotiated: where the lower skilled (who are numerically predominant) are reasonably influential, flat-rate increases are normal; where the higher-status employees are dominant, percentage increases are common. Historically, in both Britain and the United States (and recently in Sweden), higher-paid minorities have revolted against union policies of pursuing flat-rate increases. In the Irish study by Behrend *et al.*, as seen earlier, the higher paid alone were likely to volunteer a percentage figure as a fair increase for themselves. Conversely, representatives of the lower paid have recently emphasised that 'ten per cent of damn all is damn all'. In this context, however, it is necessary to bear in mind the extent to which *inconsistent* frames of reference can be applied to incomes: the same individual may partially accept the logic of the arguments for the fairness of *both* flat-rate *and* percentage increases. As Wootton (1962:139) has suggested, 'in ordinary life there are, no doubt, occasions when it is appropriate to reckon differentials in absolute terms, and occasions when percentage comparisons are more appropriate'. In such a situation, external influences may exert a crucial influence. For example, the tendency for the incomes policy norms of the 1960s to be cast in percentages appears to have set the perspectives for public discussion of pay movements. The initial formulation of the Heath government's pay restraint policy in late 1972 was in terms of a flat-rate £2 norm: later *both* approaches were combined in the £1 plus 4 per cent formula. It is too early to consider

28. At the two extremes, those earning below $400 a month named on average $76 as an 'average' increase for themselves; this represented a 22 per cent advance on their existing salaries. For those earning over $2,000, the average figure mentioned was $191 — an advance of 8 per cent.

what effect this change might have on attitudes to pay differentials and movements.

The above discussion has considered various ways in which the 'logic of the situation' appears to influence the choice of pay comparisons. Yet, as several authors have argued, such choices at times appear to have very little logic about them: custom and tradition often provide the only obvious rationale.

> There is . . . a logic and meaning to the internal rate structure. Nevertheless, there is some danger of becoming too sophisticated in our analysis. . . . There is hardly a rate for which a plausible case could not be made for at least a modest change. Because of the indefiniteness of wage standards, such a change in either direction would be approximately as logical as the existing rate. Still most workers on most jobs continue to accept existing differentials. A partial explanation is that the rate becomes so closely associated with the job that, in one sense, it is the job. One job may be a 'better' job than another simply because it pays more. The social structure in the work environment adjusts to, and builds upon, the rate structure as it has traditionally existed. Ambitions are centred upon working up the wage ladder, with complex seniority patterns woven into the promotional customs, and the social standing associated with the particular job is to a considerable degree dependent on the rate. A worker who might tear up the plant to correct a 10-cent accounting error in his week's pay might also work all his life without seriously questioning a rate for the job (Livernash 1954: 332-3).[29]

W.A. Brown (1973) documents a variety of examples from British engineering factories where what are, to the outsider, gross anomalies in relative earnings are accepted as legitimate — or at least, 'treated fatalistically' — on grounds of custom alone. At a more general level, the same rationale may also apply. Williams (1956:629-30) argues that 'when we talk . . . of comparable occupations and comparable skills, we are thinking backwards. We know that over a considerable period of time certain kinds of work have afforded similar standards of living . . .; and it is this knowledge which makes us class them together.' Thus a circularity of reasoning occurs: 'the job that once achieves high pay continues to stand high in esteem because the pay is proof that it deserves to. Equally, what costs little may be thought worth little' (Phelps Brown 1962:132-3). The conservative implications of this force of tradition — 'the authority of the "eternal yesterday" ' (Weber 1948:78) — have already been mentioned and will be considered further in a later part of this book.

29. This latter point suggests a warning that it is dangerous to exaggerate employee commitment to traditional pay relationships. At Pilkingtons in 1970, such an accounting error *did* provoke serious questioning of the established rate for the job.

Conclusion

There are many evident parallels with the findings in the previous chapter. Appeals to the notion of fairness are regularly made in the course of discussions of wage relativities. Implicitly or explicitly, such appeals assert the relevance of certain aspects of the employment situation in comparing the income of one individual or group with that of another. In other words, certain similarities or differences are cited as justifying the payment of similar or differential wages, or certain changes in earnings. Empirical evidence indicates that the choice of pay comparisons is typically unambitious and powerfully shaped by custom: major inequalities which form an established part of the incomes hierarchy are rarely a focus of contention. This is to suggest that the choice of comparative reference groups is structured by an acceptance of prevailing norms of the 'proper' rewards and status of different socio-economic groups; or at least by a belief that large inequalities are 'natural' and inevitable. To explain the prevalence of such generalised normative assumptions, it is necessary to take account of broader societal relationships of power and value-formation: topics which will be examined in Chapter 7.

However, studies also indicate that pay comparisons can generate discontent and conflict even when their focus is relatively narrow.[30] Even when comparison groups are selected from within a narrow occupational and socio-economic range, relative deprivation may still be experienced with some intensity. In so far as employee perceptions of pay contain elements of imprecision, inconsistency and volatility, the scope for conflict is further accentuated. Yet these same characteristics entail that the 'spontaneous' comparisons and perceptions of employees may be 'processed' by the various institutions of industrial relations so as to contain their disruptive potential. The operation of such institutions provides the focus for the chapter which follows.

30. This doubtless helps to explain the interpretative dispute, noted at the outset of this chapter, as to whether pay comparisons are a source of conflict or stability.

Chapter 4

Mechanisms of Adjustment

The discussion in the two previous chapters points to a degree of normative consensus underlying both the arguments and the actual practice of those involved in industrial relations. Furthermore, the values which are generally embraced tend implicitly or explicitly to underwrite the inequalities of power and material advantage in industry which were described in the Introduction. What, in effect, is the meaning of the widespread endorsement of the notion of 'a fair day's work'? That those employed in uncongenial circumstances and in conditions of subordination should recognise an obligation to obey the orders of those with managerial authority and to perform tasks designed to create profits for the privileged minority who own industrial enterprises. And what perspectives towards pay relativities stem from the normal use of the notion of 'fair comparisons'? That the main structure of income inequalities is to be taken for granted, and hence that debate should focus exclusively on perceived anomalies of a parochial nature.

To anticipate the argument of a later chapter: this may be viewed as one aspect of the more general phenomenon of ideological formation within our society. There are identifiable social processes which shape the prevailing beliefs and values in a manner favourable to social stability and the interests of those in positions of power and privilege. But at the same time, the acceptance of the prevailing values in their general and abstract form by those who are relatively powerless and underprivileged does not preclude attitudes and actions in relation to concrete and specific issues which create conflict and instability. This also is apparent in the context of industrial relations. Employees who endorse the general notion of 'a fair day's work' may nevertheless dispute particular definitions of their precise work obligations; and pay comparisons, however parochial, may still generate intense controversy, and result cumulatively in acute problems of management both at the level of the individual enterprise and the overall political economy.

The Management of Discontent

For any student of industrial relations it is obvious that a measure of normative agreement within a society is no guarantee of industrial peace. Yet equally it is plain that the potential for practical disagreement does not erupt continuously into overt conflict. Strikes are of course regularly accorded serious problem status; and sociologists regularly emphasise the far greater incidence of less dramatic and often 'unorganised' forms of industrial conflict. But industry still functions; economic life continues with only sporadic interruption, and this indicates that the conflicting interests, objectives and aspirations of different groups are for the most part sublimated and accommodated. The study of industrial relations is thus in large measure the study of those institutions and processes which contribute to this sublimation and accommodation. In this chapter we examine a number of these processes, from the informal workplace accommodations of employees and management representatives, through the official negotiations of trade unions, to the increasing interventions of governments in industrial relations.

The paradox of conflict — the dynamic whereby hostile relationships in some circumstances become, if not amicable, at least characterised by 'antagonistic co-operation' — has long been a focus of sociological interest. The insights developed at the turn of the century by Simmel (1955) have more recently been elaborated into Coser's theory (1956) of the 'functions of social conflict'. His argument is, in essence, that when conflict is openly articulated there develop institutions for its peaceful resolution. Over time the opposing parties construct mutually acceptable processes for resolving disputes and acquire a commitment to the maintenance of stable and predictable relationships. Hence conflict becomes in large measure routinised, its scope delimited, its disruptive potential attenuated.

If proposed as a general theory of conflict — an argument that openly expressed conflict *necessarily* engenders the means of its own regulation — Coser's analysis is clearly absurd. As a theory of tendencies which can in some circumstances exert a dominant influence it is far more plausible; and indeed the 'institutionalisation' of industrial conflict is regularly cited as an example of such tendencies in operation. The primary source of this institutionalisation, it is often suggested, is an ambivalence inherent in the very function of trade unions. Unions are concerned on the one hand with the articulation of employee interests in respect of income distribution and the control of production in opposition to the conflicting interests of employers; on the other with the preservation of their own organisational integrity and security, and the bargaining relationships in which they participate. Union representatives are subject to constant pressure (most evident in the case of full-time officials but no less real for lay representatives) to act, in Mills's famous phrase (1948:9), as 'managers of discontent'. They express, and in some circumstances actually stimulate, their members' consciousness of grievances; yet at the same time they seek to limit the expression of industrial conflict to forms over which they can exert control, and which do not jeopardise the arrangements and understandings developed with employers. The formally established machinery of industrial relations often serves, moreover, to transmute the very nature of employee grievances, by defining issues within a narrow focus which shapes the parameters for potential resolution; fundamental questions of principle are typically suppressed and compromise is thus facilitated.[1]

The Negotiation of Order and the Effort Bargain

In what respects does the process of 'management of discontent' impinge on potential conflict over conceptions of fairness in industrial relations? It has been seen that divergent standards of a 'fair day's work' only infrequently kindle open hostilities between employers and workers. As will be indicated, the formal institutions of industrial relations play an important part in controlling conflict over standards of work performance. But there is also considerable evidence that less formal processes of negotiation and accommodation exert a significant influence: that the 'informal system' of industrial relations in Britain, often identified as a source of

1. For a more detailed discussion of the institutionalisation of industrial conflict, see Hyman 1971b and 1972b; and for the specific implications of grievance machinery, see Hyman 1972a.

disruption, nevertheless contains tendencies which accord with the analysis of Simmel and Coser.

It is a commonplace that much workplace industrial relations in Britain is so informal that the notion of collective bargaining can be only loosely applied: the processes involved are to a large extent 'unwritten understandings, informal arrangements and customs and practices' (Clegg 1972 : 250). For some analysts, the resulting standards and conditions of work are determined autonomously by work groups in a situation where — at the point of production — their power to disrupt is greatest and the efficacy of the managerial control system most tenuous. Hence 'if the collectivity is powerful and management complaisant enough, the collectivity may be able unilaterally to establish norms of its own either in the form of explicit rules or in the form of "custom and practice" ' (Fox 1971:136). The corollary is often implied (or explicitly asserted) that any attempt to justify and legitimise such norms is merely a superficial rationalisation. Yet as Brown indicates in his study of this process (1972:60), 'shop stewards are not primarily opportunists who seize upon management aberrations in order to advance custom and practice'. The force of tradition in general — one of Weber's ideal-typical bases of legitimacy — in British industrial relations, and of appeals to 'custom and practice' in particular, indicates that the principle has a moral content which is recognised by workers and employers alike. It constitutes in effect a countervailing source of legitimacy to that of managerial authority, thus providing a respectable rationale for workers or shop stewards to raise a demand and for managers to accede to it. Moreover, the concept is sufficiently imprecise in its empirical applicability to be employed extensively; hence its use can at times represent a mere rationalisation of simple bargaining power. Nevertheless, the insincere appeal to normative criteria pays dividends only to the extent that it is parasitic on sincere usage: for otherwise the currency becomes devalued. And there is much evidence that norms and standards proclaimed as custom and practice, far from reflecting work-group initiative in the face of employer passivity, often represent the outcome of a *reciprocal* relationship between management and workers.

Here the concept of 'negotiated order' — originally applied to the study of social relations in a hospital (Strauss *et al.* 1971) — is of explanatory value. The term serves to indicate that where activities within an organisation require the co-operation of individuals and groups with divergent attitudes and interests, there is a natural tendency for understandings, agreements and rules to emerge from processes of formal and informal negotiation. The relevance of the idea of 'negotiated order' for industrial relations analysis is accentuated by the fact, emphasised in Chapter 2, that the effective functioning of contemporary economic organisations requires not merely passive compliance but active co-operation from participants at every level.

A very similar interpretation of the genesis of social norms is offered by Barth with his assertion of their 'transactional' character: they are created, he argues, through an ongoing social process involving relations of reciprocity; hence they represent 'the cumulative result of a number of separate choices and decisions made by people acting *vis-à-vis* one another' (1966:2-4). Barth illustrates this interactionist perspective with the example of the development of an 'effort bargain' in Northern Norway. In a locality where fishing was traditionally carried out part-time on a small scale by subsistence farmers, semi-permanent employment on large new trawlers was offered by outside fishing companies. The terms offered appeared so attractive to the local farmer-fishermen that waiting lists for employment developed; but labour relations on the trawlers were unsatisfactory and turnover was high. Barth argues that the balance of costs and benefits in the new employment — higher income as against loss of autonomy and leisure, and disruption of home life — could not be realistically assessed in the abstract. The fishermen could only attempt to define their ideas of a 'fair' wage when this became 'the object of transaction and choice'; and when experience showed their initial judgments to be unsatisfactory, these were 'adjusted and changed through a process of bargaining, trial and conflict over the terms of the transaction' (pp. 18-19).

The interactionist interpretation of the sources of social order, elaborated in its most ambitious form by Berger and Luckman (1967), has been applied by other writers who suggest that similar processes are apparent in microcosm in the context of workplace bargaining. Dalton (1950) was one of the first to note how first-line foremen, stripped of many of their traditional official prerogatives by the rise of union organisation and the provisions of collective agreements, 'sought to control, or at least bargain with, the union in officially unacceptable ways'. The dynamics of such 'fractional bargaining' have been analysed in detail by Kuhn (1961:118-19), who argues that 'the more freely foremen can work out local, immediate arrangements in their departments, the better can they fulfil their production goals'. The (often elaborate) grievance arrangements in American collective agreements, if ruthlessly exploited by workers and their stewards, could hamstring first-line supervision; hence foremen are concerned to minimise the submission of formal grievances by their subordinates, and to ensure the flexible application of those provisions in the collective agreement which restrict their own autonomy.

> Since the guarantees of the grievance procedures and the collective agreement restrict foremen's pursuit of both aims, they find informal problem-solving with the aid of the union representatives or, if necessary, fractional bargaining the most satisfactory method of treating shop and worker problems. Those foremen who had few complaints about grievance handling were men who treated few, if any, formal grievances but who were adept at inducing or forcing their stewards to settle problems fractionally and with but passing regard for the collective agreement.

Such 'fractional bargaining' may apply, tacitly or explicitly, to the operation of a payment by results system. Roy (1954) described the acquiescence of first-line supervision in workgroup 'fiddles' which had the consequence of facilitating the flow of production. In Britain, Lupton (1963:154) has reported a similar relationship of reciprocity. Workers in an engineering factory had clear norms of the behaviour appropriate to a foreman: he should be available when help was needed with a work problem, but should not otherwise interfere; in particular he should not interfere with practices which infringed company rules. If a foreman 'fulfilled these expectations, he received the collaboration of the operatives when he himself was faced with difficulties in fulfilling his programme. If he behaved otherwise, he forfeited his moral right to ask for help.' Similar relationships in other engineering factories have been described by Brown (1972 and 1973).

Part of the 'negotiated order' of workplace relationships may involve the trading of managerial leniency in enforcing disciplinary rules in return for the goodwill of employees and their representatives. Gouldner (1954a:173) has pointed to the ability of supervisors to use formal company rules as a bargaining counter in order to secure workers' *informal* co-operation. Rules in the plant studied were applied indulgently so long as employees remained co-operative; but the threat of more stringent rule-enforcement remained as a background sanction. Hence 'formal bureaucratic rules served as a control device not merely because they provided a legitimating framework for the *allocation* of punishments, but also because they established a punishment which could be *withheld*.' In Britain, McCarthy (1966:12-20) has noted an analogous use of formal rules as a bargaining counter; while Turner (1971:99-100) describes an interesting and more specific example relating to 'foreigners' (items made illicitly by a worker for his own use from company materials and in company time). In many engineering workshops, this practice is firmly embedded in custom; and attempts by supervisors to suppress it would probably fail or, if successful, would sour relationships. Turner cites one foreman who therefore encouraged his men to make foreigners *openly*; he hoped thereby 'to be able to retain control over them, and prevent *excessive* use of materials and time'.

These examples suggest that norms of work performance adopted by employees are likely to represent simply one element in an ongoing process of negotiated order. Such a process of negotiation is indeed inherent in Behrend's concept of the effort bargain; and she argues (1961:114) that mutual accommodation of normative standards is inevitable even where a formal system of work measurement operates. Precisely because effort-rating is a subjective exercise, the standards applied by the work study practitioner may conflict with those of the employees whose work is studied. Yet if the process is to prove acceptable to the workers, he must base his own standards on those which he judges are compatible with theirs. If he guesses wrongly, workers will object that they cannot achieve their normal earnings with their habitual level of effort; the job is then likely to be restudied and a new production standard fixed. In practice, Behrend concludes, 'setting production standards and piece-rate prices is a question of getting agreement between both sides as to what is the "right" standard and the "right" price for it. Close examination reveals that agreement on correct rates and standards is arrived at by a process of bargaining which involves the adjustment of standards to each other.'

There is much evidence, then, that the definition of work obligations in everyday employment situations can usefully be understood as an example of negotiated order. Yet what are the factors which shape the *outcome* of this process — often tacit and informal — of accommodation and agreement? Clearly important are the perceptions and aspirations of the parties among whom order is negotiated. Managerial standards of performance will be substantially modified, if at all, only if workers seek to impose a far more restrictive interpretation of their obligations; if they demonstrate, in Zweig's terms (1951:24), a 'restrictive spirit'.

> Most employers state emphatically that the restrictive spirit harms more than restrictive rules. In fact every legitimate and commonly agreed practice can become restrictive if the restrictive spirit is infused into it; then every rule and regulation will be misapplied, and work will slow up considerably. Men disgruntled or frustrated treat all the rules and instructions cynically, not caring about the job, often intending to frustrate the work of others as well as their own.

By contrast, employees may display the opposite attitude: a spirit of complete co-operation. Mathewson (1931:9) emphasised that his study of 'restriction of output' provided a one-sided account of workers' attitudes: many examples could be cited of workers voluntarily maintaining a high level of exertion without expecting special reward. (Though how extensive such 'Stakhanovism' may be is perhaps questionable.)

It is likely that the orientation displayed will reflect the *meanings* which his work holds for the employee. A sense of exploitation might be expected to stimulate the 'restrictive spirit'. 'There is no more fatal obstacle to efficiency than the revelation that idleness has the same privileges as industry, and that for every additional blow with the pick or hammer an additional profit will be distributed among shareholders who wield neither' (Tawney 1961:78). By contrast, a co-operative orientation — Durkheim's 'organic solidarity' — is most likely where work is seen as an element in a collaborative social process. What is at issue, then, is the ideology and social imagery held by employees and generated not only within work itself but in social life generally.

An adequate understanding of such social imagery — whether, for example, the structure of economic relations is visualised in primarily class terms — is impossible without analysis of the general societal processes of ideological formation; and these will be considered in a later chapter. It is true that Lockwood (1966:249) has emphasised that 'for the most part men visualise the class structure of their society from the vantage points of their own particular *milieux* and their perceptions of the larger society will vary according to their experiences of social inequality in the smaller societies in which they live out their daily lives'. Variations in such localised situations and experiences clearly help to explain some of the differences in work orientation between employee groups. (Another important factor is the 'non-rational' character of traditions as a basis for standards of work performance: this may account for otherwise inexplicable differences in behaviour in apparently identical contexts.) Yet awareness of the range of variations in employee attitudes must not be allowed to obscure the underlying uniformities. The perception of employment in explicitly exploitative terms would entail the holding of an oppositional or radical value system and is an untypical employee perspective.

Thus for reasons which will be elaborated when the general problem of ideology is considered, most employees mediate their employment experiences through a frame of reference (incorporating the concept of 'national interest' and the 'teamwork' model of the enterprise)[2] which is at least conducive to the adoption of an internalised work ethic. These experiences may indeed induce limitations and qualifications to the acceptance — previously discussed in Chapter 2 — of the legitimacy of managerial work instructions. Nevertheless, it defines the *point of departure* for typical employee perceptions of work, and thus serves to limit the challenge posed to managerially prescribed standards of performance.

It is worth noting at this point that managerial standards are themselves open to considerable variation. Two factors appear of importance here. The first is the stringency of the economic constraints under which the employing organisation operates, and hence the pressures to minimise labour costs. The second is the scope available for lower-level management — who are in immediate contact with subordinate employees — to engage in informal agreements and understandings which further their personal interests and facilitate their immediate tasks of co-ordinating production but may conflict with other (particularly longer-term) objectives of higher management. This scope will be considerably influenced by the level of managerial expertise and the sophistication of management information and control systems. The evidence suggests that these factors play a large part in determining the degree of managerial leniency in relation to discipline, work standards, payment systems, and 'custom and practice'.[3]

2. For a comprehensive survey of British studies of employees' social imagery, see Bulmer 1973.
3. See for example Gouldner 1954b; Lupton 1963; Brown 1972 and 1973.

The outcome of the process of workplace accommodation and negotiation is also likely to be influenced by the degree to which it is institutionalised through trade unionism. Here the previous discussion of the 'management of discontent' is of crucial relevance. Collective bargaining tends to accommodate employees to a status of subordination; and there are both practical and ideological reasons for this. In so far as unions' central function revolves around negotiations with employers, the limits of practical trade unionism are set by what can be achieved within an employment structure in which managers control and workers obey. At the same time, as is argued in Chapter 7, 'trade union consciousness' is structured by the prevailing social values which take for granted the inevitability and desirability of capitalist relations of production. Trade union negotiation thus focuses on the *detail* of worker obligations rather than the *principle* of hierarchically structured authority and the subordination of social relations in industry to the dictates of profit. Hence the *general* tendency of collective bargaining is to reinforce managerially defined perspectives on worker obligation.

A number of specific consequences of this tendency have been documented. Stable collective bargaining appears to be associated with a *reduction* in a variety of forms of employee interference with managerial production goals: in 'restriction of output' (Webb and Webb 1897:308-9; Leiserson 1931:163) and in 'restrictive practices' generally (Zweig 1951:21); in the use of the 'go-slow' as a pressure tactic (Hammett *et al.* 1957:127); and in industrial sabotage (Taylor and Walton 1971:237, 242). This can be readily understood in the light of the argument by Fox (1971:150-51) that representation in rule-making increases employee commitment to the resulting norms and standards, even where the substantive effect of such representation for the *content* of rules is only marginal. Hence collective bargaining can act as 'a means of restoring authority relations when they have broken down as a result of normative conflict. It restores "consent".' Those who analyse industrial relations in terms of 'institutionalisation' insist that collective bargaining transforms industrial conflict from an unorganised and destructive to an organised and constructive form, and hence helps accommodate employee actions and aspirations to the 'legitimate expectations of management'. Trade unionism permits debate around the terms of workers' obedience, while not challenging the fact of their subordination; thus while the outcome of collective bargaining can be fully acceptable to employers its consequence is typically to strengthen workers' sense of moral obligation. While 'negotiation of order within the enterprise takes place only at the margins' (Fox 1973a:219), the 'myth of achievement' cultivated by union representatives themselves and by a variety of external commentators adds to the ideological pressures on employees to observe the dominant work ethic.

In these ways, collective bargaining can increase employees' generalised endorsement of managerial authority and their own obligation to perform a 'fair day's work.' Yet it has already been emphasised that there exists a gap between such generalised values and the concrete definition of 'fair' standards of performance. This gap can itself be bridged by collective bargaining. Thus trade unions may negotiate over and agree to systems of job evaluation and work measurement; payment by results systems based on work study alone (rather than on 'mutuality' between operator and rate-fixer); measured day-work; productivity schemes which allocate a range of decisions over labour utilisation to managerial initiative or to formalised negotiation. The tendency of all such developments, as Flanders has emphasised (1970:204), is 'to strengthen managerial control over pay and work through joint regulation'. Partly this is because managerial objectives themselves are usually more explicitly and ambitiously defined in such a process; partly because the formalisation of negotiations over the effort bargain reduces the leeway which can be exploited by employee groups in informal arrangements with lower-level management; but also because such agreements involve endorsement by trade unions of the *principles* underlying managerial definitions of performance standards, and hence undermine the legitimacy with which employees can assert divergent standards. The importance of this endorsement of managerial conceptions of the effort bargain is very clearly stated by Flanders (p.202):

> If shop-floor agreement is lacking, or only grudgingly given, one has to expect that workers and their representatives will try to 'buck' or 'bend' the system to their advantage; and their opportunities are legion. Managements who assume that men will work only for money, that there are no other sanctions apart from pay for influencing work behaviour, are denying themselves other possible ways of meeting their own responsibilities. One has not to take an over-optimistic view of human nature to recognise that when job performance is governed by a set of agreed rules, and when the rewards attached to performance are thought to be justly determined, there is a much greater prospect of workers feeling a sense of obligation to give a fair day's work and of shop stewards using their influence to see that this happens. Joint regulation leads to involvement and a sharing of responsibility.

Again, it is evident that such 'sharing of responsibility' facilitates a normative integration of employees which is highly advantageous to those who own and control economic enterprises. Management, in Flanders's much-quoted phrase (1970:172) 'can only regain control by sharing it'. The unstated corollary is that employers regain control *from* rank-and-file employees by agreement *with* union representatives, whose collaboration reflects distinctive interests and perspectives. Hence the paradox, impressively documented in Herding's study (1972), of 'more union influence, less labour power'.

This leads to the final point to be mentioned as a determinant of the content of performance standards: the distribution of power. As was evident from the previous discussion of 'negotiated order', interactionist sociologists who employ this concept emphasise the extent to which those without formal authority within an organisation have power to influence its internal relationships — power of which those in authority must take account. Similarly, many commentators on industrial relations stress the power of work groups to frustrate managerial objectives if their own aspirations are neglected.

The fact that effective economic performance presupposes not merely the physical presence of the employee at the workplace but his active co-operation, initiative, and discretion clearly does represent a source of power; for the threat to withhold co-operation can constitute a potent sanction. Yet exclusive attention to the disposition of power at the point of employment involves the neglect of *broader* structures of power in the economy and society. Ownership and control of economic resources provide the power in large measure to define the structure and objectives of employing organisations, and to mould the beliefs and values of those who are employed. Thus the power of work groups is essentially defensive and reactive: if their views and wishes are ignored, employees may be able to obstruct the implementation of managerial decisions; but they are in no position to impose radically new policies or priorities. And even this negative power is constrained by the realistic appreciation within most employee groups that resistance to specific management policies which is carried 'too far' will not be tolerated — a consideration particularly salient for trade union representatives who are especially concerned to safeguard the bargaining relationship with management.[4]

4. For a particularly clear analysis of the constraints which this fundamental power

The general theoretical issues which centre around the interpenetration of power and ideology will be examined further in Chapter 7. At this stage, however, the preceding analysis may usefully be summarised. The general work ethic and the particular conceptions of a 'fair day's work' prevalent among employees are unlikely to diverge radically from managerial expectations. Normative conflict does indeed occur, but its disruptive potential is to a large extent sublimated through an ongoing process of accommodation and negotiation in the workplace, in which the reality of the external system of concentrated economic, social and political power exercises an important constraining influence. The formal institutions of trade unionism and collective bargaining also play an important part in sustaining employees' practical acceptance of their subordination to managerial control.

Collective Bargaining and Pay Comparisons

The influence of collective bargaining institutions on the formulation of standards of a 'fair day's work' is for the most part indirect; but their impact on conceptions of 'fair comparisons', as we suggested in the previous chapter, is direct and clearly apparent. If, as Clegg suggests (1971:21), 'comparisons are the basis of all ideas of fairness in relation to pay,' they constitute the bread-and-butter of trade union argument over wages. Hence it is not surprising that the role of trade unions in structuring pay comparisons is regularly emphasised, in studies of industry-wide and domestic bargaining alike.

The use of comparisons by official union negotiators has been internationally documented. Backman, for example, in his survey of criteria employed in wage bargaining, reports (1959:18) that 'wage comparisons provide the key facts relied upon by labor and management in many negotiations. . . . Comparisons with wages in other companies or in other industries frequently are the core of the material considered in collective bargaining.' In Britain, Wootton has demonstrated the parallel importance of comparability, and has noted the common practice 'of carrying comparisons far back into history' (1962:133). Within the public sector, the principle of 'fair

---

disparity imposes even on a consciously oppositional and militant shop steward organisation, see Beynon 1973.

comparisons' has for many groups been formally institutionalised, so that the earnings increases received by specified external 'analogues' are automatically matched. (We consider the role of the government in relation to pay comparisons in more detail in a later section.) The apparent influence on negotiators of the principle of comparability, even in the absence of such a formal commitment, led many commentators, a decade or so ago, to diagnose a marked uniformity in national negotiations through the ritualistic imitation of a small number of 'key bargains'. Flanders, for example, suggested (1958:118) that 'the pattern for the annual round of increases is set by one or two industries by the essentially competitive process of "coercive comparison" '. More recently it has been argued (Jackson *et al.* 1972; Jones 1973) that wage increases agreed in industries with high productivity growth set the standard for negotiators throughout the economy, with inflationary consequences.

In reality, the principle of comparisons is not so mechanically adopted as this argument suggests. The fact mentioned earlier, that comparisons may be made in either absolute or percentage terms, provides one obvious complicating factor in applying the principle: it would in any case be far too simple to suggest that the process of comparison is the only determinant of pay settlements (whether or not this is the principal basis of workers' pay *aspirations*). Hence it is significant that a detailed analysis of wage settlements by Knowles and Robinson (1962) emphasises the *lack* of uniformity in increases agreed within each 'wage round' (and indeed that the notion of a distinct wage round is itself in large measure a myth). This accords closely with the verdict of Routh (1965:152) who, while emphasising the long-term stability of wage relativities, points to 'transient advantages which may be of considerable importance to the parties concerned, and may give groups of workers advantages that are obscured in long-term comparisons'.

One explanation of this finding, consistent with the discussion in the previous section, might well be that there exists a threshold beyond which alterations in the relative positions of different industry groups are likely to become particularly salient for those adversely affected. While variations in individual settlements may be too small to generate considerable discontent among those whose relative position deteriorates, the cumulative effect over a longer period may be to breach the threshold and stimulate urgent trade union action to restore the traditional relationship. Of the many such instances in recent year, two well-documented cases may be noted. Ford employees, whose earnings during the 1960s fell progressively behind those of pieceworkers in the Midland car firms, tolerated this situation until the end of the decade when the demand for 'parity' was widely voiced. Pressure arose initially at rank-and-file level, but wage relativities were documented in detail in the claim officially submitted at the end of 1970 (TGWU 1970). The campaign for parity with the Midlands, backed by industrial action, served over a two-year period to narrow inter-company differentials considerably. In coalmining, a remarkably similar pattern occurred: over a number of years earnings fell relative to those in manufacturing industry; but pressure (again initially unofficial) for the restoration of the previous relative position developed only at the end of the 1960s. This resulted in the substantial claim of 1972, justified primarily in terms of the trends in comparative wages (Hughes and Moore 1972) — a claim which after massive strike action was largely successful.

At plant level, by contrast — precisely because of the proximity of internal reference groups — comparisons may be expected tc be applied with greater immediacy. An early post-war study (Derber 1955:56) found that, in the Birmingham area, 'in the light of continuous bargaining over job and personal rates, one of the frequent sources of grievance was the allegation of inequities between jobs'. Similarly, McCarthy (1966:17) has reported that stewards in his studies most commonly resorted to comparability arguments in support of claims and grievances. Demands for extra payments, regrading, or other improvements in conditions were justified by reference to the superior advantages of 'another individual or group in similar circumstances, or employed on similar work'. Where concessions had been made to some other individual or group, demands for parallel improvements were based on the principle of 'equity' or 'fair treatment'. And 'even if the groups or individuals concerned were clearly not employed on similar work, or were already paid more money, arguments based on comparisons could still be made on grounds of the need to maintain existing relativities and differentials between them.'

While the main emphasis in these studies is on comparisons internal to the establishment, Lerner and Marquand (1963:290) stress the successful use by engineering shop stewards of *external* comparisons. Earnings information from other workplaces was obtained from unofficial combine committee meetings and quarterly district meetings of the Engineering Union, and was then used as a basis for domestic pay claims. In this way, pressure arose for the generalisation of increases obtained in the most favourably placed factories, regions and industrial groups. Turner *et al.* (1967:138-44) have pointed to the same institutional processes underlying pay comparisons in the specific context of the motor industry. Yet while such external comparisons may provide the basis for some of the most dramatic pay disputes and pay movements at plant level, internal comparisons seem far more common in routine and domestic bargaining situations. In a study of engineering negotiations in Coventry (Hyman 1972a), comparisons with other groups within the plant were employed overwhelmingly as the primary rationale for claims for straightforward pay increases. In Lerner *et al.'s* later study (1969:51-2), the importance of internal comparisons has also been documented.[5] Turner *et al.* (1967:63 also report that in the motor industry 'very many of the strikes officially classified as due to demands for wage-increases in fact spring from differences in rates or earnings between related jobs in the same plant or firm'.

For some writers, this central importance of comparability in pay bargaining is taken as clear evidence of the impact of ethics in industrial relations. Leiserson, for example, has claimed (1966:8) that 'worker protest against the competitive market concept of the employment relationship is one of the foundation stones upon which the institution of trade unionism in the United States has been erected. It is of the essence of trade union wage policy that wage rates be judged in relation to such non-economic criteria as "fairness" and "equity" and to seek to establish wage relationships that can be rationalized in terms of non-market values.' Yet an obvious problem which arises is the *sincerity* of appeals to values in

5. From the list of claims cited — which give the rationale used to support wage claims — it would appear that internal comparisons were twice as common as external. The findings of the Government Social Survey (1968: 28, 79) are also relevant: they show that shop stewards considered internal comparisons a more important argument in negotiations than external, whereas works managers and personnel officers thought external comparisons the more convincing. This apparent discrepancy may reflect a tendency for claims based on internal comparisons to be more readily resoluble at the level of junior management; and also the preoccupation of many managers with real or assumed labour market competition.

the context of collective bargaining. What distinguishes the collective bargaining situation from the contexts normally considered by reference group theory is that pay comparisons are deliberately articulated in order to influence the perceptions of other social actors. Thus the choice of pay comparisons may reflect more practical motives than the mere avoidance of cognitive dissonance.

One of the most familiar arguments on this score has been developed by Ross (1948:51-2).

> Comparisons are crucially important within the union world, where there is always the closest scrutiny of wage agreements in the process of negotiation as well as of those already negotiated. They measure whether one union has done as well as others. They show whether the negotiating committee has done a sufficiently skilful job of bargaining. They demonstrate to the union member whether he is getting his money's worth for his dues. . . . There is an additional reason why going rates and going increases are likely to be followed. The ready-made settlement supplies an answer, a solution, a formula. It is mutually face-saving. The employer can believe that he has not given away too much, and the union leader that he has achieved enough. It is the one settlement which permits both parties to believe they have done a proper job, and the one settlement which has the best chance of being 'sold' to the company's board of directors and the union's rank and file. One can understand why wage negotiations are often stalled until an applicable 'pattern' develops, and why the employer is then reluctant to grant anything more and the union to accept anything less.

The susceptibility of managements to comparability arguments is open to a variety of interpretations. Hazard has stressed the reluctance of managers to become involved in disputes in which normative criticisms of their actions may have damaging economic or political consequences. 'A judgment is exercised, moral in nature: "Am I right enough so that big, scarce customers and big, powerful competitors will be tolerant while we have this out?" ' (1957:47). For Robertson (1970:21-2), an important factor is the influence on managers of the labour market theories of classical economics: they fear that if the wages offered fall below the 'going rate', labour supply problems will inevitably ensue. Other writers have argued that the principle of 'fair comparisons' is attractive to employers since it tends to ensure that increases in one company's labour costs apply also to those of competitors.

On the trade union side, likewise, the use of moral argument can be related to manifestly practical concerns. Standardisation of wages, a prominent concern of nineteenth-century unionism, may be viewed primarily as a means of reducing competition in the labour market and enhancing union job control: 'in the hands of the craft amalgamations, the "standard rate" represented less a principle of social equity . . . than a method of exclusion' (Turner 1962:203).

Similarly, the trends towards the narrowing of skill differentials in the present century may be interpreted less as a consequence of egalitarian sentiments than as a reflection of the internal pressures of trade union politics.[6] The use of comparisons may also be analysed as an element in the strategy of self-commitment, which forms an important element of theories of bargaining (e.g. Schelling 1956; Walton and McKersie 1965). If union negotiators shape their members' aspirations by convincing them that a particular pay comparison is appropriate and fair, the parameters of success in bargaining are thereby defined. The union representatives may then be able to convince the employer that membership expectations will not permit them to settle for less than this comparison implies. (Conversely, company negotiators may seek to persuade the union that *they* are committed to a different set of comparisons.)

It is not therefore surprising that some writers have reacted cynically to the usage in industrial relations of ethical arguments in general and the principle of 'fair comparisons' in particular. According to Ross (1948:8), 'wage policy is not explained by the hortatory slogans of the labour movement — a fair day's pay for a fair day's work, a living wage, a health and decency wage, a productivity wage, and so forth'. As we saw earlier, Wootton (1962:100-101) has also regarded sceptically 'the modern tendency to deal in ethical currency'. The implication, she insists, is not 'that wage decisions have suddenly become moral . . . but that those who make them recognise the need for their justification in moral terms . . . . Those who speak for vested interests must, in fact, as much as anybody else, use the moral currency of the community which permits the growth of those interests.' Hence it is argued that appeals to fairness and the articulation of comparisons reflect a deliberate strategy designed to add legitimacy to a negotiating position which may derive from quite different considerations. The relevance of legitimacy is that it increases the 'chances of securing willing compliance' (Fox 1971:32). Workers who are convinced of the justice of their demands are more likely to support them in strike action than workers who are not so convinced; and managements presumably are not unaware of this. Managements who sense that a demand is fair may well feel less justified in resisting than if they consider it unreasonable. Moreover, each party may seek indirectly to influence the other through an appeal to what is conventionally

6. This has been argued in detail by Turner 1952.

termed 'public opinion'; and 'the public is always better at ethics, which are warm and real, than at economics, which are cold and abstract' (Wootton 1962:100).

Yet does the pragmatic basis of normative arguments in industrial relations imply that their use is necessarily insincere? Were it universally the case that such arguments represented nothing but 'devices necessary to clothe a pragmatic position in moral respectability' (Wiseman 1956:255), their credibility — and hence their practical rationale — might be expected to evaporate. If appeals to fairness were not at times made sincerely, their insincere use would have no point. Hence, as Clegg has put it, 'any negotiator knows that half his art consists in distinguishing between those comparisons which have to be taken seriously and those he can neglect' (1971:21).

One reason for regarding ideological or normative factors as more than a cloak for a simple power relationship is the evidence that positions of power are not always effectively exploited. For some three decades a spectre haunting economic analysts has been the bargaining power potentially at the disposal of labour in the absence of mass unemployment of inter-war proportions. 'Making the labour market generally a seller's market rather than a buyer's market will increase permanently the bargaining strength of labour. . . . There is a real danger that sectional wage bargaining . . . may lead to a vicious spiral of inflation' (Beveridge 1944:199). The fear was thus that trade unions, following the logic of traditional economic analysis, would use their favourable market position to raise wages; and that this would confront employers with the choice of raising prices or accepting a relative decline in profits. Such action, it was (and is) almost universally agreed, is necessarily 'irresponsible'. What is significant is the extent to which this highly ideological notion of responsibility has indeed influenced the practice of official union negotiators for much of the post-war period. Notions of responsibility have normally ensured relatively modest wage aspirations; and the principle of fair comparisons, in this context, is likely to ensure that modest achievements are generalised. As Allen argues (1966:30), unions 'do not measure each of their acts against the possibility of maximum achievement because the whole range of their expectations is trimmed. There has developed a myth of achievement whereby unions have an illusion which magnifies fractional changes in wage rates or marginal improvements in employment conditions into resounding successes.' This is to suggest, then, that in national negotiations ethical arguments may *constrain* the use of union power rather than being cynically adopted for its maximum exploitation. This point has been neatly captured by Wootton (1966:17) in his comment that 'full employment provides the golden opportunity, ***but it need not be seized***'. To exploit an advantageous market position, what is also necessary is a 'propensity to bargain'; and it is this which prevailing ideologies of fairness characteristically inhibit.

This same argument is relevant in the context of shop-floor negotiation. As suggested in the previous chapter there is considerable evidence of situations in which employees' norms of fair comparison possess little obvious rationale. Thus minor anomalies may provoke serious discontent while (to the outsider) more glaring inequities are ignored. The chaotic structure of earnings levels and movements often reported in piecework engineering factories (e.g. Robinson 1970) appears to indicate that such restricted frames of reference impinge on the actual processes of domestic pay determination. While coercive comparisons do occur they are not applied ruthlessly and systematically. This is indeed implied in the Report of the NBPI on Payment by Results Systems.[7] In a much-quoted passage the Board commented (p. 29) that 'once a PBR system gets out of effective management control, it takes on a life of its own as individuals and groups seize on any chance of raising their earnings to the level that they think is "fair"'. Yet, conversely, as many writers have indicated, such groups rarely exploit their ability to manipulate the system *beyond* the level of earnings which they consider fair. W.A. Brown (1973) has analysed the factors internal to shop-floor union activity which serve to sustain this self-restraint; and he has also called attention to the necessity for 'bargaining awareness' before workers even begin to exploit their potential to raise earnings. And Sisson (1975) has argued that while newspaper workers have exploited their strategic position to achieve the highest earnings of any manual occupation, their notions of 'fair comparisons' nevertheless set limits to their pay aspirations.

This indicates that the interaction of power and values in the process of wage determination — of which the use of pay comparisons is merely one aspect — involves a relationship of

7. Report No. 65, Cmnd. 3627 (May 1968).

considerable complexity. Thus Flanders (1970:227-8) has insisted that while the use of comparisons in negotiations is evidently affected by the pragmatic concerns of the negotiators themselves, the 'social, indeed cultural factors' associated with workers' own normative standards can exert an independent influence. Hence 'the force of comparability seems in fact to be compounded of a mixture of considerations of administrative convenience (administrators on both sides can more easily defend a settlement which is based on an already established pattern) and of its being accepted as a rough measure of social justice (why should we fall behind the rest?)' (p. 163).

If material and ideological factors are both of importance in influencing the process of pay determination, however, it would appear that they interact in a manner singularly unfavourable to the interests of trade unionists. For as argued above, normative conceptions of their own value structure workers' pay aspirations, and also influence the confidence with which they apply their collective strength in support of these aspirations. The power workers' dispute of 1971 exemplifies the inhibiting consequences of insufficient ideological self-confidence: the limited industrial action in which they engaged clearly demonstrated the strategic power which they possessed, but the ideological onslaught unleashed in the media induced them to end their dispute on what at the time appeared highly unfavourable terms. Hence the ability to provide a convincing ethical rationale for their aspirations and actions would appear a precondition for the successful pursuit by trade unionists of ambitious pay demands; and access to such moral justification is restricted by the framework of the dominant ideology. Yet even if such an ethical rationale can be effectively applied, it is not a *sufficient* condition for success. Clegg has made this clear, in referring to government policies which have caused a relative decline in earnings in the public sector. 'Trouble has concentrated, as might be expected, where there are powerful unions' (in Hughes 1972:105). Groups with the power to cause serious disruption — or with the social status to command respect — have been most successful in achieving the implementation of 'fair comparisons'. By contrast, such groups as postal and hospital workers — whose case, even within the restrictive framework of conventional notions of fairness, was extremely cogent — found that their arguments could be ignored because of their lack of similar strategic power. To summarise: employee groups without adequate collective strength are unlikely to benefit significantly from moral righteousness; yet the limited availability of normative rationale for the pay demands of stronger groups is likely to inhibit the effective exercise of their power.

One context for the interaction of power and values in pay determination is represented by the existence of specific occupational institutions and traditions which provide *both* a public definition of a high level of worth *and* the strength to enforce a correspondingly high level of rewards. Turner (1962:111) has stressed that in many industries 'the sharp demarcation between skilled and unskilled workers . . . is largely a product of the traditional apprenticeship system, by reference to which those who may perform "skilled" tasks are distinguished from those who may not. . . . The allocation of jobs has, in effect, been adapted to a classification of workers, rather than the classification of workers being based on the nature of the jobs they do.' The 'device of restriction of numbers', as the Webbs called it, may have had its primary rationale in directly influencing the price of 'skilled' labour. Yet no less important — particularly in those occupations where apprenticeship has lost its status as the exclusive route of entry to the trade — is the *ideological* effect of the institutions of craft organisation in buttressing the mystique of skill and hence legitimising differential payment.

What is true of skilled manual occupations is of even greater relevance in the case of the professions — whose controls of job entry served as a model to traditional craft unionists and have not (unlike craftsmen's) lost any of their effect. It is here, as Mills (1951:137) has shrewdly noted, that 'the merging of skill and money' is often dramatically in evidence.

The legitimate predominance which the crafts have traditionally achieved within the hierarchy of *manual* occupations and incomes, the professions have established within the far broader hierarchy. As Johnson has made clear (1972:42-3), this represents the successful imposition of a definition — or 'mystification' — of the worth of an occupation which few groups in society can hope for. The professional institutions which underpin their members' economic power and buttress the ideology of professionalism are supported, in the last analysis, by the coercive sanctions of the state. This privileged position, as we argue in Chapter 7, can only be fully explained through an understanding of the interdependence of class and state power and ideological influence.

The more routine institutions of collective bargaining exert a less crucial but nevertheless important influence on conceptions of what are 'realistic' comparisons for the pay of less exalted occupations. Precisely because, as was suggested in the previous chapter, workers' reference groups are commonly characterised by imprecision, ambiguity and inconsistency, they are particularly open to such institutional patterning. And in so far as 'public opinion' is similarly characterised, institutionalised comparisons may pattern the prevailing notions of reasonable pay relationships between different occupations and indirectly influence the members of those occupations.

Many writers — particularly in the United States — have pointed to a tendency for collective bargaining to crystallise a limited range of shared conceptions of fair comparisons. According to Slichter *et al.* (1960:558), the reduction of controversy over pay relativities and the extensive agreement on 'rational' pay structures has been an outstanding feature of post-war American industrial relations. Leiserson has argued in similar vein that with the weakening of external labour market determination of pay levels, bargainers have been compelled to institutionalise other criteria. 'Without clearly recognizable and reasonably precise market criteria, informal wage-setting procedures inevitably generated internal wage relationships of a haphazard, chaotic nature, continually giving rise to feelings of dissatisfaction and inequity on the part of the workers' (1966:15). Yet union pressure to remedy perceived inequities 'stimulated and tended to formalise in turn the search for and use of comparative wage criteria', with the result that a 'patterning' of wage-setting became established (pp. 33-7).

The typicality of this consolidation of an agreed structure — whether intentional or otherwise — led Reder (1952:39) to comment that 'one hall-mark of a "mature" collective bargaining relation is a de facto agreement on the comparisons relevant in wage setting'.

In an influential analysis of these emergent processes of institutional patterning, Ross (1948) devised the concept of 'orbits of coercive comparison' and discussed the factors bearing on the salience of particular comparisons in collective bargaining. The local labour market, he argued, was of limited importance; the same was true of the product-market, unless standardised conditions were negotiated on an industry-wide basis. By contrast, the centralisation of bargaining within a union led to pressure to remove anomalies within the area covered; the common ownership of establishments tended to create pressures for company-wide standardisation; government involvement in pay determination provoked demands for uniformity of treatment; while unions involved in competition for membership sought to emulate and indeed exceed the achievements of their rivals.

In a later article, Kerr (1957) presented a slightly divergent analysis. Institutional policy, he argued, had virtually eliminated differentials among employees performing similar work in the same plant. Unionism had also narrowed differentials between firms in the same labour and product markets, and had had some effect on regional differentials. Their impact appeared least on differentials between occupations and industries. This pattern of influence Kerr related in part to the intensity of motivation for standardisation: as suggested previously, those differentials which are closest to hand are commonly most salient. But Kerr has also emphasised the importance of power relations in mediating these equalising pressures: 'group motivation to be effective must be expressed through the exercise of power, and this power may need to be exercised not only against "market forces" but also against the opposing power of organised employers or the state, and even against discordant factions internal to the union institution' (p. 185). Hence the elimination of interpersonal differentials might be welcomed by employers as an administrative convenience; while standardisation among firms in a labour or product market might be accepted as a means of preventing competitive 'leap-frogging'. Attempts to alter inter-occupational or inter-industry relativities, by contrast, would meet far stronger opposition. The implication of this analysis would seem to be that unions typically concentrate on those comparisons which it is most within their power to influence; and that this particular focus of union activity feeds back on the aspirations of union members.

Even within the categories analysed by Ross and Kerr, some comparisons are typically more compelling than others; and Dunlop (1957) has attempted to illuminate this fact with his concepts of 'job clusters' and 'wage contours'. The former are defined as groups of occupations within a firm among which pay comparisons are conventionally made and accepted as legitimate; they are mainly determined 'by the technology, the managerial and administrative organization of the wage determining unit, and by the social customs of the work community' (p. 16). The latter are defined as 'a stable group of firms (wage determining units) which are so linked together by (a) similarity of product markets, (b) by resort to similar sources for a labour force, or (c) by common labour market organization (custom) that they have common wage-making characteristics' (p. 17). Job clusters and wage contours are linked by 'key rates' of jobs accepted as specially relevant for both internal and external comparisons.

These analyses, while based primarily on experience in the United States, have an obvious bearing on the institutional structuring of comparisons in British industrial relations. Thus Crossley (1966:180) has cited the chain of events initiated by the reduction in the working week of 6,000 Scottish plumbers in 1962. While most of these worked for jobbing employers, some worked alongside building tradesmen on new construction. These latter claimed a comparable reduction; and after industrial action this was conceded to 80,000 workers by the Scottish National Joint Council for the Building Industry. This agreement was followed in negotiations in civil engineering, covering the whole of Britain; finally the comparability argument was successfully deployed on behalf of building workers in England and Wales. About a million workers thus gained the benefit of the original agreement. In another example, Clegg (1971:39-40) has called attention to the repercussions of the pay increases contained in the Fawley productivity agreements of 1960. These had no evident effects in the local labour market, for 'other firms in Southampton were not accustomed to taking their cue from Fawley'. But because of the institutional links between pay settlements in different oil companies, 'the Fawley agreement was soon followed by substantial pay increases in other refineries throughout the country'. Another interesting example of the effect of institutional processes on comparisons is documented by Sisson (1975). In Fleet Street newspaper offices, the most salient comparisons were traditionally between members of the same occupation in different firms. But from the mid 1960s — following the amalgamation of a number of separate occupational unions, and the negotiation of a series of 'comprehensive agreements' at company level, inter-occupational comparisons within each company became of greater significance.

It is important to note that while the conventions established by collective bargaining tend to institutionalise the salience of particular comparisons, they do not necessarily *stabilise* a pay structure. The burden of a multiplicity of studies of industrial relations in engineering, and in particular the motor industry, is that the practice of 'coercive comparisons' may generate a succession of 'leapfrogging' claims by sectional groups (e.g. Lerner and Marquand 1963; Turner *et al.* 1967; Scamp 1968; W.A. Brown 1973). A similar pattern is familiar in British shipbuilding (CIR 1971; Brown *et al.* 1972). Thus while collective bargaining may formalise and make concrete the choice of comparisons, and even consolidate a particular hierarchy, this need not extend to agreement on the exact relationship of each occupational group within the overall earnings structure. It is precisely for this reason that companies often seek to introduce formal job evaluation schemes, for their explicit purpose is to define narrowly and rigidly the criteria which may legitimately determine the pay relationships of occupational groups among whom comparisons conventionally occur.

The success of such attempts to 'rationalise' and hence control and stabilise pay structures may well depend crucially on the attitude of trade union negotiators. It has already been suggested that trade unionism tends to provide a certain generalised ideological support for a capitalist social order. Unions underwrite the existence of a wages system as natural, inevitable and legitimate by virtue of their very activity in bargaining — and at times fighting — over wages; while they add endorsement to the notion of the 'rights' of management even as they dispute the precise limits of these rights. But if unions agree to specific schemes of job evaluation (perhaps linked to a formal acceptance of management's right to impose 'scientifically' determined work standards) the advantage to employers is even greater. The typical consequence is to impose so powerful an influence on workers' perceptions of pay that 'disruptive' aspirations and behaviour are inhibited; and to give *practical* support to managerial control by precluding official union backing for rank-and-file resistance to decisions within the framework of such agreements.

Many American writers — as is apparent from the previous discussion — assume a natural trade union readiness to approve such developments. Several studies indicate that 'when a union is faced with *conflicting* pressures for adjustments of differentials from its members within one company then, unless the leaders of the union see it as in the interests of the union to stir up trouble, they have a strong motive to bring the wage structure under control' (Walker 1965:241). Such a motive might be considered particularly important in the United States, where it is normal for a single union to have exclusive jurisdiction over the whole manual labour force of a plant; in Britain, where intra-plant pay rivalries are often between members of different unions, the formal or informal stabilisation of relativities may be less readily imposed.

More general social pressures are also relevant. The ideology which condemns ambitious trade union demands as irresponsible and crudely aggresive, while welcoming timid bargaining behaviour as the embodiment of reason and statemanship, extends its definitions to trade union attitudes to procedural and institutional 'reform'. Leaders who accept (or indeed propose) structures which limit their members' ability to control autonomously their conditions of work or use workplace organisation to win pay improvements win virtually unanimous acclaim — from press, politicians, and academics — as men of vision exercising bold and effective leadership. Those who resist such developments, by contrast, are condemned as short-sighted, narrow-minded, and probably unreasonably constrained by hopelessly out-dated processes of internal union democracy. It would be surprising if such intense ideological pressure did not exert some influence; though other aspects of leadership orientations are also important, as of course are the power of the rank and file and their own responses to such institutional developments.

The factors which induce trade union representatives to seek to influence their members' reference groups have been systematically analysed by Lipset and Trow (1957). They argue (pp. 403-4)

> that political, union, and other leaders, in their efforts to manipulate the reference groups of their audiences, attempt to establish a 'sense of pertinent similarity' between the statuses of an audience and other specific groups or strata, *so that the ensuing comparisons will engender sentiments strengthening and supporting the position of the spokesman.* The consequences that follow upon such efforts may or may not coincide with the intentions behind them; but in any case, such purposeful efforts to manipulate comparisons compose a class of reference group determinants that should be taken into account. Union officials may point to an unfavourable wage differential in order to mobilize rank and file support for a strike. They may point to a favourable differential to demonstrate their own effectiveness to their members, or to unorganized workers. Labour leaders may also engage in multi-union bargaining to indicate the absence of differentials between their own contracts and those of other unions which are, for the membership, actual or potential reference groups.

In elaborating this argument, Lipset and Trow suggest that leadership attempts to manipulate comparisons are most likely in unions with an active internal political life. Inter- and intra-union conflict is likely to lead to attempts to extend comparisons. Successful manipulation of reference groups is possible only within limits: the comparisons proposed must not do violence to members' notions of legitimacy or their meaningful experience. Finally, the authors suggest, the manipulation of comparisons (possibly for short-term ends) may *permanently* alter members' frames of reference, possibly with unintended consequences.

This analysis presupposes an assumption of critical importance: that the arguments, policies, attitudes and interests of union *negotiators* need not be identical with those of rank-and-file members. Factors associated with internal union politics may inspire leadership attempts either to stimulate or to restrict the pay aspirations of their members. Such manipulation is likely to bear an intimate relation to the process of 'management of discontent' which was discussed previously: it helps ensure that members are neither too militant nor too apathetic. Thus Lipset and Trow suggest that where specific problems in the internal or external relations of union leaders may be eased by greater membership militancy, 'their manipulations of comparisons tend to emphasize the importance of general status categories as over against the spontaneous use of face to face intimates as comparative references' (p. 404). Where the desire is to 'cool out' the membership, by contrast, union leaders may seek to persuade them that only limited pay comparisons are 'realistic'. In either case, as Lipset and Trow indicate, there is a core of normative autonomy in workers' attitudes to pay which sets limits to the scope for effective manipulation: union leaders can merely influence members' reference groups within a range which is already structured. Their final point is also important: once a new comparison has been suggested to union members and embraced by them, a return to the previous restricted frame of reference may be impossible. In this manner the 'hortatory slogans of the labor movement', the importance of which Ross (1948:8) has treated somewhat dismissively, may have a powerful though indirect influence on union wage policy.

For Lipset and Trow's somewhat emotive terminology of 'manipulated' and 'spontaneous' references might be substituted a distinction between 'primary' and 'secondary' comparisons: this would indicate that the language and frames of reference of union negotiators may differ from those of the rank and file even in the absence of overt manipulative intent. Primary comparisons — those which derive from the immediate reference groups of union members or their representatives — may be regarded as important influences on the crystallisation of particular aspirations and demands, and thus as among the *motives* for the presentation of a pay claim of a particular level. Secondary comparisons, by contrast, are those which are self-consciously articulated within the bargaining context in order to *justify and legitimise* the claims which have been formulated. These may, but need not necessarily, be the same comparisons which are most salient in stimulating the claim in the first place; different arguments may be selected because they appear to possess greater cogency or plausibility in the bargaining context.

Where primary and secondary comparisons diverge, this may well indicate a tension between the reference groups spontaneously adopted by trade union members and the 'vocabularies of motive' accepted as appropriate within the institutions of collective bargaining. There are, however, good reasons to expect a reasonable degree of congruence between the two. For on the one hand, as has been argued, the institutions themselves exert a considerable influence over the choice of reference groups at employee level. Any disparity would be among the factors influencing union officials to seek to manipulate their members' frames of reference — often successfully. Conversely, where effective manipulation is impossible — as for example, when new orbits of comparison come to exert a powerful influence on the rank and file — then union negotiators will be subject to compelling pressure to accommodate their members' aspirations within the official bargaining processes.[8]

8. A recent example from British industrial relations is the demand by Ford workers for 'parity' with earnings in the Midlands motor industry. This same example demonstrates the importance of lay activists as a mediating force between rank and file and official leadership. Beynon (1973: 94) documents the contrast in attitudes between shop stewards and ordinary members at the Halewood plants, which spearheaded the parity campaign: 'while the majority of the sample of members based their evaluation of the firm upon their own immediate experience of the labour market on Merseyside, the stewards consistently tended to take a wider view. Frequently they based their evaluation of wage rates upon what they felt the company could *afford* to pay, supporting their arguments by reference to profits and the rates paid by other motor manufacturers in the Midlands.' These stewards played a crucial role in influencing union attitudes both upwards and downwards: crystallising more ambitious

The distinction between primary and secondary comparisons can be of considerable value in analysing whether the immediate aspirations of the members or the priorities of the negotiators are of greater importance in the formulation and pursuit of particular pay demands. But the two are so evidently reciprocally conditioning that there is little value in seeking to isolate the primacy of the one or the other in the general and long-term development of pay contributions in collective bargaining.

The same is true *a fortiori* of any distinction in terms of spontaneous and manipulated comparisons. For the burden of all the preceding discussion is that reference groups are never selected 'spontaneously': their choice is structured by a complex of material and ideological pressures. While union leaders seek at times to influence workers' reference groups deliberately and in accordance with their own particular interests, the same is true of employers and politicians. And such intentional manipulation itself occurs only within the restricted range left open by the more general and persuasive processes of ideological formation.

The analysis of these more general influences must await a later chapter. The broad conclusions of the previous discussion may however be summarised at this point. Pragmatic considerations of restricted power, together with possible normative considerations of legitimacy, inhibit those in subordinate occupational positions from posing any general and explicit challenge to the prevailing social and economic hierarchy. Thus the basic principles of a highly inegalitarian income structure are not seriously and extensively questioned: discontent focuses on more parochial grievances. The pressures towards a restricted frame of reference in evaluating incomes are both reflected in and reinforced by the official institutions of collective bargaining. Reference groups are unambitiously selected; and pay comparisons focus more commonly on *movements* in the pay of the reference group than on the absolute

comparisons and aspirations among their members, and compelling official negotiators to take account of these enhanced expectations. Such cases — of which there have probably been many in recent years — underline the danger of treating work-group attitudes to pay as stable and homogeneous. It is interesting to contrast recent official union responsiveness to more ambitious rank-and-file aspirations with experience in the United States, where union leaders have often proved insensitive to changing rank-and-file expectations (perhaps because of the bureaucratic isolation of centralised 'international' negotiators). The consequences have at times been explosive : see Seidman 1970.

level of earnings. They are thus applied in a manner which is primarily conservative, in terms of underwriting established relativities; and such conservatism is reinforced by the commitment to the institutionalised processes of 'realistic' compromise and accommodation which is central to the normal dimensions of trade union wage policy. Conflict and change are not, indeed, precluded: on the contrary; and such change and conflict may at times threaten serious political and economic instability. Yet from the perspective of the overall structure of economic inequality, the conflict and change inherent in the operation of pay comparisons cannot be considered more than marginal.

Fairness and Public Policy

There is, moreover, a further source of normative accommodation: for the mechanisms of adjustment in industrial relations comprise not only the autonomous arrangements of employers and unions but also the various forms of intervention by the state. In recent years this has of course involved comprehensive attempts to influence the process of wage determination. Traditionally, however, government policy in Britain has been characterised by 'voluntarism': a reluctance (except in the special conditions of wartime) to interfere directly with the operation of collective bargaining.[9] Yet for many years the state has been involved at least at the margins of British industrial relations. Perhaps most significantly, the notion of fair wages has long formed part of the official vocabulary of Great Britain and several other English-speaking nations; and the manner in which the concept has been officially defined has served to reinforce those modest perspectives which have been previously analysed.

In the 1880s 'fair wages' was the slogan of the successful trade union campaign for the inclusion of clauses in local authority contracts requiring private contractors to observe union wages and conditions; by 1894, according to the Webbs (1920:399) 'a hundred and fifty local authorities had adopted some kind of "Fair Wages"

9. This abstentionism reflected a pragmatically based trade union suspicion of legislative interference, a strong employer commitment to *laissez faire*, and the fact that trade union actions and aspirations could be accommodated without too much difficulty with the economic objectives of employers and governments.

resolution'. The first of a series of 'Fair Wages Resolutions' adopted by the House of Commons in 1891 obliged the government to include a somewhat weaker clause in its own contracts.[10] The Canadian legislature followed suit in 1900 while the principle of 'fair wages' was enshrined in early compulsory arbitration legislation in Australia and New Zealand (Burns 1926).

From the outset the official interpretation of fairness was based on two criteria. The first involved the notion of a *standard* wage — that prevailing in analogous employment, normally under a trade union agreement; the second, that of a *living* wage — the minimum necessary to support a socially defined standard of subsistence, in contrast to a 'sweated' or 'starvation' wage (Snowden 1912; Burns 1926; Bayliss 1962; Ford 1964). The original Fair Wages Resolution of February 1891 declared 'that in the opinion of this House it is the duty of the Government in all Government contracts to make provision against the evils of [sweating] . . . and to make every effort to secure the payment of the rate of wages generally accepted as current for a competent workman in his trade.'[11] Sydney Buxton, in opening the debate, insisted that 'all that is asked is that the Government shall accept as fair wages those which are fixed in the particular trade by negotiations between employers and workmen'. This implied reference to collective bargaining was made explicit in March 1909, when it was resolved that 'the Fair Wages' Clauses in Government contracts should . . . provide as follows: the contractor shall . . . pay rates of wages and observe hours of labour not less favourable than those commonly recognised by employers and trade societies . . .'.[12] These formulae enshrine the principles that were to predominate in official British wage policy for half a century: that fairness is represented by the 'normal' or 'standard' rates established through market forces mediated by the processes of collective bargaining;[13] while in exceptional circumstances where the wage established by such processes (or in the absence of collective regulation) prove inadequate, a more acceptable minimum should

10. For an account of the development and legal status of Fair Wages Resolutions, see Kahn-Freund 1954.
11. *H. C. Deb.*, Vol. 350, col. 647.
12. *ibid.*, Vol. 2, col. 425. This resolution was considerably elaborated and extended in 1946.
13. This principle was reflected not only in the Fair Wages Resolutions but also in the practice of wartime compulsory arbitration and the Terms and Conditions of the Employment Act, 1959, which replaced it.

be set by statutory machinery.[14] In practice, it should be added, a narrow definition is normally applied both to the scope of a particular set of 'standard wages and conditions', and to the minimum requirements of a 'living wage'.

A further reflection of these same principles is in the operation of Courts of Inquiry, official arbitration machinery, and other forms of government intervention. As has often been noted, such intervention has traditionally been somewhat marginal to British industrial relations: 'statutory machinery for the settlement of disputes is always subsidiary, always only a "second best", and intended to do no more than fill the gaps left by autonomous negotiation and arbitration' (Kahn-Freund 1954:89). Such intervention is indeed doubly marginal, in that the *principles* traditionally applied have been those which appear to underlie autonomous collective bargaining.[15] An early study (Fisher 1926:264-6) concluded that in so far as any general principles underlying arbitration awards could be detected, they were those already discussed: 'insistence on the payment of a minimum living wage'; and above this minimum, 'the wage level determined by competition'. A more recent analysis (Ford 1964) has pointed to the increasingly explicit use of comparability arguments, but otherwise draws very similar conclusions. Arbitration and inquiry have not generated 'a settled and consistent body of principles'; and this, argues Ford, is 'for the best of reasons: these bodies are not called upon to decide whether film stars should be paid more than shop girls, or doctors more than dockers, but to adjudicate on particular disputes about the amount by which an existing wage or salary, high or low should be somewhat increased or decreased'. More specifically, their role is to reach decisions on the basis of submissions made by the parties to the dispute themselves: submissions which typically 'assume the broad relationships between the various grades of employment as they are found in the market' (pp. 95-6).

The conservative implications of this mode of operation are

14. This principle underlies the Trade Boards Acts, 1909 and 1918, and the Wages Councils Acts, 1946 and 1959.
15. For a survey of the operation of arbitration machinery and related forms of government intervention, see Fisher 1926; Sharp 1950; Lockwood 1955; Ford 1964; Guillebaud 1970. The analysis by McCarthy and Clifford (1966) of the operation of Courts of Inquiry comes to conclusions similar to those cited in the text; they also point out that such inquiries have proved 'uncompromisingly hostile' to any rank-and-file action which challenges the authority of managers or union officials.

readily apparent. As Ford comments (1964:116), 'the awards of courts and the recommendations of committees accept and reflect, if they do not actually strengthen, the social values and social hierarchy of contemporary British society'. These institutional agencies of 'public policy' are grounded, in effect, on the conventional principle of fair comparisons; and the restrictive import of this principle has already been indicated.

It is not surprising that British governments — committed by the Fair Wages Resolutions to oblige contractors to observe comparability with the outside labour market — should long have regarded similar standards incumbent in their dealings with their own immediate employees. The anti-sweating spirit of the first of the Resolutions was applied to naval dockyards in March 1893 when the House of Commons resolved that 'no person . . . should be engaged at wages insufficient for proper maintenance'. The principle of comparability was extended to government munitions factories in 1904 with a resolution that unskilled workers should receive 'not less than the standard rate of wages for similar work in other employments in the respective districts'. A further resolution of March 1910 applied to government employees generally: their conditions 'should be in every respect at least equal to those observed by the best private employers or by local public authorities doing similar work.' Yet the concrete specification of comparable employment provided a source of persistent dispute. In the debate of March 1904, John Burns had argued that ' "Fair" was an unsatisfactory term, and might be interpreted in one way by a generous employer, and in another by a mean employer. The same remark applied to "current rate of wages" and "standard rate of wages".'[16] The common charge was that government departments, subject to tight Treasury control, were indeed mean employers. In 1916, for example, it was alleged that the War Office 'had taken the wages of jobbing blacksmiths, agricultural labourers and gardeners' as the basis of comparison for non-craft employees in rural areas.[17]

The implementation of the principle of 'fair comparisons' in the public sector in a manner acceptable to the unions concerned is a comparatively recent phenomenon, and moreover has been achieved mainly as the prerogative of the more advantaged sections of public

16. *H.C. Deb.*, Vol. 132, cols. 569-70.
17. G. Dallas, Workers' Union Triennial Conference, June 1916. See also Shepherd 1923.

servants. The most important landmark was the recommendation of the Royal Commission on the Civil Service in 1955 that comparability should be institutionalised in the non-industrial civil service.[18] Subsequently the unions affected reached agreement with the government that salaries should be determined by 'fair comparison with current remuneration of outside staffs employed on broadly comparable work, taking account of differences in other conditions of service'; and the Civil Service Pay Research Unit was created to compile data for use in the process of pay determination. In 1960 two further Royal Commissions, on the medical and dental professions and the police, proposed substantial salary increases on comparability grounds which set influential precedents for the treatment of these groups.[19]

Low-paid manual workers in the public sector have for the most part been less fortunate: in the absence of sympathetic Royal Commissions they have faced serious problems in achieving the acceptable application of 'fair comparisons'. Conflict has occurred both over the choice of external 'analogues', and over whether wage rates or actual earnings should be compared. The problem of analogues has been a recurrent problem in the postal service, and despite a Committee of Inquiry in 1964 was never satisfactorily resolved. In the industrial civil service, while analogues were formalised in agreements in 1956 and 1959, the comparison was made with wage rates which were substantially below the actual earnings of the analogues. The public sector manual group which achieved the most favourable application of 'fair comparisons' was perhaps the railwaymen, following the Guillebaud Committee of Inquiry of 1960; but in 1966 they were the first victims of the reaction against comparability, discussed below, in the report on their pay by the National Board for Prices and Incomes.[20]

It may be concluded that where the principle of 'fair comparisons' is institutionalised, the substantive question of fair pay for a specific occupation is delegated, in effect, to the decision-making authority of those external forces (market or otherwise) which determine the pay of analogous outside occupations. Controversy is thereby limited to the largely technical question (which can, in many cases, be

18. The Priestley Report, Cmd. 9613.
19. The Willinck Report on Doctors' and Dentists' Remuneration, Cmnd. 939, and the Pilkington Report on the Police, Cmnd. 1222.
20. Report No. 8, Cmnd. 2873 (Jan. 1966).

ultimately resolved by arbitration) of how the comparison process is to be implemented; whether the structure of external incomes can be *justified* is a question excluded from debate. (It is, presumably, taken for granted that the 'impersonal' operation of the outside labour market necessarily sets a 'fair' level of wages.)

Yet the principle of comparability, if rigorously and extensively applied, would eliminate flexibility in relative incomes; it might also require considerable increases in earnings levels for public employees whose bargaining power is weak. This helps explain the ambivalent application of the principle in government employment, particularly to the lowest paid; and also the growing government disenchantment in recent years with comparability as an element in incomes policy.

The notion that where pay in two industries or occupations has traditionally borne a definite relation, changes in one should automatically be matched in the other, necessarily precludes any government strategy to *alter* established relativities. In 1948 the government considered such alteration essential to encourage inter-industry labour mobility, and therefore in its *Statement on Personal Incomes, Costs and Prices* argued that

> the last hundred years have seen the growth of certain traditional or customary relationships between personal incomes — including wages and salaries — in different occupations. These have no necessary relevance to modern conditions . . . . These old relationships of income must, where necessary, be adapted to conform to the national interest. Relative income levels must be such as to encourage the movement of labour to those industries where it is most needed.[21]

Similarly, the 1962 White Paper *Incomes Policy: the Next Step* — while conceding that 'comparisons with levels or trends of incomes in other employments . . . will still have a part to play' — insisted that 'more regard will have to be given to . . . general economic considerations.'[22] The policy enunciated in 1965 added productivity and low pay as additional factors which might require modification of the principle of comparability. To explore these qualifications to 'fair comparisons' it will be necessary to turn explicitly to the role of incomes policies as mechanisms of accommodation in the process of pay determination.

21. Cmd. 7321 (Feb. 1948).
22. Cmnd. 1626 (Feb. 1962).

Incomes Policy and Social Justice

Ethical argument has played an important part in recent discussion of incomes policy, and its themes have involved the notions not only of fairness but also of justice. As we suggested in our Introduction, these two concepts imply distinct levels of judgment: while questions of fairness arise primarily in the limited context of the treatment of specific individuals or groups, questions of justice (and in particular 'social justice') submit to scrutiny the rules and definitions of rights and duties which underlie the social structure. Moreover, notions of social justice are typically employed with critical intent, to support claims for *redistribution* of rights or rewards. In the words of one political philosopher, 'the term "social justice" tends to issue from the mouths of reformers, and to be regarded with suspicion by those who are satisfied with the social order' (Raphael 1970:170).

This dimension of critical scrutiny and practical reform has been inherent in the rationale of the elaborate exercises in incomes policy devised by both Labour and Conservative governments. The Joint Statement of Intent signed in December 1964 opened with the declaration that 'the Government's . . . social objective is to ensure that the benefits of faster growth are distributed in a way that satisfies the claims of social need and justice'. Given the bitter opposition of the Labour Party and the trade unions to the Conservative policy of 1962 — including the refusal of the latter to co-operate with the National Incomes Commission — this rationale was clearly essential to win the support of the labour movement for the policy. The rhetoric of 'creating a socially just and defensible society' was used to great effect by George Brown in 1965 in persuading the TUC that his policy had 'nothing in common with the wage restraint policies of previous Conservative Governments'.[23] Similar language was adopted by the Conservatives after their reversal of attitude towards incomes control in 1972; the standstill legislation was presented to the Commons by the Chancellor as the first step towards a 'fair and just long-term policy'.[24]

The shift from the narrowly economic rationale of previous incomes policies is noteworthy. Historically, such policies emerged primarily (often, indeed, solely) as an anti-inflationary device in circumstances of national emergency. In the First World War, the

23. Conference of Executive Committees, 30 April 1965.
24. A Barber, *H.C. Deb.*, Vol. 845, col. 1009.

government made somewhat ineffectual efforts to restrain the level of wage increases. In the Second, government intervention — more systematic though less rigorous — was 'perhaps the most successful of all the attempts at an incomes policy in Britain' (Clegg 1971:1). The first explicit peacetime policy was launched in 1948 in a context of economic crisis. The government specified a single objective: 'to prevent the development of a dangerous inflationary situation'. Thus the government proposed (though it assumed no powers to enforce) a general standstill on incomes; the only exception specified was 'where it is essential in the national interest to man up a particular undermanned industry and it is clear that only an increase in wages will attract the necessary labour'.

Subsequent exercises in incomes policy were also framed within a predominant strategy of overcoming short-term economic crisis or long-term economic malaise. The Conservative government presented its 'pay pause' of 1961-2 solely as a stabilisation device, designed to keep money incomes from rising faster than the volume of national production. Exceptional treatment was considered justifiable only as part of an explicit productivity agreement, or to remedy or prevent a general labour shortage in an industry; or — subject to considerable qualification — out of regard to established principles of comparability. The terms of reference of the National Incomes Commission, defined in a subsequent White Paper,[25] incorporated a similar set of priorities. The only ethical question to be considered by the Commission was 'the desirability of paying a fair reward for the work concerned'. As argued above, such a reference to fairness could be — and was — interpreted in such a manner as to involve no interference with the established structure of incomes.

Yet the notion of incomes policy as an instrument of social justice had found influential advocates long before the Labour government came to office in 1964. Referring to the first post-war experiment, Wootton had commented (1962:108-9) that 'the 1948 White Paper is exceptional in its exclusive emphasis on what may be called old-fashioned economic criteria. . . . [It] represents a remarkable victory of economics over ethics. Such an attitude was, however, out of harmony with the mood of the times.' One indication of a changing 'mood' was Flanders's (1950) proposal — published as the trade union support which had allowed the government a brief

25. Cmnd. 1844 (Nov. 1962).

period of success for its strategy was disintegrating — for a national wages policy to be administered by a National Wages Board. In certain respects his suggested institutional machinery foreshadowed closely the National Board for Prices and Incomes, created in 1965. Wages policy itself, he insisted, should not be conceived 'only within . . . limited, economic terms of reference. It should also be related to the demands of social justice' (p. 6). More specifically, he suggested as objectives 'the simplification of the wage structure, which means the elimination of unnecessary and fortuitous wage differentials'; 'the establishment of a national minimum'; and 'a greater national standardisation of other conditions of employment'. Once these objectives were achieved, he concluded, 'it becomes possible to examine the remaining wage differentials rationally, that is according to their economic and social justification' (pp. 25-6). This particularly lucid presentation of the 'social justice' argument for incomes policy may be said to have defined the terms for much of the subsequent debate both on the general principles and on particular policy proposals.

We have seen that the strategy enunciated in 1964-5 was the first official endorsement of this perspective. Yet what were the practical consequences of a verbal commitment to the goal of social justice? The first White Paper defining the Labour incomes policy[26] specified a norm for wage increases of three to three and a half per cent, but specified four circumstances in which exceptional treatment might be justified.

(i) where the employees concerned, for example by accepting more exacting work or a major change in working practices, make a direct contribution towards increasing productivity in the particular firm or industry. Even in such cases some of the benefit should accrue to the community in the form of lower prices;

(ii) where it is essential in the national interest to secure a change in the distribution of manpower (or to prevent a change which would otherwise take place) and a pay increase would be both necessary and effective for this purpose;

(iii) where there is general recognition that existing wage and salary levels are too low to maintain a reasonable standard of living;

(iv) where there is widespread recognition that the pay of a certain group of workers has fallen seriously out of line with the level of remuneration for similar work and needs in the national interest to be improved.[27]

Much of this formulation parallels very closely the proposals of the

26. *Prices and Incomes Policy,* Cmnd. 2639 (April 1965).
27. These criteria, and their application, have been extensively discussed; see for example Clegg 1971 and 1972; Corina 1966; Jackson 1967; Fels 1972; Molhuysen 1971.

previous Conservative government. The first two 'economic' criteria echo those of its 1962 White Paper. The fourth criterion has practical implications very similar to those of the 'fair reward' clause in the terms of reference of the National Incomes Commission. It is the 'low pay' criterion for special treatment which represents the main innovation, and was proclaimed as the factor which transformed incomes policy from a negative mechanism of restraint into a positive weapon of reform. In subsequent formulations of the policy the same rationale was fervently articulated. 'Improvement in the standard of living of the worst-off members of the community is a primary social objective.'[28] 'The challenge which faces us as a socially just society is what steps we can now take to improve the lot of the low paid in an increasingly affluent society.'[29] The support of trade unionists for the policy was thus explicitly canvassed on the grounds that their own restraint would directly benefit the poorest and weakest sections of employees.

The practice, it is generally agreed, failed to match these pretensions. The National Board for Prices and Incomes (NBPI) interpreted the criteria for exceptional treatment in a restrictive manner, and the 'social' criteria especially so. The comparability formula — most readily interpreted in the conservative sense of maintaining traditional 'fair comparisons' — received short shrift.[30] In one of its earliest reports the NBPI rejected the Guillebaud formula for comparability on the railways;[31] while the discussion of pay in its first General Report was devoted almost entirely to an attack on the 'convention of comparisons' (1966:14-17). Thus the NBPI articulated strongly the qualifications to the doctrine of comparisons which were noted in the previous section: in so far as an aim of incomes policy was to alter established relativities, it was essential to reduce the force of comparison in wage determination.[32]

28. *Prices and Incomes Standstill: Period of Severe Restraint,* Cmnd. 3150 (Nov. 1966).
29. *Productivity, Prices and Incomes Policy after 1969,* Cmnd. 4237 (Dec. 1969).
30. The treatment of comparability in the 1965-9 White Papers and the Reports of the NBPI is discussed at length in Fels 1972.
31. Report No. 8, *Pay and Conditions of Service of British Railways Staff,* Cmnd. 2873 (1966).
32. The rejection of comparability was however never total: while it 'nearly always refused to recommend pay increases for one group because other groups had received *increases* . . ., the NBPI was in certain circumstances prepared to take account of comparisons of *levels* of pay' (Fels 1972:119). Moreover, the relaxation of government policy from 1969 was reflected in a more favourable disposition towards comparability arguments.

Yet this commitment to flexibility in the national wages structure was not seriously oriented to the redress of poverty and unemployment. The productivity goal held sway, and it was the Board's contention that productivity improvements would in themselves provide the source of such earnings increases as would solve the problem of low pay.[33] These priorities were incorporated in the White Paper *Productivity, Prices and Incomes Policy in 1968 and 1969*,[34] which defined productivity as the sole criterion for increases above the three and a half per cent ceiling. In consequence the NBPI was obliged to report that a seven per cent increase awarded to agricultural workers (the lowest-paid group in the country) was not permissible under the terms of the policy.[35]

One problem in applying the 'low pay' criterion was its lack of clarity or specificity: 'the definition of a "reasonable standard" is open to any interpretation' (Corina 1966:31). Yet as Clegg has pointed out (1971:21), whether there existed 'general recognition' that the pay of a group of workers was too low was a question which *could* have been tested empirically. The members of the NBPI, relying on their own intuitive judgment, found the whole question most perplexing. While conceding that 'anyone whose pay is scarcely above the level of national assistance is low paid', they went on to argue that 'by and large . . . the concept of the low paid is a relative rather than an absolute one; the most that can be said in most cases — and even this is difficult — is that pay is too low, or alternatively too high, in relation to somebody else's. What is at issue, therefore, is the question of differentials' (1967:15).

From this perspective, it is not surprising that the NBPI was less than optimistic in its view of the low pay question. In its first Report on agricultural workers it had set out the argument that no concrete definition of low pay was possible: any definition of 'standards of need' would involve 'highly arbitrary assumptions'; and need would in any case vary according to such factors as family size.[36] Defined as a question of relativities rather than of poverty, the problem of low pay appears to lose much of its urgency as a social issue, and becomes correspondingly more vulnerable to economic objections. 'If pay increases are confined to those at the bottom of the scale,

33. The Board also insisted that problems of labour shortage should be resolved through productivity improvements.
34. Cmnd. 3590 (April 1968).
35. Report No. 101, Cmnd. 3911 (1969).
36. Report No. 25, Cmnd. 3199 (1967).

there may be no incentive to others to acquire the necessary qualifications and skills needed to supervise them' (1967:15). Even when the NBPI, in its last specific Report (devoted to general problems of low pay), finally offered a concrete definition of the low paid as the bottom ten per cent of full-time manual employees, its view of the prospects for improvement remained pessimistic. 'Differentials are clearly not easy to change, and there are sound economic reasons why they exist and may even, in some cases, need to be widened' (1971:43). It was thus natural that the Board should be reluctant to assign any special priority to the low paid: 'except in a minority of instances . . . we consider that the improvement of the position of the low paid can be subsumed in the general problem of improving efficiency' (1969:21).

While all the Board's arguments possess some validity, cumulatively they constitute a general tendency to regard low pay as a very subordinate element in incomes policy. The Board expressed, in Hughes's terms (1972:165), a 'gradgrind philosophy'. There is evident logic in the contention that low pay can be defined only in relative terms (even if comparisons are implicit rather than explicit), and that the identification of low-paid workers requires empirical investigation of earnings. Yet the NBPI consistently presented data which appeared to *minimise* the severity of the low pay problem, by comparing for example lower-paid women with higher-paid women, lower-paid manual workers with higher-paid manual workers — when the majority of workers in these categories are at the lower end of the hierarchy of *all* earnings. Had the Board considered income differentials within this *broader* context, it might have found it far less easy to assert their economic justification. Moreover, the Board's emphasis on the historical stability of wage relativities appeared to suggest — intentionally or otherwise — that the scope for change was severely limited:[37] whereas the professed rationale of incomes policy was, by ending the traditional 'free-for-all' in collective bargaining, to permit a radical reform of pay relationships.

It could indeed be argued that the intractability of the problem of low pay derived less from the specific difficulties mentioned by the NBPI — for the implementation of *any* major social or economic reform inevitably confronts such obstacles — as from more

37. See, for example, NBPI 1971:40: 'the experience of this country and of others shows how difficult it is to improve low pay in relation to other pay'.

fundamental ideological and political constraints. The Board's own frame of reference clearly owed much to orthodox economic analysis: witness its emphasis on the importance of differentials as an 'incentive' to the acquisition of qualifications and skills. Such arguments totally ignore the *non-economic* advantages of higher-status occupations, a factor to which we shall refer in later chapters when we discuss the various influential attempts by economists and sociologists to justify economic inequality. Yet perhaps even more crucial is the failure to raise the question of *machinery of political control*: as many trade unionists have emphasised, no procedure exists whereby restraint on higher-paid employees might lead to the transfer of resources to the lower-paid, rather than simply to their own employers. To establish such machinery would be to attack a fundamental aspect of the structure of the political economy.

Hence it is not surprising that, as Clegg argues (1971:26), 'the Board did not really make sense of the low-paid criterion'. Or as the historian of the Board concluded (Fels 1972:132):

> The NBPI and the prices and incomes policies, both accorded a lower priority to low pay than to other wage problems. . . . The NBPI was less vociferous about low pay as a social and economic problem than about other wage problems. This illustrates a general theme which applies to nearly all of the NBPI's work. It did not regard the alteration of the existing distribution of income as one of the main purposes of incomes policy, unless greater efficiency or wage stability was likely to result.

The practical consequences were predictable. 'In view of the paucity of effort put into helping the low paid it is not surprising that the figures should show that they have not made relative gains since 1964. . . . So far from reducing inequities in relative pay, incomes policy has in its operation in the public sector increased them' (Bosanquet 1969:10). The Board's own statistics indicate that, over the period of its existence, the relative position of the low paid in general deteriorated; while Hughes suggests (1972:173) that 'within bargaining units, the lower paid have been accorded more priority since the collapse of incomes policy than they had during it'.

The orientation towards inequality of the Conservative government of 1970-74 was in no way more radical. Among its first actions were the introduction of tax changes which were specially favourable to the highest income groups; and the creation of a review body with exclusive concern with 'top salaries'. It endorsed the opinion of the latter that pay increases of up to £2,500 a year for Chairmen and Board members in nationalised industries (giving salary scales of up to £27,500) were 'the minimum required if confidence in fair treatment for the public sector is to be maintained'.[38] This was closely followed by the introduction of an incomes policy the first phase of which froze even-handedly the incomes of rich and poor alike (indeed arguably the higher-paid and higher-status groups were the least stringently affected, having access to promotions, increments and fringe benefits which were either exempt or could not be effectively policed during the freeze). The second and third phases of the policy (with their ceilings on increases of £1 per week plus 4 per cent, and £2.25 or 7 per cent) provided for some narrowing of percentage differentials but for their widening in absolute terms. The policy on relativities, enunciated at the beginning of 1974, envisaged alterations in the position of *individual* employee groups within a hierarchy the fairness of which was not itself in question. The problem was defined as one of exceptional groups which might persuasively argue a case for special treatment (Pay Board 1974); that there might be a *general* problem of inequality and low pay was implicitly denied. Despite the language of its supporters, the possibility that 'fairness' might require alterations in the broad structure of inequality (including, perhaps, reductions in the advantages of specially privileged strata), and not merely marginal improvements in the relative position of a limited number of special cases, was excluded from discussion.

Recent experience thus suggests that while some reference to social justice is apparently an essential element in the public relations which surround incomes policy, such considerations may have little visible effect on its actual content. Even where a genuine egalitarian commitment exists, this is likely to be subordinated to the traditional aims of government policy: the management of the economy *as it is at present structured*. Hence in the period of Labour government, the professed long-term social objectives were neglected as soon as they appeared to conflict with short-term economic ones. Flander's comments (1970:104-5) are particularly apposite.

> We come nearer to the truth of the matter and cut through the layers of cant under which it is submerged, once we recognise that impending balance-of-payments difficulties have been the principal factor in pushing governments into action over wages. Whatever theoretical arguments may be advanced on behalf of a national incomes policy, the practical considerations that have forced it into the foreground of public attention have usually sprung from this source. Labour costs in export industries — rather than earnings in general or still less wage rates as such — have

38. Review Body on Top Salaries, Report No. 2, Cmnd. 5001 (1972).

been the nub of the problem, and the main objective of government intervention has been to keep them competitive in relation to costs and prices abroad.

The implication would seem to be that — however sincere may be some advocates of incomes policy as an instrument of reformative justice — the rhetoric of equity is employed within public policy as a more or less cynical attempt to achieve worker and trade union support for restrictions on their bargaining activities. In this respect, notions of fairness and social justice are used for unashamedly ideological purposes.[39]

For our present purposes, the most significant point about such ideological usage is its relative efficacy. A policy which requires that wages and salaries should rise no faster (or even more slowly) than total production, and that individual increases should be subject to a more or less uniform norm, takes for granted the equity of the prevailing inequality.[40] As Shonfield (1969:217-19) has remarked, what is 'presented as a simple piece of economics is, in fact, a highly political argument'. The presupposition is that 'the existing division of wealth and the income derived from it [are] basically fair'; hence when its endorsement of the policy is required, 'labour is asked to give its consent to a particular type of social order'. For reasons which will be explored more fully in a later chapter, such consent *is* in large measure given. Trade unionists in general adopted the main premise of Labour's incomes policy: that a radical attack on major economic inequalities was out of the question; it was within this perspective that support was initially granted and subsequently qualified. These same assumptions appeared to underlie the tripartite discussions of 1972 which preceded the introduction of the Conservative policy; the talks broke down on matters of detail rather than on fundamentals, and trade union verbal opposition did not extend to a basic criticism of its primary rationale.

39. There are interesting parallels with the Redundancy Payments legislation introduced by the Labour government at the same time as its incomes policy was launched (though largely drafted by the previous government). While presented as catering primarily to the social needs of employees, Fryer (1973) has demonstrated that it was designed primarily to serve the economic needs of employers.
40. This characteristic is not peculiar to British incomes policies. Turner (1957a:19) concluded, from an extensive international survey, that 'whatever their methods, National Wage Policies have apparently included certain common features. First they have apparently accepted the existing range and structure of wage-differentials . . . . Second, such wage-policies have usually assumed the existing level of wages, and have aimed to stabilise it in some way.'

It might appear that proposals for incomes policy have acquired a more radical dimension with the agreement between Labour and the unions on a 'social contract' which places the issue of inequality on the political agenda. Yet it is significant that the notion of a social contract assumed central importance in British political theory, in the seventeenth century, as a device *to justify a social and political order which stabilised the existing distribution of property* (Macpherson 1962). Whereas the original version assumed the *imposition* of the social contract on the mass of the population, deprived of political rights through their lack of substantial property, its revival in the 1970s may be viewed as a bid for the active consent of an organised working class whose potential for economic disruption is self-evident. Yet the programme of reforms offered workers for their restraint involves only the most marginal challenge to the powers and privileges of capital; set in the context of the broad spectrum of inequality (in wealth, income and general life-chances, and in the whole complex of conditions, character and status of work) which were detailed earlier, the projected measures of equalisation are modest indeed.[41]

There can be little doubt that extensive acceptance of the 'fairness' of policies which confirm existing inequalities has an effect on the attitudes and aspirations of ordinary employees. The main effect of recent incomes policies has been to focus debate on the justification of *minor changes* in the structure of relative incomes rather than on the rationale of the structure itself. While empirical research is limited, Behrend's findings (outlined in the previous chapter) indicate that the rhetoric of equity has successfully influenced attitudes to pay: has reinforced those tendencies, already analysed, towards modesty in employee aspirations.

Conclusions

The importance of the various mechanisms of adjustment which

41. Fox exposes the spurious character of such attempts to contain workers' actions and aspirations within the limits set by the existing socio-economic order. 'The more government upholds a social system which, through its institutions of private enterprise, profit-seeking, market relationships and massive inequalities, sanctifies and institutionalises material and status self-seeking through power, the less the participants in such a system can be reached by moral appeals from government to restrain their own hand "for the common good" ' (1974: 169).

have been discussed lies in the fact that a considerable degree of normative consensus, particularly at the abstract and general level, is no guarantee against the occurrence of conflict. There are, however, evident tendencies for conflict in industrial relations to become institutionalised. This can occur, informally, through processes of 'negotiation of order' within the workplace; though its most obvious manifestation is in the activities of official trade unionism. While informal processes are probably most important in creating and maintaining an 'effort bargain' in face of the pressures of economic and technological change, the formal machinery of collective bargaining is of particular significance in structuring pay comparisons.

Yet while established collective bargaining relationships tend to institutionalise particular, more or less restricted, comparisons as the appropriate limits of employee aspirations, the structure of incomes is not necessarily stabilised; a process of 'leapfrogging' claims and settlements may well occur. It is in this context that government intervention reinforces the stabilising pressures. 'Public policy' embraces a conservative conception of fairness, shaped by an acceptance of the overall structure of the political economy. In the context of incomes policy this particular conception exerts a powerful ideological influence, and helps contain those unintended challenges to the structural stability of economic inequality which are inherent in the sectional processes of 'free collective bargaining'.

Chapter 5

Inequality and Economic Theory

Our discussion so far has been largely descriptive. The empirical studies we have surveyed have indeed been presented within an interpretative framework, but this framework has involved only a low level of abstraction, and has involved little attempt to transcend the perspectives of the participants in industrial relations. The aim of this second part of the book is to raise the level of analysis, considering the broader theoretical issues necessarily involved in a fuller explanation of what has gone before. The detail of the preceding chapters thus gives way to analytical generalisation. The focus of enquiry is as follows: what theoretical perspective serves best to make *comprehensible* the structure of rewards and deprivations in industrial employment, and the complex of attitudes towards this structure? In what manner can the confused detail of this aspect of social life be made meaningful without inflicting too much violence on reality?[1]

The academic discipline with the most obvious credentials to explain the dimensions of inequality in industrial life is economics. Engels made this point when he raised the question: what is meant by 'a fair day's pay' and 'a fair day's work'?[2]

> How are they determined by the laws under which modern society exists and develops itself? For an answer to this we must not apply to the science of morals or of law and equity, nor to any sentimental feeling of humanity, justice, or even charity. What is morally fair, what is even fair in law, may be far from being socially fair. Social fairness or unfairness is decided by one science alone — the science which deals with the material facts of production and exchange, the science of political economy.

1. Any theory, and any classificatory concept, involves *some* distortion of the complexity of reality; but such distortion is indispensable in order to make any kind of sense of the real world. The criterion for judging any theoretical interpretation or generalisation must therefore be: what is the cost in over-simplification, and what is the gain in comprehensibility? The problem of theory is considered further towards the end of this chapter.
2. *Labour Standard* (May 1881).

Within a capitalist society, labour is treated as a commodity like any other, hence its price is determined by forces of supply and demand: on this point, classical economists[3] and their Marxian critics were agreed. Marx's well-known formulation of this point in *Wage-Labour and Capital* was echoed, almost a century later, by Hicks in *The Theory of Wages*: 'The theory of the determination of wages in a free market is simply a special case of the general theory of value. Wages are the price of labour; and thus, in the absence of control, they are determined, like all prices, by supply and demand' (Hicks 1963: 1).

The central premise of classical theory is that competitive forces generate pressures towards a determinate equilibrium wage in each occupation, this equilibrium being defined by the intersection of schedules of demand and supply. The earliest theorists paid greatest attention to the supply of labour, developing many of the insights propounded by Adam Smith in 1776 in *The Wealth of Nations*.[4] A sophisticated theory of the demand for labour was elaborated a century later as part of marginal productivity theory, while Marshall provided a synthesis in his concept of 'efficiency wages'. Leading economists could still publish expositions of classicism, with minimal reservations, as late as the 1930s (see, for example, the works of Hicks and Douglas, both confidently entitled *The Theory of Wages*). Despite the volume of recent assaults on the traditional formulations, their assumptions remain central to textbook presentations, and in the last decade have been re-asserted with great vigour in more exalted contexts.

Despite (or perhaps because of) its age, Smith's theory of relative wages remains highly influential; it 'appears and reappears, sometimes refurbished but often clothed in the identical garb, not only in works offered as histories of economic thought but in works devoted to analysis of contemporary economic behaviour' (Salkever 1964: 17). Smith's basic proposition is that under competitive conditions 'the whole of the advantages and disadvantages of the

3. It is conventional to distinguish between 'classical' and 'neo-classical' economics; though the precise differences are not always clear, the introduction of marginalist analysis is normally taken as the dividing line. Common to both, however, is the competitive-utilitarian paradigm; and for the sake of simplicity we often refer to both as classical.
4. Smith's work represents less a coherent and integrated doctrine than a number of not altogether consistent principles on which a theory of wages could subsequently be founded.

different employments of labour and stock must . . . be either perfectly equal or continually tending to equality' (1937:99). The fact that persistent inequalities can be observed in the earnings of different occupations reflects (where government interference with competitive 'liberty' is not responsible) differences in the non-pecuniary advantages and disadvantages of these occupations. Relevant factors listed by Smith are the relative agreeableness and social esteem of an occupation; the costs involved in learning the trade; the security of employment; the responsibility demanded of the worker; and the chances of success or failure in a particular career. According to Smith's thesis, the effect of income inequalities is to equalise the *net advantages* of each occupation. This is an inevitable argument in view of the postulate of *laissez faire* utilitarianism that unequal remuneration must attract an increased supply of labour in high-paid occupations and reduce supply in the low-paid until equilibrium is restored.[5]

Smith's analysis of the determinants of the *level* of wages is less precise. The contract between employers and workers is structured by the superior power of the latter.[6] Employers cannot reduce the wages of the lowest class of labour, for any considerable time, below subsistence level; but minimum wages might rise significantly above this level in certain circumstances — as, for example, when economic expansion increased the demand for labour. A maximum is however set by 'the funds which are destined for the payment of wages' (p. 69).[7]

The notion that the wages of the lowest class of labour tend towards the level of bare subsistence (often related to the theory of the 'wages fund' which Smith outlined) dominated much of

5. Some writers appear to treat this proposition as tautological, hence protecting it against empirical disproof but at the same time depriving it of any reference to the real world. This point will be considered again in a later section.
6. 'In all . . . disputes the masters can hold out much longer. A landlord, a farmer, a master manufacturer, or merchant, though they did not employ a single workman, could generally live a year or two upon the stocks which they have already acquired. Many workmen could not subsist a week, few could subsist a month, and scarce any a year without employment. In the long-run the workman may be as necessary to his master as his master is to him, but the necessity is not so immediate' (p. 66).
7. The notion of a fixed 'wages fund' was popular throughout the first half of the nineteenth century. Given the economic context of the time — a relatively primitive organic composition of capital — it possessed a plausibility which the expansion of industry was to destroy. See, for example, Stark 1944.

nineteenth-century economic theory.[8] It was adapted by Marx as the centrepiece of his theory of exploitation. The price of wage-labour is determined by the same factors as the price of any other commodity: namely, the cost of its production (in Marxian theory, the socially necessary labour time). Yet for the unskilled labourer, 'the cost necessary for his production is almost confined to the commodities necessary for keeping him alive and capable of working. The *price of his labour* will, therefore, be determined by the price of the necessary means of subsistence' ('Wage Labour and Capital' in Marx and Engels 1958: I, 88). Marx explicitly rejected the thesis that there existed an 'iron law of wages' (though many writers still reveal their ignorance of Marx by attributing this doctrine to him). He recognised, first, that the definition of subsistence was subjective in character; hence the labourer's wage 'depends not merely upon the physical, but also upon the historically developed social needs, which become second nature' (1962:837). (Thus beliefs and values could shape economic processes.) And second, collective organisation and struggle could achieve some — though in the view of Marx only limited — success in keeping wages above the subsistence minimum.[9]

It is a commonplace that Marx carried Ricardo's labour theory of value to its logical conclusion — a task in which he had been preceded, though less systematically, by such early socialist theorists as Thompson and Hodgskin. If the unequal power concentrated in the hands of owners of capital ensures that workers are paid less than the value of their contribution, then exploitation is clearly central to the employment of labour. The uncongenial quality of this insight for any economist committed to capitalist relations of production helps explain the equivocation of the Ricardian school. Marx, through his relentless exposition of its necessary but previously suppressed implications, effectively destroyed the labour theory of value as an acceptable component of economic orthodoxy. This led, in the decade following the publication of *Capital,* to the independent elaboration of marginal productivity analysis by such writers as Jevons in Britain, Walras in Switzerland, Menger and Böhm-Bawerk in Austria, Clark in America; and their formulations

8. This proposition is, of course, particularly associated with Malthus. It should be seen in the context of the unprecedented increase in population — and hence labour supply — of the period.
9. For an elaboration of these points, see Hyman 1971b.

were hastily transplanted into classical wages theory.[10]

Marginalist analysis is founded on the postulate of the 'law of (eventually) diminishing returns'. In the context of production this involves the assumption of the diminishing marginal productivity of each factor of production, i.e. that successive equal additions to the amount of each factor of production employed will yield diminishing increments in output. On this basis it is argued that the rational entrepreneur will employ each factor of production in such an amount that its cost is equal to the value of its marginal net product. Equilibrium requires the identity of factor price and marginal product value: for if the prevailing price is above or below this level, demand will decline or increase until identity is established. In respect of wages, marginalism thus entails a tendency for their level to equal labour's marginal productivity.[11] From this perspective, 'normal' wages are determined not by the unequal power of

10. In view of the critical comments which we direct at neo-classical orthodoxy, it is perhaps necessary to emphasise that our intention is neither to assert the unqualified adequacy of the labour theory of value nor to deny all credit to the analytical insights of the marginalists. As a framework for the analysis of the *production function* the labour theory is unsuited to a developed industrial society with substantial variations in the capital-output ratio and the organic composition of capital between industries and enterprises, and with a high input of fixed capital in at least some sectors of the economy. Marginalism, despite its spurious pretensions to scientific precision (and despite other inadequacies which we note below), is of obvious heuristic value in this context. Yet from the onset (with such pre-classical pioneers as Locke) the labour theory was intended to characterise not primarily the process of production but the structure of *distributive entitlement*. What a man produces by his own labour, Locke argued, is his by right. As Macpherson (1962) cogently argues, Locke escaped the conclusion that workers were exploited by assuming a right to alienate one's labour and the equivalence between wages and the value of the worker's performance. This perspective persisted until Marx demonstrated the existence of *surplus* value, and hence the exploitation of workers not only as individuals but also as a class.

    The critique of the labour theory of value as a framework for the analysis of productive efficiency has no necessary bearing on its force as a theory of distributive justice. The need to recognise fixed capital within the production function by no means entails that capital should be privately owned and that owners should receive a specific proportion of production as their own. Yet precisely this conclusion is typically drawn from marginal productivity theory. Clark (1886:109) made the point explicitly: 'these questions tend, if rightly answered, to public order; if wrongly answered, to communism; and, if unanswered, to agitation and peril'. The dramatic rapidity with which marginalism was embraced as a theory of production is explicable only by its apparent efficacy as a legitimation of the incomes of the rich.

11. More accurately, wages should equal the net value of the marginal physical product, or net marginal revenue product.

employers as against workers but by labour's own *efficiency*; hence they may well be above subsistence level.[12] The concept of 'efficiency wages' was popularised by Marshall (1920:549), who systematised the application of marginalist analysis to both supply and demand functions of labour. The fact that the level of wages resulting from the designated process was assigned the label 'normal' — a term with obvious evaluative as well as descriptive connotations — implied a degree of moral approval which some economists made explicit by *defining* 'fair wages' as those determined in accordance with marginalist theory.[13]

Three features of classical wage theory must be noted. First, it presupposes a highly specific model of rational economic activity. Second, the theory is based on the assumption of more or less perfect competition. And third, it is essentially a theory of *long-run* tendencies: in the absence of 'equilibrium' wages, no classical economist seriously suggested that there could be immediate adjustment either on the supply side (workers moving from occupations with low to those with high net advantages) or on the demand side (employers reducing or increasing their labour force in response to wages above or below the value of the marginal productivity of labour).

As a theory of long-run tendencies or forces, classical theory thus involves a high level of abstraction. By excluding explicit consideration of the beliefs, values and intentions of managers and workers it is unable to offer any insight into the *processes* through which equilibrating forces allegedly operate. Leiserson (1966: 55) has made the point that

> the power of competitive wage theory in the analysis of broad long-run developments in wage-employment relationships . . . depends upon a structure of assumptions which are also the source of its weaknesses in other contexts. By abstracting from the actual structure and character of decision-making processes and by concentrating on equilibrium relationships, traditional theory is unable to throw much light on the dynamic processes of wage setting and the significance of changes in institutions and organizational relationships in the economy.

The concept of marginal productivity itself contributes significantly

12. Marginalism could thus offer an explanation for the rise in real wages in many industrialised countries during the second half of the nineteenth century: a trend not readily explicable within the categories of the classicists.
13. This is discussed in a later section. Marginalists have tended to gloss over the continuing implication of exploitation within their theory: for the *average* productivity of labour is higher than that of the marginally efficient worker, yet all receive wages equivalent to the value of the latter.

to the abstract character of the classical approach. For whatever the theoretical elegance of marginalist analysis, in practice the marginal productivity of a factor of production is not open to measurement by anything but the crudest means. Hence employers lack the information on which to base 'economically rational' wage and employment policies, even were they otherwise committed to the prescriptions of classic economic theory.[14] Thus classical theory is doubly incapable of illuminating the actual processes of wage determination.

The explanatory utility of classical theory is further undermined by its assumption of a competitive economy: the interaction of a multiplicity of atomistic buyers and sellers of all commodities (including labour power), none of sufficient size or influence to exert a significant individual impact on the conditions of the market.[15] Yet economists have been increasingly compelled to take account of the existence of concentrated economic power, and of a range of other 'imperfections' which vitiate the competitive model. Hence the classical theories both of wage structure and wage levels must be regarded as less than persuasive.

'Revisionism' in Economic Theory

The perceived lack of realism in the presuppositions of classical theory has provoked a variety of responses in contemporary labour economics. On the supply side, the whole concept of a labour market has received critical scrutiny. On the demand side, marginal productivity theory has been extensively questioned. The fact that, over a wide sector of employment, wage rates are determined collectively between managements and trade unions has also stimulated a variety of theories of bargaining.

The classical conception of the labour market assumes that the 'net advantages' of each occupation will be equalised by the responsiveness of labour supply to any deviation from competitive equilibrium. But the difficulty of applying this analytical framework to the actual structure of incomes in Britain (or any other economy)

14. As is suggested in the following section, the classical model of employer decision-making has been questioned by recent 'theorists of the firm'.
15. This assumption was perhaps more plausible in the 1870s, when marginalism evolved, than in any other period: see Stark 1944 and Tolles 1964.

has long been appreciated. Wootton (1962) has argued with particular vigour that high earnings, far from compensating for unstable or unpleasant employment, are typically associated with secure and congenial positions. Classical theory, she insists, can merely attribute the 'economic curiosities' of British pay structure to 'imperfections' in the competitive process, and hence abdicates any attempt at explanation.

This contention neglects one element in classical theory:[16] for differential rewards may be treated as a reflection of the varying costs of acquiring occupational skills. In the short run, the scarcity of possessors of particular skills or qualifications may permit their earnings to include an element of quasi-rent; though a long-run tendency to its elimination is assumed, through the attraction of new recruits to acquire the necessary skills. The proposition that, in the long run, differentials are attributable to costs of training and education is considered critically in a later section. Of immediate relevance is the implication that, in the short run, plumbers and physicians do not compete in the same labour market. This recognition, apparent in tentative form in Smith's writings, was made explicit in 1874 in Cairnes's notion of 'non-competing groups': an insight of which subsequently 'some version . . . is, more often than not, incorporated into the explanation of wage structure, whether the author is a classicist, a marginalist, a neo-classicist, an institutionalist or what have you' (Salkever 1964: 61-2).

Yet if one major qualification to the postulate of competition is accepted as necessary in the interest of realism, a similar claim can be made for others. Classical theory assumes a tendency for competitive pressures to equalise net advantages in the short term within even if not between occupational groups. Yet this presupposes both mobility and information on the part of employees, and recent studies have pointed to limitations in respect of both. Many workers are unaware or misinformed of rates of pay for their occupation in other firms in their locality; others fail to move to more advantageous positions of which they do have knowledge. Employers can often pay substantially below the norm in their local or occupational labour market without experiencing serious problems of labour supply;[17] thus the very notion of a labour

16. For an economic critique of Wootton, see Phelps Brown 1955.
17. From a range of studies see for example Reynolds 1951; Robinson 1970. See also the final section of this chapter.

market seems somewhat misleading.

A different qualification to conventional economic assumptions is implicit in the argument that (for certain sectors of the labour force at least) pressures of supply and demand are mediated and constrained by customary conceptions of appropriate wages. Piore, for example, has recently suggested (1973: 379) that workers' normative commitment to specific conceptions of fair wage relationships 'is intrinsic in the process through which the supply of labour is generated and, hence, it is difficult to generate a set of competitive pressures which will undermine it'. The underlying motivational problematic of economic theory is here placed in question: an issue to which we return below.

The demand parameter of classical wage theory has been assailed by writers who deny the salience of labour's marginal productivity for managerial employment policy. Systematic criticism of the neo-classical theory of the firm, on the basis of empirical research, dates from the 1930s. The evidence indicated that in much of the economy, prices were not given by the market but could be determined within limits by companies (partly because of monopoly power, partly because of product differentiation); firms did not in practice seek to equate prices with marginal cost and marginal revenue, but normally applied a standard percentage mark-up on average cost; indeed, managers were typically ignorant of the cost and revenue at the margin of their various products. This same perspective was applied by Lester (1946) to wage theory, with the argument that wage levels and movements do not appear to exert a major influence on the production and employment policies of managers. Despite the serious methodological weaknesses of Lester's study — vigorously exposed by Machlup (1946) — it demonstrates effectively that marginal productivity analysis does not normally enter into the explicit rationale of employers' labour policies.[18] In the absence of empirical counter-evidence, classical theory can be regarded as no more than a model of long-run tendencies and constraints. But if this is so, the pretensions to precision inherent in marginalist analysis are unwarranted. The elaborate and imposing analytical edifice appears bereft of much of its specificity and refinement when applied to real employment situations.[19]

18. 'Machlup won the battle but Lester won the war' (Corina 1972: 62-3).

19. 'The weakness of deductive analysis in the wage field is that its findings are

Three other considerations affect the cogency of the neo-classical theory of labour demand. One is that, in many employments, recruits to particular occupational levels are drawn not from the external labour market but from among existing employees of the company. Within such a structure of recruitment, conventional pressures of supply and demand are likely to be modified.[20] Secondly, it may be argued that in any complex productive system the notion of marginal productivity is not merely empirically imprecise but in principle vacuous: economic activity is essentially a *collaborative* process in which the specific contribution of individuals cannot be isolated.[21] Thirdly, recent decades have made increasingly evident the hiatus between classical micro-economic analysis of wages and employment, and more modern theories of aggregate demand. Mass unemployment between the wars effectively exploded the plausibility of the notion of a self-regulating labour market. Wages did *not* so decline as to restore equilibrium; and underconsumptionist theory, incorporated since Keynes into macro-economic orthodoxy, would insist that general wage reductions in a situation of inadequate aggregate demand would necessarily fail to remedy, and might well exacerbate, unemployment.[22] More recently, Ross has argued (1948: 80) that 'the real employment effect of the wage bargain is lost in a sea of external forces. The volume of employment associated with a given wage rate is unpredictable before the fact, and the effect of a given rate upon employment is undecipherable after the fact.' Conversely, in a condition of full employment the firm (in a context of monopoly capitalism) may be able to adjust prices to a wide range of wage levels without any employment effect.[23]

---

impossible to prove or disprove by appeal to the facts. The marginal-productivity theory of wages, for example, was arrived at almost wholly by deductive means many years ago; yet to this day it lacks any solid factual underpinnings, since it embodies concepts which defy empirical verification. In this connection one cannot help being struck by the rigor with which writers of a theoretical bent analyze wage relationships deductively in contrast to the extremely casual, unscientific methods they employ in checking their findings against the facts' (Pierson 1957 : 7).

20. See for example Kerr 1959.
21. For a recent argument on this point, see Nell 1973.
22. 'There is . . . no ground for the belief that a flexible wage policy is capable of maintaining a state of continuous full employment' (Keynes 1936 : 267).
23. Indeed Hicks (1955 : 391) has referred to the operation of a 'labour standard' whereby the contemporary economy adjusts to the prevailing level of wages: instead of actual wages having to adjust themselves to an equilibrium level,

Dissatisfaction with classical formulations of the supply and demand schedules for labour underlies (implicitly or explicitly) recent discussion of the impact of combination, rather than pure competition, in the labour market. As Douglas has noted (1934: 79), marginalist theory

> assumes that labor is composed of relatively minute units which are distinct from and independent of each other. They feel no more loyalty to each other than do particles of water, and, like the water, they move in such a way as to restore the equilibrium whenever it may be disturbed. Trade-Unionism, on the other hand, combines these workers in large groups and declares that they must be taken or left as a group.

Smith himself was aware of the importance of combination; but writing in the context of extreme legal repression of trade unionism, he assumed that it was combination among *employers* which was alone of economic significance.

> The masters being fewer in number, can combine more easily, and the law besides, authorises, or at least does not prohibit their combinations, while it prohibits those of the workmen . . . . Masters are always and everywhere in a sort of tacit, but constant and uniform combination, not to raise the wages of labour above their actual rate (1937 : 66-7).

Employer collaboration remains an important (though often neglected) factor in wage determination; but the rise, since Smith's day, of large-scale trade unionism means that the power of employers is no longer wholly unchecked. This led Marshall to argue that 'if the employers in any trade act together and so do the employed, *the solution to the problem of wages becomes indeterminate*'.[24] Economic constraints merely set upper and lower

---

monetary policy adjusts the equilibrium level of money wages so as to make it conform to the actual level. (Ironically, this tendency within recent macro-economics would appear to represent a reversion to the labour theory of value.) The earliest systematic attempts to relate neo-classical orthodoxy to the realities of 'monopolistic competition' include Chamberlin 1933 and Robinson 1933. See Baran and Sweezy 1968 for the argument that the concentration and centralisation of capital have societal consequences far more profound than the mere supersession of marginalist models of competitive equilibrium.

Recent scepticism towards classical conceptions of the demand for labour is well exemplified by the conclusion of Robinson's study of local labour markets (1970:269-70): 'While this study does not make a general claim that economic forces coming from the external labour market exert no pressure on an internal wage structure, it does seem to be the case that in certain situations external economic pressures are weaker than the internal institutional pressures coming from within the company. This suggests that the firm rather than being a helpless victim of economic forces beyond its control, has a margin of opportunity within which it can adjust its internal position and take independent decisions regarding its wage structure and wage levels. This margin of opportunity may be considerable in scope and extent.'

24. As recent writers have emphasised, it is not the outcome but the theory which is indeterminate.

limits to wages; but within these limits the actual level is fixed 'by higgling and bargaining . . . tempered somewhat by ethico-prudential considerations' (1920: 827-8; emphasis added).

Hence even the classical theorists were aware that, however precise the operation of economic laws in the context of their idealised assumptions, in the real world there existed an area of economic indeterminacy. Within this area the values, beliefs and assumptions of the actors (as well as the distribution of power amongst them) might be of considerable effect. Marshall presaged more recent approaches to wage determination when he wrote of pay being set 'by bargaining, supplemented by custom and by notions of fairness' (p. 626).

Modern labour economists have adopted several strategies in an attempt to relate their theories to the realities of collective bargaining. The most popular approach treats bargaining merely as the *process* through which competitive forces are mediated. This presupposes the view, cogently argued by Lindblom (1948: 409) that there is 'no necessary antithesis between the bargaining-power theory of wages and the theory developed in modern price analysis, although careless statements of either may create an antithesis'. Ethical appeals, it is implied, are effective only to the extent that they accord with economic constraints. An early argument to this effect was used by Hicks (1963: 80):

> Demands for a rise in wages come, in the first place, because a rise appears to be 'fair'. And the principal motive in an employer's mind when he concedes such a rise may be a desire that his wage-policy should not appear to be an 'unfair' one. The same argument which is used by the workmen to support their claims for a rise is used by employers to justify a reduction. But although this appears to be the motive for a very large proportion of wage-changes, it is not their real reason. These rules of fairness and justice are simply rough-and-ready guides whereby the working of supply and demand is anticipated.

If employers and workers followed the appeals of fairness where these conflicted with the constraints of supply and demand, the dire consequences predicted by classical economic theory would ensue. This was also the argument of Douglas (1934): if unions attempted to enforce wage levels above those dictated by marginal productivity, the inevitable result would be unemployment of union members; union bargaining power would then be weakened, and wages would resume their 'normal' level.

More recently, a similar interpretation has been offered by Reder. Students of industrial relations, unlike economists, are primarily interested in the *processes* through which wages are set; and 'on such questions as these, the competitive hypothesis has little to say'. It is true, he agrees, that 'most wage-making *decisions* are made by employers trying to conform to the demands of a variety of social, political, ethical and union pressures. Conscious profit maximization (or loss minimization) is operative only to the extent that it imposes rather broad limits upon the course of action taken.' Yet the economist who accepts the marginalist/competitive hypothesis would insist that 'however wages are determined, their behaviour will conform (to what is predicted by the hypothesis) if enough time is allowed for adjustment' (1958: 71).[25] Perhaps the best-known advocate of this position in modern labour economics is Dunlop, who insists that trade union wage policy is best understood in terms of an 'economic model'.

> The view that wage fixing under collective bargaining is fundamentally to be examined in a political context reveals considerable ignorance of the habits of mind of labour leaders and the intimacy of their knowledge of the technology and economic facts of an industry . . . . There is no denying that wage determination under collective bargaining is different from wage fixing under non-union conditions. But the difference is not as great on the record to date as has been assumed. Most of the same wage making forces operate through the institutions of collective bargaining (1950 : iv).

The argument is thus that economic orthodoxy can explain the long-run outcome of the activities of collective bargainers, whatever their own subjective intentions and perceptions. (Indeed Dunlop's thesis is that the bargainers are *consciously* motivated by economic considerations, and that these are the most salient influence on their actions.) Yet doubt is cast on this assertion by the criticisms of classical theory which have already been reviewed: the forces of

25. Reder offers the following example (p. 86): 'Let us suppose that relative wage rates are set in an arbitrary way without reference to market forces. But once they are set, economic processes begin to operate: (1) firms that pay more than the market requires are either driven out of business or tend to become more efficient labor users than others. Such firms will tend to shed labor intensive processes, either subcontracting them to lower wage firms or abandoning product lines that require them. And, even if abandonment were too difficult, such firms would tend at least to avoid producing new labor intensive products; over a long period, this would have roughly the same effect as abandonment. (2) Because such firms pay relatively high wages they will be better able to select and keep superior workers than others. Consequently, even though the desire to adopt severe hiring standards were distributed independently of a firm's wage level, the ability to maintain them would not be, and so high wages and high labor quality would tend to become associated.'

supply and demand, even if not inscrutable, at least permit a significant range within which agreements may be struck without predictable consequences for employment. Within this margin, it would appear, trade union wage policy can exert an influence. And against Dunlop's thesis (somewhat modified in his more recent writings) that union policy is itself best conceived as a form of economic maximisation, Ross (1948) has argued plausibly that an analysis in terms of internal 'political' pressures is more illuminating. Of particular theoretical importance is his assertion (pp. 4-5) that collective organisation makes possible the *conscious control* of economic forces which in a less structured market situation would themselves exert a controlling influence.[26]

In the face of the assaults of the critics of classical and neo-classical analysis, and the reservations of its defenders, contemporary wage theory is in a state of disarray. 'Labour market or wage specialists have all been most uncomfortable with "received" theory. There have been no unabashed defenders in this group' (Dunlop 1957: 12). In Pierson's summary (1957: 31), 'theorists are now saying that wage determination cannot be reduced to a single rule of behaviour, that in so far as economic influences as such are concerned, there is an element of uncertainty or even indeterminateness in wage setting, which earlier economists were inclined to minimize'. Indeed, for some labour economists this element of indeterminacy bulks so large that there is a tendency to virtual theoretical despair.

> The incomes system is far from the static and 'perfect' market world of elementary textbooks, and fails to sort out incomes on a rational basis. Instead of subjection to the free play of the market, income distribution reflects the irrationalities of an

26. Ross argues as follows: 'It is commonplace that wage rates are now determined by conscious human decision rather than by impersonal market forces. In a formal sense, this has always been true; even the most impersonal forces can operate only through human agencies. A more significant question is whether the human agencies are the servants or the masters of the market forces. In an unorganized economic society, they are likely to be the servants. But there is a persistent tendency toward rational organization in sufficient strength to achieve a degree of mastery. Prominent in many phases of economic life, rational organization operates not only through private associations, but also through the coercive authority of the state. Mastery of market forces requires the power of consolidated decision. A little decision is merely the choice to be swept along in a stream; a big decision can redirect the stream itself. Hence the large business unit, which endeavours to control supply, create demand, and shape the institutional environment in which it does business. Hence also the labor union, and the other evidences of consolidated decision-making power over the "terms and conditions of employment".'

'imperfect' market. Income distribution is the result of the disorderly interplay of many factors: the strengths of worker and employer organizations, bargaining opportunities, union aggressiveness, the varying monopolistic positions of employers, ignorance, social class, the pattern of property distribution, the role of Government, and myriad obstacles to the flows of labour and capital (Corina 1966 : 49-50).

Similarly, Levinson (1966: 276) has pointed to 'the extraordinarily complex nature of those factors that determine the outcome of any major collective bargaining negotiation, a complexity that presents formidable conceptual and empirical problems'. (Yet other writers have insisted that a relatively simple theoretical framework can illuminate the interaction of economic and non-economic influences; thus Ross (1948: 12) summarises his own perspective in 'the central proposition . . . that a trade union is a political agency operating in an economic environment'.)

A variety of attempts to transcend the problem of economic indeterminacy and specify analytically the outcome of individual bargaining situations are commonly subsumed under the heading of bargaining theory.[27] Some developments in this area involve the application of the insights and paradigms of games theory; others focus on the construction of utility functions[28] and risk valuation schedules for the parties to bargaining such that the outcome of their interaction is theoretically determinate.[29] The accommodation which such approaches offer between the classical perspectives of 'rational' individualistic economic decision-taking and the realities of industrial relations contains a number of important insights. Nevertheless, current economic theories of bargaining confront a serious dilemma. Either their formalisation of the bargaining process excludes analytically a range of 'non-economic' influences

27. One indication of the somewhat confused state of current labour economics is the controversy over the status of 'bargaining theory'. Pen (1959 : ix) insists that his own contribution 'derives its inspiration from economics and not from sociology or psychology'. Yet he adds that 'it seems useful to point out that this study is primarily about men and not about things; about goals as they exist in human minds; about the way decisions are formed in order to reach these goals; about the limitations of knowledge and their influence; and especially about the psychological impact of threats'. Other writers have treated 'bargaining theory' explicitly as an alternative to economic analysis. Yet others have declared it a 'most distressing error' (Lindblom 1948 : 398) to suppose that bargaining is anything but one element in an essentially economic process.
28. Pen follows Pareto in preferring the term 'ophelimity' to 'utility'. It is not clear that this terminological innovation signifies a genuine escape from the dubious motivational assumptions of utilitarianism: see the discussion below.
29. See for example Zeuthen 1930; Hicks 1963; Pen 1952 and 1959; Walton and McKersie 1965; Coddington 1968.

on its outcome: in which case 'in embarking on an extravaganza of model-building one faces a great danger of becoming so intrigued and enchanted with the workings of the models that one loses all contact with reality' (Coddington 1968: xv). Or else their parameters of risk and utility *incorporate* assumptions regarding the subjective preferences, normative standards, control of resources and so on, on the part of the bargainers, without seeking to analyse and explain their character; hence key interpretative problems are forced into the background.

Recent bargaining theories, it might be argued, reflect an antinomy inherent in contemporary labour economics. At one extreme there is a tendency to defend the disciplinary credentials of economic analysis through a re-assertion of the first principles of classical orthodoxy. This is the perspective of recent attempts to refine classical theory in a manner which retains its essence while taking account of modern criticisms.[30] Yet as Corina (1972: 3) has pointed out, 'it may be argued that the so-called revolution (counter-revolution?) in labour economics which developed during the 1960s, is neither so coherent nor so conceptually original as some of the extreme neo-classicists claim'. Corina's extensive documentation need not be recapitulated here; but in brief, it can plausibly be asserted that those writers who have attempted to 'save' the main structure of classical theory remain open to the same criticisms raised previously when the formulations of the classic theorists themselves were considered.

The opposite tendency, premised on the acceptance that the limitations of marginalist/competitive theory are (in an era of monopoly capitalism at least) incorrigible, carries with it a serious danger of eclecticism. Among those willing to discard a large measure of the classical theoretical edifice, recent debate has centred to a large extent not on *whether* wage theory should take account of non-economic as well as economic determinants but on which should be accorded theoretical *primacy*. The existence of an area of economic indeterminacy within which the values and beliefs and the strategic or organisational power of workers and employers can exert an influence is not seriously contested; at the same time, little effort has been made to relate theoretically the ideological influences in industrial relations to their economic context or to the broader structural realities of power. Corina's conclusion (1972: 14)

30. In Britain see, most notably, Fisher 1971.

appears justified: 'as a corrective to the rigidities of neo-classical assumptions, the "institutionalist" approaches have provided varied insights into the possibility of a theory combining "economic" and "non-economic" behaviour; but, as yet, appear to have thrown up no powerful analytical substitutes replacing the classical economic tools themselves'.

The Value Problem in Economic Theory

Classical economic theory, we would wish to argue, rests upon conceptual foundations which 'institutionalist' economists evade without fully escaping. 'The fundamental problem facing labour market theories', Corina writes (1972: 11-12), 'is . . . not one of their own faulty generality or shaky premises: it stems from economic analysis itself — the fundamental problem of axiomatic "rationality" . . . .' In appraising the limitations of economists' accounts of inequality, we must therefore scrutinise their underlying analytical assumptions.

One problem which confronts the critic at the outset is the fact that economists are commonly far less ready than other social scientists to assert that their theoretical formulations relate directly to events in the real world. Many claim merely to demonstrate what *would* happen given a specific set of assumptions the unreality of which they will, when pressed, admit.[31] Hence to complain that economic theory presents an inaccurate picture of reality is to invite a charge of naivete: no serious economist, it may be replied, ever suggested otherwise. Yet this is a somewhat facile response. In their perspectives on reality, economists commonly fall victim to their own abstractions; as Wootton has put it (1962: 12), 'innocent though these models are of any claim to representational accuracy, the fact that they are used as the point of departure has . . . profoundly affected the conception of the real world that has resulted from their use'.

Economic interpretations and explanations of inequality are beset by the value problem in economic theory. One may indeed speak not of one value problem but of three, all of which have a bearing on our

31. Hence the unfortunate student is often required first to master the doctrines of classical theory, then to learn how these fail to apply in concrete economic situations.

discussion. These three value problems involve, respectively, the influence of social values and ideologies on the structure and content of economic thought; the treatment within economic theory of the subjective values of economic actors; and the attribution of value to the various goods, services and relations which are the focus of economic analysis.

Early students of political, economic and social affairs were for the most part content to combine analysis and prescription overtly in their writings. But for over a century — coinciding roughly with the popularity of the notion of a social *science* — it has been customary to insist that the two processes can and must be separated. The task of the social scientist, *qua* social scientist, is to describe and analyse with objectivity and detachment; the evaluation of the facts and the formulation of policy belong to a distinct area of problems which concern the social scientist, if at all, only in his extra-mural capacity. The goal of value-free academicism — passionately proclaimed by Weber in his lecture on 'Science as a Vocation' (1948: ch. 5) — has been more fervently embraced by economists, perhaps, than within any other social discipline.

We regard the goal of value-freedom as misconceived: for the values prevailing in the social environment impinge on intellectual activity (especially, it might be argued, in the social studies) in a variety of identifiable ways. This occurs, at the outset, in the choice of an area of study. Since it is possible to investigate only a minute fraction of knowable reality, the focus of enquiry represents the outcome of a process of selection (conscious or otherwise). The 'problems' to be studied are not objectively given, but are determined on the basis of subjective criteria of relevance: they entail a value-judgment. As Myrdal has written (1953: vii), in a criticism of his own former assumptions, the 'implicit belief in the existence of a body of knowledge acquired independently of all valuations is, as I now see it, naive empiricism . . . . There is an inescapable *a priori* element in all scientific work. Questions must be asked before answers can be given. The questions are expressions of our interest in the world, they are at bottom valuations.'

Once the initial choice of an area of investigation has been determined, ideological factors are again involved in structuring the way in which the object of enquiry is conceptualized. Social reality does not fall naturally into categories: these are *imposed* on reality. A concept represents an abstraction from reality: a decision that certain features of phenomena are to be treated as relevant and others as irrelevant for the purposes of classification and analysis. 'The value connotation of our main concepts represents our interest in a matter, gives direction to our thoughts and significance to our inferences. It poses the questions without which there are no answers' (Myrdal 1958: 1). The choice of a particular conceptual framework presupposes but also underwrites a specific orientation to reality: it can never be neutral or value-free. [32]

To develop this argument further: the choice of an area of study and the interpretation of reality provided are possible only on the basis of theoretical assumptions and hypotheses. 'Human "facts" never speak for themselves but yield their meanings only when the questions put to them are inspired by a philosophical theory of the whole' (Goldmann 1969: 133).[33] Simply piling fact upon fact brings confusion, not enlightenment: the student of society who denies the relevance of theory merely reveals that his own theoretical presuppositions are unrecognised (and hence probably confused). And even if, as is sometimes argued, 'facts are neutral', theories unquestionably are not. Yet theories which are merely implicit and unscrutinised are particularly subject to the structuring of external social influences.

It is thus of crucial importance to consider explicitly the social origins of the criteria which determine the choice of a field of enquiry, a conceptual framework, and a set of theoretical assumptions: in other words, to investigate academic production as ideology.

In the absence of explicit recognition of the irreducibly evaluative foundation of academic analysis, this normative basis will be uncriticised and unscrutinised; and the illusion of value-freedom is likely to cloak the encapsulation of the taken-for-granted ideological assumptions of the social milieu. And this in turn — to anticipate the argument of Chapter 7 — can easily render academic theory a

32. Perhaps even more devastating is the criticism which Streeten has made of the principle of value-freedom (1958:xliii): that it embodies its own refutation, being itself evaluative. 'For no observation or logical analysis can *discover* that we *ought to* separate values from facts, or ends from means. No amount of description or deduction can show that we can fully analyse actual political and moral choices without introducing values into our analysis.'

33. E. H. Carr (1964: 11) has applied the same insight to historiography: 'the facts speak only when the historian calls on them : it is he who decides to which facts to give the floor, and in what order or context'.

legitimation of the existing order of social relations and the structure of power and privilege which it incorporates. Hence the paradox that those who are committed to the necessity of academic objectivity may 'mean what they say, yet they never practise it' (Streeten 1958: xii). This contradiction is manifest, in the case of economics, in the employment of ostensibly objective categories with profound evaluative content. The value-laden character of modern economic terminology has been clearly exposed by Myrdal (1953: 19-21): such concepts as 'productivity', 'equilibrium', 'balance', 'adjustment', 'function', 'utility', 'welfare' — and indeed 'value' itself — are Janus-faced, incorporating both description and normative judgment; they 'represent involved structures of metaphysical ideas which are firmly anchored in our tradition of thought'.

To consider a specific instance more closely: the concept of 'national income', so fundamental to macro-economic analysis, is presumed to represent an objective index of economic 'welfare'. Yet it is possible to aggregate a discrete set of goods and services only by accepting the valuation of the market, through the medium of money: transmitting qualitative differences into quantitative, segregating 'productive' activities from 'non-productive' (all unpaid work, including for example that of housewives). If a justification for this procedure is to be offered, it is presumably that market valuations mediate the decisions of the 'sovereign consumer' engaged in maximising his utility. Hence to utilise such neutral-sounding concepts as 'national income' (and derivatives such as 'economic growth') is to embrace the values of a specific economic system.

This example may serve to bridge the *general* value problem in economic theory — the ideological content of economic analysis — with the more specific problems of the treatment of the subjective values of economic actors and the exchange values of the market.

It is a noteworthy fact that whereas sociologists recognise the importance of providing some theoretical account of values, and sociological orthodoxy assigns them key explanatory salience, economists have traditionally attempted to *exclude* them from analysis. The established premise of economic theory is that, whatever the intentions of the human actors, economic behaviour is mediated by objective factors ('economic laws', 'market forces', or even the 'unseen hand') such that the end result is independent of their wills. It is thus the generation of specific *objective consequences,* rather than the nature and origin of *subjective meanings and intentions,* that is the centre of scrutiny for the economist.

Yet economic analysis can exclude explicit consideration of values only because these are already built into its own framework of concepts and assumptions. Thus the notions of 'economic rationality' and 'economic man' presuppose that economic activity is pervaded by an (in every sense) peculiar set of values. Single-mindedly devoted to the 'maximisation of utility', the paradigmatic economic actor derives from the classic utilitarian model, engaging in a calculative and narrowly individualistic pursuit of precisely defined objectives through a tidy hierarchy of means and ends. In so far as economists treat 'economic rationality' as the *only* true form of rationality, it is possible to neglect the centrality of a specific and bizarre set of normative assumptions.

The model of the human actor as a rationalistic hedonist, most elaborately articulated in Bentham's felicific calculus,[34] represents the core theoretical link between the marginalists and the preceding classical tradition.[35] Yet the motivational presuppositions of utilitarianism are almost wholly without foundation in empirical research: they represent, as Myrdal has ironically remarked, a notable example of British empiricists indulging in armchair theorising. Unsatisfactory even as a model for *consumer* behaviour, *homo oeconomicus* is a particularly inappropriate stereotype for the analysis of productive and employment relationships. For although, in a capitalist economy, labour power is treated as a commodity like any other, it is nevertheless a commodity with peculiar charac-

34. The doctrine of utility, by reducing everything to instrumental value, begs the whole question of the ends pursued by men. Bentham's philosophical hedonism fails to resolve this problem: the postulate that happiness is the only human objective, if not tautological (and hence a mere reformulation of the problem) is patently false. It is well known that the attempt to appraise the ends of human action obliged the last classic utilitarian, J. S. Mill, so to amend and qualify the utilitarian problematic as effectively to destroy it. The fallacy of utilitarianism derives in part from the assumption that ends and means can be clearly differentiated, and form a tidy hierarchy; for a cogent presentation of the argument that ends and means interpenetrate see Streeten 1958:xxii-xxiii.
35. Myrdal (1953) notes that many marginalists attempted to evade the implications of their intellectual dependence on Benthamite hedonism — even abandoning the very concept of utility — yet failed to provide an adequate alternative motivational basis for their theories. Myrdal's study represents one of the most devastating critiques of the utilitarian foundations of modern economic orthodoxy.

teristics. Normally it is physically inseparable from the seller of labour power: work requires the presence and application of the worker throughout a prescribed period of time, and his subordination to a structure of managerial control. Moreover, a person's occupation provides a major point of reference for those with whom he interacts in social life. Hence far more is involved in employment than a simple economic exchange (a fact emphasised by Lockwood (1958) in his differentiation between the market, work and status situations of employees). These various facets of employment necessarily affect the beliefs and attitudes of employees, influencing both their choice of work and their performance within work. It is significant that the range of problems associated with work performance and effort levels, discussed in detail in the previous chapters, are scarcely considered within economics; for the traditional model of economic man is blatantly inadequate for the analysis of such questions. Yet if economic theory can contribute little to the understanding of the *deprivations* inherent in employment (including the inegalitarian structure of these deprivations), its credentials to explain the structure of *rewards* must appear somewhat dubious.

The disposition of economic analysis in relation to this second aspect of the value problem links closely to the third. The motivational model of economic man both derives from and reinforces a presumption of the objectivity of the market as a medium of evaluation. The solution offered to both problems by economic theory represents the hypostatis of the principles inherent in the rise of the capitalist political economy. The debt owed by the classical theorists to the *practice* of the triumphant bourgeoisie was repeatedly emphasised by Marx. 'The apparent stupidity of merging all the manifold relationships of people in the *one* relationship of usefulness, this apparently metaphysical abstraction arises from the fact that, in modern bourgeois society, all relations are subordinated in practice to the one abstract monetary-commercial relation' (Marx and Engels 1970: 109). The approach of the early economists provided, in essence, a systematisation of prevailing consciousness in which money constituted 'the representative of the value of all things, people and social relations' (Marx 1959: 110). This *Weltanschauung* found its logical extreme in the formulations of Jeremy Bentham: yet Bentham's utilitarianism merely made brutally explicit the prevailing assumptions that 'the only force that brings

[men] together and puts them in relation with each other is the selfishness, the gain and the private interests of each' (Marx 1959: 176); and that what each man pursued could be reduced to a simple calculation of utility. 'The individual carries his social power, as well as his bond with society, in his pocket. Activity, regardless of its individual manifestation, and the product of activity, regardless of its particular make-up, are always *exchange value*, and exchange value is a generality, in which all individuality and peculiarity are negated and extinguished' (Marx 1973: 157).

Utilitarianism also formed the basis of a specific conception of *political* relations: the notion of 'civil society', a political structure based solely on the pursuit of self-interest by each individual. This conception of political relations in purely market terms underlay the model of the social contract developed by Hobbes and Locke in the seventeenth century. Just as utilitarian economic theory viewed the employment relationship as a free exchange between equals, so utilitarian political theory viewed subordination to political authority as the voluntary action of free and equal citizens. Hegel (in the *Phenomenology*) commenced a critique of utilitarian political philosophy which Marx and Engels developed into a radical analysis of political power and institutions as the forms of protection of sectional, economic power. What is particularly significant in the present context is the manner in which this insight illuminates the rationale of the early social contract theorists. As Macpherson (1962) has so sensitively demonstrated, the seventeenth-century pioneers of utilitarian political theory worked within a framework of assumptions which he terms 'possessive individualism'. Within these assumptions, the common interests of those who possess property *as against* the propertyless gave the former a need for institutions of political control over the latter, and thus a motive for accepting the consequential restrictions on their own individual autonomy. Without these assumptions, the notion of a social contract is a device so unrealistic as to be of minimal explanatory utility.[36]

The inadequacy of this perspective is laid bare in Marx's famous analysis (in *Capital*) of the 'fetishism of commodities', indicating

36. It follows that by making these assumptions explicit and revealing their ideological nature the limitations of the utilitarian conception of politics may be transcended. It is through a critique of the utilitarian categories of social reality that, as O'Neill puts it (1972:191), 'the attempt to base the social and political order upon the postulate of the natural identity of interests is broken once and for all'.

how a particular structure of economic relations leads men to *misconceive* its nature. The exchange value of commodities derives from the social relations between men as producers and consumers; yet men regard the structure of commodity exchange as natural and immutable, and hence treat exchange values as the intrinsic properties of the objects of exchange. 'A definite social relation between men . . . assumes, in their eyes, the fantastic form of a relation between things' (1959: 72). Yet men within capitalist society view their economic relations in a mystified, reified[37] manner *because* of the nature of these relations: the essentially social relations of economic activity being obscured by the mechanics of a market system.

In the form of society now under consideration, the behaviour of men in the social process of production is purely atomic. Hence their relations to each other in production assume a material character independent of their control and conscious individual action . . . . Since the producers do not come into social contact with each other until they exchange their products, the specific social character of each producer's labour does not show itself except in the act of exchange. In other words, the labour of the individual asserts itself as a part of the labour of society, only by means of the relations which the act of exchange establishes directly between the products, and indirectly, through them, between the producers. To the latter, therefore, the relations connecting the labour of one individual with that of the rest appear, not as direct social relations between individuals at work, but as what they really are, material relations between persons and social relations between things (pp. 73, 92-3).

This means, as Geras (1972:295) has clearly demonstrated, that reified consciousness is not simply 'false' consciousness: 'it is not that something imaginary has been endowed with the quality of reality'. What is implied is that the irrational consequences of a *specific form of social organisation* are regarded as natural and inevitable. And it is precisely this perspective which economic orthodoxy incorporates: the uncritical acceptance of the valuations of the marketplace, which transmute the qualitative richness of human life into a single quantitative measure. Indeed, this perspective is often extended beyond economic relations conventionally conceived to social life generally, making the reified model of commodity exchange the paradigm for all social relations. An early version of this philistinism was assailed by Marx in the 1844 manuscripts:

Political economy conceives the social life of men, their active human life, their

37. To reify is to attribute an objective and independent identity to social processes and institutions which are in reality the product of human activity — thus diverting attention from the human agencies involved.

> many-sided growth towards a communal and genuinely human life, under the form of *exchange* and *trade*. Society, says Destutt de Tracy, is a series of multilateral exchanges. It *is* this movement of multilateral integration. According to Adam Smith, society is a commercial enterprise. Every one of its members is a salesman. It is evident how political economy establishes an *alienated* form of social intercourse, as the *true and original* form, and that which corresponds to human nature (1963 : 179).

Nevertheless, this approach remains influential; it has indeed recently spread from economics to sociology, in a variety of related doctrines described as 'exchange theory'.[38]

The incorrigibility of market valuations is an essential presupposition if utilitarian economics is to transcend the methodological dilemma inherent in its individualistic problematic: for how can the discrete utilities of each economic actor be *aggregated* and hence provide the basis for social- or macro-economics? Only through the postulate that exchange is the objective measure of all utilities. This solution is facilitated by an assumption of a harmony of interests which, as Myrdal (1953) has documented, has so often provided utilitarians with an escape from grievous logical perplexities. For a harmonistic perspective facilitates the conception of the market at face value as the medium in which individuals freely exchange equal for equal.[39] Economists adopt 'a characteristic mode of analysis, in which the economy is divided horizontally, so to speak, into "agencies", or institutions which, whatever their other differences, always operate on the same side of the market and so respond in roughly similar ways to market incentives. Thus Rockefellers and share-croppers are both households, GM and the corner grocery are both firms' (Nell 1972: 76). Classical economics cannot envisage the market as a medium of *domination*, the economically powerful dominating the market and through the market dominating the powerless.[40] Not only does orthodox economics suppress consideration of inequalities of resources between and within the categories of producers and consumers; its problematic precludes systematic analysis of the

38. See for example Homans 1961; Blau 1964.
39. As was seen above, the same blending of utilitarian and harmonistic premises typically underlies political theories based on the notion of social contract.
40. Weber followed Marx in rejecting this mystification of market relations; he insisted (1968: 942, 946) that 'the control over economic goods, i.e., economic power, is a frequent, often purposively willed, consequence of domination as well as one of its most important instruments . . . . Because of the very absence of rules, domination which originates in the market . . . may be felt to be much more oppressive than an authority in which the duties of obedience are set out clearly and expressly.'

implications of the power disparity between employers and employees. On the contrary: the presupposition is that 'each enters into relations with the other, as with a simple owner of commodities, and they exchange equivalent for equivalent' (Marx 1959: 176). The *asymmetry* of the labour contract, deriving from the concentrated social power inherent in the ownership and control of the means of production, disappears in the mystifying categories of commodity exchange.

As with the general political theory of possessive individualism, so with its specific application to employment relationships, it is only on the basis of a critique of the utilitarian paradigm that it is possible satisfactorily to analyse the reality behind the formal equality and freedom of the labour market: to recognise 'that utility is subject to appropriation in the form of capital which is then able to command the services of others to their disadvantage whatever the circumstances of a formally free contract' (O'Neill 1972: 192). For *within* this paradigm there is no problem of exploitation, only a problem of allocative efficiency. A typical labour economics textbook introduces its discussion of the labour market as follows:

> The allocative process . . . must not only sort out labour resources for their most effective use but must also determine the best combination of the various factors of production, given present conditions of supply and demand and current technology. In our economy we rely almost completely upon the pricing system and free markets to reach these decisions. They do not always produce the first jet aircraft, the first penicillin, or the first Sputnik, but in the interest of achieving a flexible, productive, and dynamic economy in a manner consistent with our moral and political values, this is an effective means of allocating resources and distributing commodities (Cartter and Marshall 1967: 205).

Nell's comments (1972: 95) are apposite: 'orthodox economics tries to show that markets allocate scarce resources according to relative efficiency . . . . It is good to know about efficiency, but in our world, it tends to be subservient to power.' Failing to integrate this power dimension into its analysis, economic theory easily becomes (often, as in the previous quotation, quite openly) a simple legitimation of the prevailing structure of economic relations. Economic theories of distributive inequality exemplify this tendency admirably.

Economic Theory and Inequality

The perspectives of economic orthodoxy have often led to the proclamation of the *fairness* of the existing structure of incomes.

'What is a fair distribution?' enquired Marx in the *Critique of the Gotha Programme.* 'Do not the bourgeois assert that the present-day distribution is fair?' (Marx and Engels 1958: II, 21). This point was elaborated by Engels in his critique of the slogan 'a fair day's pay for a fair day's work' (*Labour Standard,* May 1881):

> Now what does political economy call a fair day's wages and a fair day's work? Simply the rate of wages and the length and intensity of a day's work which are determined by competition of employer and employed in the open market . . . . The fairness of political economy, such as it truly lays down the laws which rule actual society, that fairness is all on one side — on that of Capital. [41]

The most explicit attempt to equate fairness with the principles of capitalist political economy is associated with the writings of Marshall and Pigou. For Marshall (1887: ix-xiv), what was ethical was to be judged by what was possible, and what was possible by what actually existed. Hence fair wages were those regarded by the economist as 'normal': in other words, those prevailing in the labour market and assumed to represent the natural outcome of the workings of supply and demand. In discussing the fairness of wages paid to workers in different occupations, Marshall admitted with remarkable candour,

> we are not inquiring whether the social system which permits great inequalities in their usual rates of remuneration is the best possible: but taking the present social system as it is, we want to know whether those with whom we are dealing are doing their part to make it work smoothly.

This same starting point allowed Pigou to argue that wages which were 'normal' from the perspective of economic theory were imbued with moral propriety. In an early work he did indeed admit (1905: 42) that only if wealth were evenly distributed could it be automatically assumed that 'the natural or competitive solution of the wages problem is . . . ethically the best'. Yet on the grounds that the achievement of any other structure of wages would be

41. More recently, Coates (1967:83) has developed the same argument: 'If the fundamental system of present values is contradictory, there can be no continuous valid standard of what is fair. It is perfectly fair, within capitalism, for Capital to seek to maximise its returns. To do this, it is not only fair but necessary to seek to buy labour at the cheapest possible price consonant with productivity. It is equally fair, within the same framework, by the same ethics, for Labour to seek for itself the highest possible return. "While there is a free for all, we are part of the all", says Mr. Cousins. But more than this is true. The rights of Capital, here, and the rights of Labour, there, confront one another, head on. There is, as Marx pointed out, an antinomy, right against right. "Between equal rights, force decides," he added. To force, we might add cunning. And cunning has been largely concentrated at one corner in this century-long combat.'

impracticable, this reservation was ignored. Hence by the time of his *Economics of Welfare* (1920) he chose to *define* fair wages as those equal to the worker's marginal net product (Marshall's 'efficiency wages').[42] Interference with the competitively determined 'fair wage' could be justified only in the exceptional circumstances of a vicious circle of exceedingly low wages, impoverishment and hence inefficient workers. Wages raised through 'artificial' intervention might then, through enhanced worker efficiency, become self-sustaining.

Whilst this conception of fairness is no longer often explicitly articulated in economic theory, its basic assumptions (slightly modified to take account of the reality of collective bargaining) have proved extensively influential. Of these the most significant are, first, that any given structure of incomes is to be appraised principally in terms of its contribution to allocative efficiency; and second, that the existing pattern of earnings differentials *is* largely explicable in conventional economic terms.

Most current economists — in line with the prevailing doctrine of value-freedom — refrain from animadverting on the ethics of income distribution (hence the virtual disappearance of the concept of fairness from the economist's vocabulary). Those who do pass explicit value judgments commonly profess a *prima facie* commitment to equality but — adopting the premise of the French revolutionary assembly in 1789, that 'civil distinctions . . . can be founded only on public utility' (Paine 1969: 132) — go on to offer a utilitarian justification for inequality.

In one form or another, such justifications can be traced back to the pioneering analysis of Adam Smith. His theory of 'equalising advantages' took account of the education and training required for the exercise of particular occupations. 'A man educated at the expense of much labour and time,' he argued (1937: 101), was comparable to 'any expensive machine . . . . The work he learns to perform, it must be expected, over and above the usual wages of common labour, will replace to him the whole expense of his education, with at least the ordinary profits of an equally valuable

42. That this was indeed intended as a *definition* of fairness was made explicit in Pigou's 4th edition (1932:549): 'provided that the wages paid to workpeople in all places and occupations were equal to the values of the marginal net product of their work . . .there would be established between different people's wages a certain relation. *This relation I define as fair.*'

capital.' This aspect of Smith's theory received particular emphasis in the writings of Nassau Senior (1836: 133-4):

> A very small proportion of the earnings of the lawyer or the physician can be called wages. Forty pounds a year would probably pay all the labour that either of them undergoes, in order to make . . . £4000 a year. Of the remaining £3960, probably £3000 may in each case be considered as rent, as the result of extraordinary talent or good fortune. The rest is profit on their respective capitals; capitals partly consisting of knowledge, and of moral and intellectual habits acquired by much previous expense and labour . . . .

The resulting 'capital theory of labour', though receiving rather less emphasis after the mid-nineteenth century, has enjoyed an important revival in recent years — often as a highly sophisticated rationalisation of inequality. 'Investments in human capital — e.g., formal education, on-the-job training, or migration,' it is argued, can explain 'such diverse phenomena as interpersonal and interarea differentials in earnings, the shape of age-earnings profiles . . . and the effect of specialization on skill' (Becker 1964: 153).[43] In explaining differentials at the highest income levels, reference is also commonly made to another factor emphasised by Smith: the responsibility attached to different positions.[44] In its most sophisticated form, current human capital theories offer explicit accounts of both the supply of and demand for labour of different kinds: occupational earnings levels are explained as reflecting, on the one hand, the costs to the employee in terms of education, training and responsibility; on the other, the contribution of his specific aptitudes to productive efficiency. (Forces of supply and demand ensure in equilibrium, so it is argued, a single determinate wage level for each occupation in each place.)

The adoption of such an analytical framework implies evident policy conclusions even if (out of concern for 'value-neutrality') these are not explicitly stated. It follows from such interpretations that existing inequalities are both functional and inevitable: equalisation of incomes, even if desirable in the abstract, 'is restrained by the long-run operation of the market' (Ford 1964: 117-18). As Guillebaud (1967: 18) insists, differentials which appear to offend against principles of equity are essential 'to induce labour voluntarily to shift from one industry to another in accordance with

43. For an application of the 'human capital' perspective to the British economy, see Fisher 1971 and 1973.
44. The structure of incomes in Britain is interpreted by Lydall 1968 as the outcome of the combined effect of human capital and responsibility.

the changing needs of the economy'. Indeed, on the premise that 'the function of the price mechanism is to attract resources to the activities in which they will be most beneficially utilised and most efficiently exploited,' it has even been argued (Merrett 1968) that the differentials enjoyed by managers in private industry — the highest paid of any occupational group — should be increased still further. Without such incentives, the argument runs, the appropriate individuals will not invest in the requisite development of their personal human capital or apply their capacities in the most economically efficient situation and manner.

The verdict of economic orthodoxy has proved extensively influential. Analysis along such lines has become so firmly entrenched in the conventional wisdom — particularly among those who *benefit* from a highly inegalitarian society — that scrutiny of its empirical basis is rarely considered necessary. A wholly uncritical orientation towards conventional economic theory is displayed in sociology, for example, in the famous statement of the 'functional necessity of stratification' by Davis and Moore (1945). They insist that without income differentials nothing would motivate individuals to acquire the skills and perform the duties associated with positions of high 'functional importance'. 'Social inequality is thus an unconsciously evolved device by which societies ensure that the most important positions are conscientiously filled by the most qualified persons' (p. 243). Even philosophers, supposedly radical in their treatment of received ideas, often take for granted such apparently commonsensical judgments. Hence a by no means insensitive analysis of political philosophy (Raphael 1970: 188) can state baldly that 'inequality of pay and status in . . . social arrangements is due to economic considerations of utility and scarcity. High pay and high status are given to doctors because the work of the doctor is highly useful and because relatively few people are capable of doing it.'

The characteristic judgment of those who adopt this perspective is that economic inequality, more or less in its existing form, is a necessary evil.

> They all think equality in itself to be desirable. They all wish the conditions of well-being to be more widely diffused among the masses of the people. On the whole, however, they still maintain that inequality has to be tolerated as a necessary evil, on the ground that equalization would tend to discourage effort, decrease saving and, by lessening efficiency, diminish the total available for distribution, and so would not benefit those for whose benefit it is advocated (Ginsberg 1965: 99).

Yet such accounts of inequality are put in question by the criticisms of classical theory which were outlined in the opening section of this chapter. Routh (1973) has recently pointed to 'a curious schizophrenia in the thought of many of the great economists'. In *The Wealth of Nations*, for example, the elaboration of the theory of 'equalising advantages' is interspersed with 'empirical observations showing that the world is not like that at all'. Yet Smith, like many of his famous successors, suppressed the awkward counter-evidence in his systematisation of competitive theory. More recently, the compartmentalisation of interest between theorists and empiricists has facilitated a divorce between 'the pure abstractions which come over in the modern textbooks' and the findings of research into actual pay structures and pay movements. In fact, many studies have cast doubt on both the necessity and the effectiveness of wage differentials as an economic allocator. 'There is . . . a growing body of evidence indicating that re-allocation of labour depends very little upon widening differentials. . . . Very substantial changes in the distribution of labour have been secured with relatively small changes in relative wages . . . . There is obviously a considerable capacity in the economy for effecting changes in labour force distribution without changes in wage structure' (Alexander 1970; Reddaway 1959; Hunter 1967).[45]

Such findings place in question the precise heuristic status of classical wage structure theory and the modern 'human capital' variants. The specification of occupational 'costs' in terms of investment and responsibility involves immense methodological problems (as does the specification of marginal productivity or functional importance); and measurement is open to manipulation in order to 'fit' a particular structure of earnings. Hence such theories may become near-tautological.[46] Or else the theorist may admit a lack of fit between the real world and his analytical formulations, but seek to save the theory through a variety of *ceteris paribus* and 'as if' qualifications. Yet the comments made at the outset of this section must be repeated: economists have often

45. For similar arguments see Fogarty 1961: ch. 6; Jackson 1967.
46. The same argument applies to those *sociological* explanations of inequality which borrow from economic orthodoxy. Thus Davis and Moore, having analysed income differentials as a reflection of 'functional importance', confess that 'unfortunately, functional importance is difficult to establish'. For a more general critique of functionalist theories of inequality, see Tumin 1953; Goldthorpe 1969.

disregarded their own qualifications and have exaggerated the representational accuracy of their models. And as Wootton has insisted, a theory which treats much of the *actual* structure of incomes as a deviation from the competitive model (and hence inexplicable within its own categories) is of limited explanatory utility.[47]

More fundamentally, we would suggest that the general motivational assumptions of economic theory are revealed at their most implausible in the context of income relativities. 'Suppose surgeons and engineers began to be paid no more than porters and street-cleaners. What would happen? . . . Men would withdraw from occupations in which the relative pay no longer seemed to compensate for the disadvantages, and line up to enter others where the balance between pay and drawbacks had now swung the other way' (Phelps Brown 1962: 148). The typical textbook repetition of Smith's formula involves a remarkably narrow conception of the 'net advantages' of occupations. 'Most well-paid jobs are more, not less, interesting than ill-paid ones,' comments Lipton (1968:99). 'If the pay of a professor or a cabinet minister were less than that of a dustman, would a single university, or government, department lose its chief to the trash-cans?' He goes on to ask: 'Even if we need some incentive payments (for overtime and scarce, price-elastic skills), do the huge present differentials reflect incentive requirements alone?' Economic theorists typically understate the non-material advantages of most high-paid work (in terms of both intrinsic job satisfaction and social status or prestige),[48] and also neglect the extent to which career aspirations and decisions are structured by social background and educational socialisation.[49] Normally they pay little attention to the facts that (in most European countries at least) the costs of education and training are borne by other persons and institutions than the recipient of the investment; and that opportunities for such investment in human capital are to a large extent constrained by class background. The model of the schoolchild as a rational economic calculator, discounting the costs of prolonged education as

47. For more detailed criticism directed specifically at recent 'human capital' theorists, see Salkever 1964:48-51; Corina 1972:52-5.
48. Thus if there existed genuine equality of opportunity to acquire the relevant qualifications and achieve entry into high-status occupations, Adam Smith's formula might imply the need for the ***highest*** pay in the most menial occupations in order to attract a sufficient supply of labour.
49. A rare exception is Pen (1971:39).

against more rapid job entry, misrepresents both the career choices available to most prospective employees and the considerations underlying such choices as are made.

A final criticism which must be levelled against economic interpretations of inequality is their subordination of the analysis of income distribution to that of productive efficiency.[50] A particular structure of rewards is explained (and hence, implicitly or explicitly, justified) as the necessary outcome of market forces in allocating factors of production in the most efficient manner. Leaving aside the various criticisms which may be made of the conventional economic conception of 'efficiency' (arguments which were touched on in our earlier discussion of utilitarianism), it may still be questioned why a large volume of national production distributed in a highly unequal manner must necessarily be preferred to one which is smaller but more equal. Or it is possible to enquire: might not the same allocation of productive resources be achieved, not by relying on the provision (through the market) to their owners of a particular set of material inducements, but through direct intervention in the ownership and control of these resources? Conventional economics tends to assume that the question of distribution can be subsumed under that of efficiency, in part through its reliance on the traditional utilitarian fallacy of the aggregability of utilities; in part through taking for granted the existing structure of ownership and control of economic resources; in part through a belief in the impersonal and immutable character of the principles which happen to underlie existing market relationships. Economists tend to neglect Tawney's advice (1964: 53-4): to remember that 'economic laws' do not state invariable relations, 'but describe how, on the whole, under given historical and legal conditions, and when influenced by particular conventions and ideas, particular groups of men do, as a rule, tend to behave . . . . They indicate the manner in which, given certain historical conditions, and a certain form of social organization, and certain juristic institutions, production tends to be conducted and wealth to be distributed.' Hence the distribution of wealth and income, while mediated by 'impersonal' economic processes, ultimately stems from a structure of social institutions the character of which 'is determined, not by immutable economic laws, but by the values, preferences, interests and ideals which rule at any

50. The importance of this subordination has received detailed attention by Myrdal 1953; Meade 1964.

moment in a given society'.

To develop the analysis of inequality beyond the relatively superficial specification of 'market forces' it is therefore necessary to investigate the environing institutions of power and ideology. A critical analysis of the *political economy* of inequality is however alien to the traditions of economic orthodoxy. Though some writers (e.g. Ginsberg 1965; Rawls 1972) have explicitly recognised that a utilitarian defence of economic inequality must not simply specify the labour market processes through which income differentials purportedly contribute to economic welfare, but must also justify the political economy which structures these processes, such authors are not primarily economists. Moreover, the analyses which they provide at this second level are typically naive and simplistic. Rawls, for example, argues (p. 304) that 'income and wages will be just once a (workably) competitive price system is properly organized and embedded in a just basic structure'; but his defence of the principle of a 'competitive price system' is remarkably cursory, and the implications of such a system for the distribution of power in society are largely ignored. In effect, such modern defenders of an inegalitarian political and economic structure tend to follow closely the perspectives of utilitarianism's major prophet: 'Equality ought not to be favoured, except in cases in which it does not injure security; where it does not disturb the expectations to which the laws have given birth; where it does not derange the actually established distribution . . . . When security and equality are in opposition, there should be no hesitation: equality should give way . . . . In consulting the grand principle of security, . . . the legislator . . . ought to maintain the distribution which is actually established' (Bentham 1838: 303, 311).

Here, the *ideological* character of economic theory again requires emphasis. Most of the classical pioneers, by virtue of their personal economic interests, or at least their membership of a privileged stratum, were sympathetically disposed towards the political economy which they sought to analyse. One need only consider, for example, Locke, the wealthy speculator who 'invented the idea, so wonderfully convenient for the merchant, that whatever price was paid was *ipso facto* just' (Routh 1973: 13-14); Bentham, with his 'almost superstitious reverence for the existing institutions of private property' (Myrdal 1953: 118);[51] Senior, whom 'the manufacturers

51. This reverence even structured Bentham's attitude to the proposed abolition of

elected . . . as their champion' (Marx 1959: 224), and who defended their profits as the reward for 'abstinence' while opposing the 10 hours movement as a threat to these same profits reaped in the 'final hour' of the working day.

The personal position of most modern economists provides little motive to develop a radical analysis of the institutions which generate inequality. And unlike their classical predecessors, considerations of academic politics provide them with a powerful motive for the continued insistence on the explanatory potency of a narrow analysis of forces of supply and demand. There are few incentives, and many disincentives, for economists to devote critical attention to the relationship between the disposal of property, the exercise of social power, and the structure of inequality. Hence the prevailing doctrines deny that power is inherent in economic processes. As Galbraith comments (1973: 6, 11), this 'is not merely to avoid the reality. It is to disguise the reality . . . . Such an economics is not neutral. It is the influential and valuable ally of those whose exercise of power depends on an acquiescent public.'

Conclusion

The perspective of economic theory is that labour (power) is a commodity, the price of which therefore represents the outcome of forces of supply and demand. The wages of ordinary labour were originally assumed to tend naturally towards subsistence level; later the marginalists introduced the notion of 'efficiency' wages, equating their level with labour's marginal productivity. The basic problem of both the classical and the neo-classical approaches is that the level of abstraction involved in their formulations prevents attention to the detailed processes of wage determination; while empirical evidence suggests that these processes (at least in a context in which competitive assumptions apply only tenuously) do not accord with the theoretical models.

Institutional analysts of labour market operations have documented the various deviations from economic theory, and have

---

slavery: 'The same attention ought to be paid to the rights of property; the operation should be gradual, and the subordinate object should be pursued without sacrificing the principal object' (1838: 312-13).

suggested explanatory hypotheses more plausible than its own competitive-utilitarian premises. Yet as the familiar cliché insists, it takes a theory to kill a theory; and we have argued that institutional labour economists have failed to develop an alternative theoretical framework which escapes the inherent limitations of economic orthodoxy. We do not suggest, of course, that forces of supply and demand are *irrelevant* to an explanation of economic inequality; but that an analysis of these forces must be integrated within a broader sociological and political framework. In Chapter 7 we sketch our own approach; but first we turn to a number of alternative attempts to interpret wage-determination processes from outside the problematic of economic theory.

Chapter 6

Alternative Perspectives: Social Psychology, Functionalism and Pluralism

There is some recognition, even among economists, that the phenomena described in the first part of this book cannot be adequately understood within the perspectives of economic theory alone. Thus Pen (1971), while insisting that marginal productivity is 'a plausible starting point for the explanation of most incomes', also stresses that 'some incomes — mainly top incomes — reflect a social value system, and we can understand them only if we know the standards that lie behind them'. The total earnings structure thus represents the outcome of 'the interplay of the market and social convention'. Another economist (Turvey 1971: 199-200) has asserted that, in analysing the recent British experience of inflation, 'we are left with phenomena which we as economists are not competent to investigate'. 'A very important driving force behind the current wage inflation,' he suggests, 'in other countries as well as this, is a strong feeling of social injustice, feelings about the appropriateness of differentials. It is not for the economist to explain these, unless he is to be more of a polymath than in the past.' He concludes that 'it is a question of relative deprivation and the perception of social injustice which is the key to understanding what has happened'. Turvey's reference to relative deprivation points to questions discussed previously, in Chapter 3. To clarify the theoretical issues involved it is necessary to examine more closely and critically the implications of reference group analysis.

Reference Group Theory and its Limitations

Since we have previously described the main outlines of reference group theory, it is unnecessary to set out its perspectives in detail here. To recapitulate briefly: the core postulate of reference group analysis is that the individual's evaluation of his situation (or a particular aspect of this situation), and hence his sense of satisfaction or dissatisfaction, typically involves a process of *comparison*. The conventional presuppositions are, further, that such comparisons are typically structured in a relatively stable, coherent and explicit manner; and that the identification of comparative reference groups involves few methodological problems of importance. Within this problematic, relative deprivation is uniquely defined by the following parameters: 1) the objective situation (or the relevant elements of this situation in terms of the balance of rewards and deprivations) of the subject; 2) the relevant comparative reference group and the subject's orientation towards it (whether he believes his status justifies equal, superior, or inferior net advantages); 3) the subject's perception of his own objective situation and that of the reference group.

In our view the social-psychological perspectives of much reference group analysis (particularly in the specific context of pay comparisons), while facilitating some important insights, contain a number of serious limitations and weaknesses. Inherent in the assumptions outlined above is a tendency to exaggerate the coherence and stability of reference groups. As we have suggested in previous chapters, and will reiterate in that which follows, attitudes and aspirations in respect of pay — particularly on the part of subordinate and underprivileged occupational groups — typically display an important element of imprecision, inconsistency and volatility; and this in turn may be related to the salience of *contradictory* frames of reference for members of such groups.[1] Insensitivity to the structural sources of contradiction and instability in comparison processes is, regrettably, a hallmark of most applications of the concept of reference group.[2]

1. The ideological processes underlying such contradictory frames of reference are discussed in our two concluding chapters.
2. This tendency is reinforced by the typical reliance on attitude surveys as the central research technique of reference group analysis. The basic limitation of such surveys is that they involve, in the words of Cicourel (1964: 5), 'measurement by fiat'. The presupposition that attitudes are simple in character and are readily articulated — and that, in the case of fixed-choice questionnaires, they can be articulated in one of a limited range of standardised forms — does violence to the complexity of social attitudes and their subjective meanings. This is a particularly serious problem in the present context, for if a respondent's values are ambiguous and only semi-articulated, such a research method may

Two associated weaknesses create particular problems for the study of pay comparisons. The first is methodological: the ability to identify the choice of reference group *independently* of a specific pay judgment or aspiration. For some writers, it is almost tautological that a specific pay comparison *follows from* the pre-existing salience of a particular reference group for the individual or group concerned. Yet such a causal relationship cannot be taken for granted: in industrial relations, for example, a desire for higher pay might encourage the selection of a specific comparison group in order to justify the pre-existing pay aspiration (which may itself reflect such extraneous factors as price inflation). Here, the choice of reference group (if indeed the concept, on normal social-psychological usage, can properly be applied to such a case) is not cause but consequence of dissatisfaction with pay. The burden of our discussion in Chapters 3 and 4 was that in many industrial relations situations, *both* directions of causation are in practice intermingled. Nevertheless, reference group analysis normally assumes a unidirectional process of causality, without offering a satisfactory means for its empirical validation.

At times, this methodological weakness is allied to (and indeed facilitated by) an assumption that employees will be predisposed to *endorse* their position in the hierarchy of rewards and deprivations, and will naturally embrace comparisons which minimise or eliminate relative deprivation. This premise is widespread among exponents of 'equity theory', to which reference was made in Chapter 2. The basic perspective of such writers is that a person will regard his pay as equitable if the ratio of his pay to that of another person with whom comparison is made is congruent with the perceived ratio between their respective contributions (Adams 1963 and 1965) or any other attribute considered relevant in evaluating pay (Patchen 1961). Where the two ratios are discrepant, however, the situation will be considered inequitable, and the perception of inequity will increase the larger is the discrepancy.[3]

---

well tap merely the conventional responses encouraged by the prevailing ideology. Such techniques cannot indicate how strongly a particular opinion is adhered to, how consistent it is with other values which the respondent holds, and how it relates to his actions in a specific social context.

3. As was seen in Chapter 2, equity theorists have assumed that where comparison indicates to an individual that he is *over*paid he will experience inequity. It is unnecessary to rehearse here the arguments on this point; our discussion concentrates on comparisons which may indicate underpayment.

Equity theorists attempt to relate this analytical framework to the theory of cognitive dissonance. In its classic formulation (Festinger 1957: 3), the theory asserts that where an individual holds inconsistent opinions or attitudes, or where his beliefs conflict with his actions, the situation will be 'psychologically uncomfortable and will motivate the person to try to reduce the dissonance and achieve consonance. When dissonance is present, in addition to trying to reduce it, the person will actively avoid situations and information which would likely increase the dissonance.' Adams in particular has suggested that this tendency is inherent in pay comparisons: consciousness of inequity creates tensions, which the employee will necessarily attempt to reduce. The implication is that if he is unable to influence directly either his own pay or his work contribution he will restore a sense of equity by selecting an appropriate reference group or by 'cognitively distorting' his perception of his own or the comparison person's ratio of pay to contribution.

A major weakness of equity theory is its individualistic and idealist bias. The presuppositions of the argument that the typical employee will seek to avoid the cognitive dissonance involved in perception of inequitable payment are, first, that such a perception is corrosive of self-esteem; and, second, that the employee confronts his work and pay solely as an individual — and can therefore achieve little real change in his objective situation yet can readily alter his subjective perception of this situation. Neither assumption can be considered universally applicable.[4] First, a sense of underpayment is likely to be corrosive of self-esteem only where the employee feels personally responsible for his pay position. Patchen's study (1961) indicates that where this is the case, an employee will indeed avoid choosing a comparison which encourages relative deprivation; but where management or 'the system' can be blamed, adverse comparisons are not resisted. Where employees are members of formal or informal collective organisations, they may well consider that inequitable payment is open to potential remedy through collective action: while adjustment of reference groups and hence perceptions of pay may not be readily effected if such perceptions are themselves structured by group norms.[5]

4. Indeed both reflect the atypical context of most empirical applications of equity theory. These have relied heavily on the employment — real or hypothetical — of students on individual tasks.
5. The interrelationship of normative and comparative reference groups was considered in Chapter 3.

The Liverpool University study of Manchester dockworkers (1954: 144) is an interesting example of the persistence of acute discontent with pay in a form apparently inexplicable within equity theory: 85 per cent of men interviewed were dissatisfied with their own earnings, while as many as 95 per cent expressed grievances related to the payment system. Such grievances could be attributed, however, to the Dock Labour Board and (to some extent) their union; and they could be seen as remediable through strike action. Hence attitudes which, to the theorist of pay comparisons, might appear dissonant, were in fact *consonant* with the dockers' more general orientations to their employment situation. Again, Patchen's analysis takes account of the possibility of such situations: if a worker is 'motivated to be dissatisfied, he will choose dissonant comparisons from among those available . . . . When a man blames his misfortunes on others, the choice of dissonant comparisons can serve to bolster his claim for higher status' (1961: 17, 109).[6]

Yet most writers on equity theory are less sensitive, apparently assuming that employer-employee relations are in general harmonious, so that dissatisfaction with pay is necessarily dissonant with other aspects of workers' attitudes. This is in turn associated with a consensual perspective on social relations and social values. Such a perspective, indeed, pervades reference group analysis more generally, though normally implicitly: for most theoretical and empirical contributions in this area are innocent of overt sociological concerns. As Merton has commented (1968: 335), 'When experimental research and theoretical inquiry into problems of reference groups once got under way, they centered largely upon study of the determinants of selection of reference groups by individuals and the consequences of this for the personality.' The early emphasis of Merton on the need to relate reference group theory to social-structural analysis has been largely neglected; in consequence, the structural and historical sources of frames of reference are conventionally scarcely scrutinised.

Not all students of reference groups, it is true, confine themselves to the narrowly psychological problematic of individual personality and primary group processes; some add a broader sociological focus. But their sociology has typically involved the perspective of

6. This comment is in line with our previous suggestion that a particular choice of comparison may often represent a consequence rather than a cause of dissatisfaction.

structural-functionalist orthodoxy, with its assumption of normative social integration. Either way, the adoption by subordinate employees of restricted and unambitious pay horizons is not conceived as a major problem for analytical elucidation: it is regarded as normal and natural. Neither focus, moreover, is well adapted either to explore the *contradictions* in employees' attitudes to their position in the incomes hierarchy; or to explain the *changes* in aspirations and perceptions which some observers (as noted at the outset of this chapter) regard as underlying recent British experience.

Structural-Functionalism and the 'Common Value System'

The above remarks are familiar to sociologists, since they relate to a central theoretical debate of recent decades. The theoretical approach particularly associated with the more sociologically oriented of reference group studies is commonly identified with the writings of Talcott Parsons. This is not accidental: for it would appear that Parsons's conception of the social system, which owes much to a form of psychological reductionism, is particularly congenial to the social-psychological disciplinary attachments of most students of reference group processes. The Parsonian model is based on an analysis of the hypothetical interaction of 'ego' and 'alter', two individuals suspended in a social vacuum. He concludes that an orderly relationship is possible only where ego and alter each have stable and compatible expectations of the other's behaviour. This in turn he considers possible only on the basis of shared values. In Parsons's inimitable prose: 'The problem of order, and thus the nature of the integration of stable systems of social interaction, that is, of social structure, thus focuses on the integration of the motivation of actors with the normative cultural standards which integrate the action system . . .' (1951: 36).

This formulation provides the basis of structural-functionalist orthodoxy in sociological theory. The central premise is that, at root, societies are characterised by the possession of an integrated set of norms and values — or 'culture' — common to all except a possible minority of 'deviants'.[7] Subsidiary assumptions are that normative

7. In his first major work, *The Structure of Social Action*, Parsons argues that the

stability is maintained through various processes labelled 'socialisation' or 'social indoctrination'; and that social integration is reinforced by the existence of interdependent social 'roles', the behaviour appropriate to each being unambiguously and uncontroversially defined.[8] Finally, social institutions are assumed to exist and persist because they are 'functional' — because they contribute to the attainment of the 'goals of the society'; a society is thus regarded as a self-maintaining 'system'.

An unusually clear statement of this perspective can be found in Davis's well-known textbook *Human Society*. According to Davis (1948: 79), 'social norms . . . are an essential part of what we call social order'. He goes on (p. 143):

> It is the possession of common-ultimate ends that gives the key to the integration of ends in human societies. Such ends stand at the top of the hierarchy of ends and hence control and regulate the rest. It is in terms of them that a distributive order is sanctioned and maintained. It is on the basis of them that a standard is found for judging the relative merits of lesser ends as held by different individuals.

The same approach is exemplified by a popular British textbook: Cotgrove's *The Science of Society*. Key emphasis is placed on 'the culture of a society': it is stressed that 'the shared norms and values of members of a social system are a most important aspect of a society' (1967: 15). Indeed 'culture' is utilised as *the* central analytical factor. In his first discussion of a specific social institution, Cotgrove treats shared norms and beliefs as the primary explanation of patterns of family relations; his secondary explanation focuses on the way in which 'family and kinship systems also perform important functions in the social system' (pp. 40, 49). In discussing educational institutions, Cotgrove notes that 'every society is faced with the need to ensure adequate preservation and transmission of culture'; he concludes that 'the model which seems most useful for describing the relations between education and society is of two systems each of which is functionally related to the other by feed-back mechanisms' (pp. 67, 110). Shared values structure social behaviour and underpin an integrated system of social institutions, which in turn sustain shared values.[9]

---

notion of a common value system is one of Durkheim's main contributions to sociological theory.

8. The possibility of 'role conflict' may indeed be admitted; but this is treated as essentially marginal to the social structure.
9. The above writers are cited merely as typifying orthodox sociological theory. Such examples could easily be multiplied.

One major problem within such a perspective is how to provide a plausible account of power. Some writers within the Parsonian tradition (such as Cotgrove) attempt a discussion of power — usually very brief — but fail to integrate this into their preceding theoretical framework. Others simply ignore the whole issue. Hence a well-known *Dictionary of Sociology* (Mitchell 1968) contains no entry on 'power'. Smelser (1963) lists 'sanctions', as well as 'values' and 'norms', as important bases of social order, but scarcely explains how the use of sanctions is generated; 'power' is not thought to deserve an entry in his index. Neglect of power may be explicitly justified. As Lockwood has noted (1956: 141), 'that sociology should deal with a particular set of problems within the theory of social systems is the position taken by Parsons in his discussion of the division of labour between the social sciences. Here sociology is defined as having to do with the process of institutionalization of normative patterns . . . . The sphere of "power", economic and political, precisely the factual social order, is delivered for safe keeping to the economist and political scientist'.[10]

There have, however, been serious attempts to consider power within a structural-functionalist framework. Often, it is assumed that the exercise of power is confined to a specific 'political sub-system' of society; and that this 'sub-system' merely serves the function of reinforcing the common values. Thus Davis writes (1948: 145):

> The mores and laws are effective partly because they are enforced by political authority, which can compare the ends of individuals arbitrarily, and also because they have been internalized and thus transformed into ends, values, and sentiments in the minds of the people. Such ends and values are common in the sense that they are noncompetitive and ultimate in the sense that there are no other ends above them. One individual does not lose by another individual's observing the mores and the laws. On the contrary, he gains; it is to his interest to see that others obey. Behind political authority, therefore, stand the sentiments of the people which justify the authority in the name of the ultimate common ends; and justifying the ultimate common ends in turn, are religious belief and practice.

This line of analysis has been developed by Parsons himself in some of his later writings. His starting point is a redefinition of the

10. The neglect of power is not peculiar to adherents of structural-functionalist orthodoxy. Many who consider themselves 'radical' sociologists are equally reluctant to discuss power. In particular, phenomenologically oriented sociologists, with their emphasis on the 'taken-for-granted' rules and understandings of everyday life, often parallel at a more trivial level the Parsonian focus on shared values.

concept of power. He criticises those sociologists (specially Wright Mills) to whom power, following ordinary usage, 'is not a facility for the performance of function in, and on behalf of, the society as a system, but is interpreted exclusively as a facility for getting what one group, the holders of power, wants by preventing another group, the "outs", from getting what it wants'. 'What this conception does', Parsons insists, 'is to elevate a secondary and derived aspect of a total phenomenon into the central place' (1960:220).

Parsons's formulation 'deliberately brings legitimation into the very definition of power, so that, for him, there is no such thing as "illegimate power" ' (Giddens 1968: 260). Just as value-consensus is central to his theory of social order, so legitimacy is central to his theory of power: the *right* of those in positions of domination to exercise control is, for Parsons, necessarily endorsed by their subordinates. The harmonistic presuppositions of classic utilitarianism, discussed in the previous chapter, facilitate Parsons's conceptual sleight-of-hand. Power is defined, in highly abstracted fashion, as 'the generalized capacity of a social system to get things done in the interest of collective goals'; and these in turn derive from 'the values of society' (1960: 181, 187). The remarkable postulate that all power is legitimate gains a certain plausibility against the background of a reified 'society' in which the interests, values and goals of all are in agreement.

By the same token, it is natural that for Parsons *who* has power is of of merely secondary importance. Unequal power is simply one dimension of the societal division of labour, a reflection of 'differential responsibility for effective performance of functions which are held to be, for the system in question, "affected with a public interest" ' (1960: 183). Precisely because power is conceived as nothing but a resource for achieving collective goals, Parsons can regard its distribution as of minor sociological significance.

Structural-functionalist theory has been subject to extensive criticism, and its account of the relationship between power and values is one of its most vulnerable aspects.[11] The most fundamental flaw derives from its idealist bias: founding its explanation of social order upon value-consensus, structural-functionalism lacks any developed account of the social basis of value-consensus itself. It

11. Criticisms include Lockwood 1956; Mills 1959; Rex 1961; Giddens 1968; Coulson and Riddell 1970; Gouldner 1970.

would be an exaggeration to suggest that *no* writer in this tradition has ventured an explanation of the origin of norms and values; but no explanation proposed carries great conviction. Thus Davis (1948: 144) suggests that 'the possession of common-ultimate values by the members of different societies arose in the process of societal evolution. It resulted from a process of natural selection on a societal basis.' Cotgrove's solution to the problem is to posit a process of 'feed-back' between the social system and the educational system. Yet such explanations involve one of two assumptions, both of which are open to objection. Firstly, the genesis and maintenance of value consensus may be attributed to the operation of social forces independent of human decisions: 'society' or 'the social system' is regarded as a supra-human agent whose 'unseen hand' guides the actions of men.[12] This is to reify social relations and social processes: to treat abstractions ('society', 'the social system') as real, active entities.[13] Or, secondly, the processes and institutions which generate and sustain value-consensus can be attributed to the intentions of the members of the society — to the goals of real people, rather than to the 'goals (or needs) of society'. The educational system perpetuates a specific set of values because this is the wish of the members of society. Yet this is to explain value-consensus as the outcome of value-consensus: the argument is patently circular. This is a regress which can be broken only by the assumption of a natural harmony of interests among all members of society.

Precisely the same difficulty affects the functionalist account of the sources of the unequal distribution of power within society.[14] For Parsons, this unequal distribution simply 'comes to be'. Presumably institutions of control emerge, and specific individuals achieve

12. Alternatively, as with Davis, social processes may be conceived as the wholly arbitrary operation of 'natural selection': a crude transposition of Darwinism to human societies so unsatisfactory methodologically as to have been almost wholly abandoned even by functionalists in the present century.
13. Or else it is to commit the fallacy of teleology : to assume that the consequence of a social process or institution represents its cause. In astronomy, an example of this fallacy would be an argument that the movements of the planets are caused by the 'need' of the solar system to maintain itself in equilibrium. Similarly, a teleological explanation in sociology might treat a particular family pattern or structure of property ownership as a consequence of the 'needs' of society or the social system. Such assumptions are involved, explicitly or implicitly, in most varieties of functionalist sociology.
14. The same argument applies to the functionalist theory of economic inequality, discussed in the previous chapter.

positions of power, as a natural response to 'societal needs'. Again, the perspective is either the 'unseen hand' or else the 'social contract'. Neither explanatory device is particularly plausible. We would therefore assert the need to bring the analysis of power — the differential distribution of control over and access to resources and sanctions, both material and ideological — into the centre of the analysis of social values and inequality. Against the simple idealism of functionalist theory we posit a dialectic in which the structure of power helps shape the prevailing beliefs and values, and these in turn help reinforce the unequal distribution of power and material advantages. This perspective we elaborate in the following chapter.

In brief, functionalist theory displays the following key characteristics: 1) common values are treated as the *primary* basis of social relations and social order (hence idealist and harmonistic perspectives are integral to its problematic); 2) the unequal distribution of power, deprivations and material advantages is treated as a *derivative* of consensually defined social goals; 3) inequality is at the same time treated as *functional,* as ultimately advantageous even for those whose immediate situation is highly disadvantageous. Where reference group analysis is pursued, explicitly or implicitly, within this framework, attention is inevitably diverted from the interdependence of economic power, political control, and processes of ideological formation, and the implications of this interdependence for the generation of subjective attitudes to the social hierarchy in both its material and its less tangible forms.[15] Against this theoretical background, empiricist attention to (and often trivialisation of) subjective attitudes and aspirations as of major sociological significance in their own right and without reference to their social origins, represents a noteworthy example of the ideological usage of sociology. Such an application of reference group theory serves to legitimise a grossly inegalitarian social order through the implication that the underprivileged and oppressed themselves 'spontaneously' endorse its fairness.

A related tendency (though rarely involving a full and explicit commitment to Parsonian social theory) may be discerned in the

15. The neglect of this interdependence is reinforced, in the case of Runciman (1966), by a simplistic application of Weber's trichotomy of social stratification. Whereas Weber recognised the interaction of 'class', 'status' and 'party', Runciman applies a rigid compartmentalisation, accentuated by his narrow definition of the concept of power.

analyses of some writers who have counterposed 'social values' to 'market forces' in seeking to explain the unequal structure of employment obligations and rewards. Thus Lupton and Hamilton (1970: 268-9) write that 'in British society, a status hierarchy of occupations exists which is part of the culture and there is a wide consensus about the ranking within it'. They continue:

> The status hierarchy is a cultured norm learnt in the socialisation process and reinforced by consensus used to order the unequal distribution of economic rewards in a legitimate way; the higher an occupation's position in this hierarchy, the more economic resources are in general allocated to it for discretionary use . . . . The influence of this hierarchy as a norm operates through two mechanisms: the socialisation process and public opinion, the one reinforcing the other. The first is present in reward allocating procedures, e.g. wage negotiations, because the individuals taking part are members of the same society who will use that society's culture as an agreed frame of reference. The latter introduces influences from outside the immediate interpersonal relations into the allocating procedures.

While explicitly denying that occupational status and hence income level are a simple reflection of 'functional relevance to the society', Lupton and Hamilton nevertheless echo the structural-functionalist perspective of inequality as the outcome of a consensual value system the origins of which are unscrutinised.

Somewhat similar is the analysis of Pen (1971), in what is in many respects a highly sensitive study of income distribution. An economist who nevertheless appreciates the importance of 'the symbolics of the social hierarchy', his discussion of the 'social value system' displays many affinities with Parsons. Pen insists, for example, that 'consensus' on the pay structure 'comes about in a complicated process of consultation, pressure, opinion-shaping'; he refers to 'the collective expression of an accepted scale of values'; and he argues (with a typically Parsonian reification) that 'society feels that a secondary-school teacher *ought* to earn more' than a primary teacher.[16] The influence of inequalities in socio-economic power and privilege on the prevailing system of values is extrinsic to the problematic of such authors; hence the notion of 'social values' all too easily serves, implicitly or otherwise, as a 'democratic' rationale for inegalitarianism, while at the same time suppressing

16. pp. 40, 101, 288. Pen indeed writes (pp. 98-9) that the salaries of professionals reflect in large measure 'the social ranking as it is seen by society *or at least by that part of society that has a say in this*' (emphasis added). Yet this cryptic addendum is nowhere elaborated: the possibility that those who benefit from an inegalitarian value system might have a disproportionate say in its formulation and perpetuation is not discussed.

attention to *contradictions* in social attitudes to inequality.[17]

Industrial Relations Pluralism

A related perspective underlies much of the literature discussed in Chapter 4: the analysis of the institutional processes involved in collective bargaining and their impact on wage determination. Much writing in industrial relations has indeed adopted an empiricist and avowedly atheoretical approach; yet as we suggested in the previous chapter, empiricism ensures not that analysis is devoid of theoretical presuppositions but merely that these are suppressed. This is particularly apparent when analysis is explicitly problem-centred; for problems, as we argue below, exist and can be identified only given a prior definition (or theoretical judgment) of objectives.

The underlying value-orientations of pragmatism in industrial relations may be indicated in the first instance by a consideration of the *Report* of the Royal Commission on Trade Unions and Employers' Associations, the Donovan *Report*. The Commission's terms of reference required it 'to consider relations between managements and employees and the role of trade unions and employers' associations in promoting the interests of their members and in accelerating the social and economic advance of the nation, with particular reference to the Law affecting the activities of these bodies' (1968: iii). This constituted a far from clearly defined subject of enquiry, and 'for its own guidance' the Commission compiled a highly significant 'survey of the field covered by its terms of reference' (p. 303). The following definitions were offered (pp. 303-4):

'The *social advance of the nation*' is taken to indicate such matters as:
(a) improvements in the standard and extent of education;
(b) greater liberty and opportunity for the individual to lead a fuller life;
(c) more adequate leisure and the proper use of it;
(d) diminution of class distinction;
(e) willingness on the part of the citizen to take his share in civic duties;
(f) reform of oppressive laws;
(g) the awakening of the public conscience in relation to wrongs suffered by any

17. See our discussion of such contradictions in Chapters 2 and 3. Pen's fervent advocacy of job evaluation, and faith in the possibility of its national application on a consensual basis, may be contrasted with our own remarks in Chapter 3 on the normative basis of job evaluation.

section of it.
'*The economic advance of the nation*' is taken to indicate such matters as:
(a) increase in the national wealth, in real terms;
(b) increase in the citizens' standard of living;
(c) adoption of new and more efficient methods of production and distribution . . . .

It may be noted that first priority was assigned to the question of 'accelerating the social and economic advance of the nation', and that no *critical* evaluation of this formulation was attempted. There can be no *a priori* grounds for assuming that actions or policies which promote the 'social and economic advance' of one section of society will prove similarly beneficial to other sections. Indeed it is obvious that policies which *redistribute* income, wealth or power will tend to benefit one group or class *at the expense of* others. Simply to speak of 'the nation' is to evade the whole question of conflicting interests; and it follows from the argument which we develop in the next chapter that such evasion will normally be of ideological advantage to those in positions of social and economic dominance, since their interests will tend to be identified as those of 'the nation as a whole'.

The use of such notions as 'the nation', or 'national interest', in a manner which diverts attention from the structure of *conflicting* interests, closely parallels the Parsonian reification of 'society'.[18] A similar convergence with functionalism is apparent in the automatic identification as 'problems' of those activities and processes which interfere with the objectives of those who exercise control in industry and society. In the Donovan *Report* it is taken for granted that industrial relations problems are self-evident: strikes, 'wage drift', 'the inefficient use of manpower', the erosion of managerial control over the work process. Yet none of these can be said to represent self-evident problems for all members of the community. As is today widely recognised by sociologists, it is not simply the existence of a specific state of affairs which constitutes a 'social problem'; to the objective situation must be added a social process through which it becomes generally *identified* as a problem. 'A "social problem" consists not only of a fixed and given condition but the perception and definition by certain people that this condition poses a threat which is against their interests and that

18. This tendency to reify was mentioned above. The affinities between functionalism and the prevailing approaches to industrial relations analysis, discussed below, are considered in greater detail in Hyman and Fryer 1974.

something should be done about it' (Cohen 1971: 14). Hence strikes, in so far as they raise wages and provide a means of resistance to uncongenial or oppressive managerial control, are highly advantageous to workers who *go* on strike. 'Wage drift' clearly benefits those workers who in its absence would enjoy an inferior income. 'The inefficient use of manpower' may be merely a derogatory label for a situation in which men successfully pursue job security, humane working conditions or a measure of control over the production process, rather than submitting to the blind dictates of profitability. The erosion of management control may be viewed, conversely, as the assertion by workers of *their own* control. Even if such practices can be shown to obstruct 'economic efficiency' (itself a highly value-laden concept) it does not necessarily follow that their elimination is in the overall interests of the workers concerned: in other words, they need not represent 'problems' for them.

It is in line with the implicit assumption that the interests of workers are fundamentally the same as the (managerially defined) 'national interest' that the Commission provided its interpretation of 'the interests of [union] members' (p. 309):

> '*Interests*' here is taken to mean the interests of the members of a trade union as such members. Such interests will include:
>
> (a) wages and conditions of work;
> (b) effective consultation with managements at national, district, and shop level;
> (c) 100% trade union membership;
> (d) participation in the conduct of the union's affairs, at all levels;
> (e) fidelity to union rules and decisions;
> (f) help in personal problems;
> (g) help in dealing with grievances;
> (h) help in legal matters;
> (i) maintenance of full employment;
> (j) maintenance of the real value of wages.

What is immediately apparent is the extreme narrowness of this conception of trade unionists' interests. The rule books of many unions refer not simply to the aim of improving terms and conditions of employment *within* a capitalist society, but specify the objective of *transforming* the social and economic basis of that society and with it the whole status of labour. Despite the constraining influence of their normal preoccupation with routine collective bargaining issues, trade unionists do on occasion discuss such questions as how they might redress the glaring inequalities of wealth, income and power which characterise our society; how the priorities of industry might be consciously determined on the basis of social need, rather than subject to the vagaries of a profit-based market economy; how workers might transcend the status of mere instruments of production and make work a genuinely creative activity (Hyman and Fryer 1974). The TUC General Council itself commented on the narrowness of the Donovan perspectives (*Annual Report* 1968: 409): 'The Royal Commission had become primarily a Royal Commission on collective bargaining. Very little was said about the role of trade unions in relation to the formulation of economic policy, or in relation to their participation in economic planning, or in general in relation to their wider social purposes.'[19]

It is not surprising that a Royal Commission should so define trade unionists' interests as to exclude such questions from consideration. Yet the Commission's general orientation has close affinities with the perspective of many leading academic writers on industrial relations.[20] In the latter case, predictably, the analytical presuppositions are often expressed with greater sophistication. Most influential, perhaps, is Dunlop's characterisation of industrial relations as 'an analytical subsystem of an industrial society', the defining feature of which is the process of 'rule making and administration' that impinges on work and employment. Dunlop borrows openly from the systems theory of Talcott Parsons, building

19. It is interesting that the Commission's perspectives were narrower even than was implied by its own definition of its terms of reference. For example, concern with 'fidelity to union rules and decisions' might be thought to require some attention to the rule-book statements of trade union objects. Thus the Transport and General Workers' Union referred (Rule 2, section 2 (i)) to 'the furthering of the interests of labour, trade unionism, or trade unionists, including the securing of a real measure of control in industry and participation by the workers in the management, in the interests of labour and the general community'. The Amalgamated Engineering Union defined its first object (Rule 1, section 2) as 'the control of industry in the interests of the community'. Yet there is no discussion of the control of industry in the Donovan *Report*. Even the issue of 'workers' participation', normally interpreted in so limited a sense as to avoid any real interference with the structure of control in the capitalist enterprise, was outside the Commission's narrow focus of interest and was dismissed in four pages.

20. It would of course be quite wrong to suggest a consensus among academics who specialize in industrial relations: controversy is often acute. Yet such controversy normally occurs within a framework of common presuppositions. Thus McCarthy and Ellis (1973:29) assert the convergence between 'traditionalist' (or 'unitary') and pluralist perspectives: 'neither side seeks to deny that problems exist and something needs to be done about them — indeed there is a remarkable degree of agreement as to the features of the British industrial relations system they set out to remedy'.

on the same premises of functional integration and a common value system. Thus 'the idea of an industrial-relations system implies a unity, an interdependence, and an internal balance which is likely to be restored if the system is displaced'; while harmony is reinforced by ideological consensus, 'a set of ideas and beliefs commonly held by the actors that helps to bind and integrate the system together as an entity' (1958: 16, 27). Systems analysis, it would thus appear, 'offers an ideologically acceptable alternative to those who embrace the perspectives of the pragmatist but eschew his unsophisticated language and concepts. The selfsame problems of efficiency, practicality, constructive adaptation to change and the 'orderly' reform of industrial relations can be tackled in either framework. The principal concerns of Parsons' sociology parallel closely the chief worries of those in authority in industry' (Hyman and Fryer 1965).

Not all who embrace the popular concept of an industrial relations system would accept a commitment to Dunlop's functionalist premises. Particularly influential in Britain is the approach of Flanders. While disavowing the assumptions of Parsonian social theory he agrees with Dunlop that 'a system of industrial relations is a system of rules', and hence argues that 'the study of industrial relations . . . may . . . be described as a study of the institutions of job regulation' (1970: 86). Yet this approach involves certain problems. If the notion of industrial relations system is employed without the postulate of a *determinate relationship* between the elements of the system, the danger is that these elements will represent no more than a check-list of actors, influences and institutions. In abandoning the functionalist paradigm, the concept of industrial relations system is thus often drained of theoretical content and explanatory utility.

It may in any case be questioned whether the redefinition of the concept in fact wholly escapes the connotations of functionalism. For the focus on particular *institutions* of job *regulation* has two important implications. First, it shares the traditional concern of conservative sociology with the 'problem of order'. The interest is in how industrial conflict is contained and regulated rather than in why it occurs: 'the emphasis tends, therefore, to be put more on the consequences of industrial dispute than on its causes' (Margerison 1969: 273). This in itself involves a one-sided perspective towards industrial relations. But in addition, while a theoretical preoccupation with order need not in principle involve a 'conservative ideological bias' (Cohen 1968: 18), in practice — as will be shown later — the perspective carries with it an assumption that 'orderly industrial relations' are by their very nature desirable.

The second implication is that the institutional processes of job regulation receive far more attention than the broader framework of power and ideology which shapes these processes.[21] In part the neglect by most students of industrial relations of broader social, economic and political analysis reflects the logic of the academic compartmentalisation discussed in the previous chapter. Yet as was argued there, this is to take for granted the overall structure of society.[22]

Another influential qualification to Dunlop's original formulation of industrial relations systems theory is open to parallel criticisms. This second variant, industrial relations pluralism, is elaborated by Fox (1966a)[23] in contradistinction to what he terms the 'unitary frame of reference'. This latter, Fox argues, postulates an identity of interests within the industrial enterprise and the nation as a whole; the enterprise is viewed according to a teamwork analogy, with 'one source of authority and one focus of loyalty . . . . Each accepts his place and his function gladly, following the leadership of the one so appointed.' Where industrial conflict occurs, those who embrace this ideology will naturally attribute it 'to faults among the governed — to stupidity, or short-sightedness, or out-dated class rancour, or

21. Even at the level of the individual enterprise or workplace, the focus of orthodox industrial relations is notably restricted. In Britain in 1971 there were 268,832 reported accidents at work, 525 of these being fatal; in addition there were 2,612 deaths from the industrial diseases of pneumoconiosis, asbestosis and other forms of fibrosis (HM Chief Inspector of Factories. *Annual Report 1971*, Cmnd. 5098 (London: HMSO 1972). Almost certainly, these figures seriously understate the extent of the problem: see Kinnersly 1973). A major factor underlying this everyday violence towards workers in the 'sheer indifference of some companies to the safety of their workers' (*ibid.*, p.ix). Yet this aspect of the relations between employers and workers is not normally considered any part of 'industrial relations'.
22. Derber (1967:158) castigates most writers in the field for accepting as their starting point 'that the prevailing values of the society and of its chief components — government, corporations, unions — are intrinsically sound and that the problems are primarily technical in nature'. Whether or not the prevailing social values are explicitly endorsed, the very fact that broader social issues are conventionally dismissed as irrelevant to industrial relations entails that the central focus is how workers and their organisations *adjust to* the structure of power and inequality which is taken for granted. Independently of the authors' intentions, most research in industrial relations thus has an inevitably manipulative character.
23. Fox has subsquently altered his position in significant respects; see Fox 1973a.

an inability to grasp the basic principles of economics, or the activities of agitators who create mischief out of nothing'. And inevitably, a commitment to the unitary frame of reference carries with it an ambivalent — if not downright hostile — attitude to trade unionism.

Against the unitary perspective, with its obvious affinities with functionalism and systems theory, Fox insists that the enterprise is 'more plausibly viewed as a coalition of interests, a miniature democratic state composed of sectional groups with divergent interests . . .' (p. 2). This divergence of interests provides a legitimate basis for union activity: firstly in protecting workers' *economic* interests where these conflict with those of the employer, but secondly in defending them against the arbitrary exercise of *managerial* authority — management action 'in deploying, organising and disciplining the labour force, after it has been hired' (p. 7). The pluralist recognises that 'conflict is endemic to industrial organisation'; hence 'instead of assuming disruption to be due to the impact of the more regrettable aspects of human nature upon an otherwise harmonious system, we see it instead as an outcome of group structure, group relations and group policies' (pp. 8-9).

Despite the important contrasts between the two perspectives which Fox outlines, industrial relations pluralism[24] is notable for its ambiguity. Fox's characterisation of conflict as the 'outcome of group structure, group relations and group policies' fails to specify what is the nature of the group processes involved, whether the divisions within each enterprise extend across the whole political economy, and how fundamental are the resulting conflicts of interest. The possibility that the structure of ownership and control within capitalist industry may generate an *irreconcilable* conflict of interest between employers and employees is not confronted. The very adoption of the label 'pluralism' would appear to imply, on the contrary, an orientation which parallels the dominant approach in recent political theory: the assumption that contemporary society, and political relations within that society, are characterised by the

24. The comments of Fox himself are relevant to the present discussions: 'In describing an ideology there is always the difficulty presented by the existence of many individual variants. Some adherents accept while others may reject each given item of the syndrome. Only a generalized picture can therefore be offered. This means that a person subscribing to any one particular pluralist belief presented here cannot be regarded as necessarily identifying with, or even being aware of, the others' (1973a : 192).

competition of numerous sectional groups of which none possesses a disproportionate concentration of power.[25] Pluralism is the political equivalent of the presuppositions of utilitarian economics: just as the market is assumed to mediate neutrally between the interests of the various economic actors, so the political process is assumed to generate a 'negotiated order' which accords tolerably with the interests of all. Utilitarian economics and political pluralism both admit the existence of conflicting aims and preferences on the part of the members of society: but both are predicated, explicitly or implicitly, on the existence of an underlying balance of power and interests. For in the absence of such balance, what is conceived as a negotiated order would rest in actuality on coercion or manipulation.[26]

This same presupposition of balance is basic to industrial relations pluralism. The pluralist perspective, as Fox has expounded it, insists that 'co-operation . . . needs to be engineered by structural adaptations in work organisation, work rules and work practices, and that direct negotiation with work-groups is an essential part of this process' (1966a: 14). It is an act of faith that workers' willing co-operation is forthcoming, so long as managements appreciate the existence of a divergence of interest which renders legitimate the activities of workers' organisations, both within and without the workplace. This presupposition of the resolubility of conflicts of interest is, however, plausible only if it is assumed that these conflicts are less fundamental than the underlying area of common aims and interests.[27] Fox has conceded this point in a later and more

25. The doctrine of political pluralism has been widely criticised; see for example Miliband 1969 and, for a review of American literature, Playford 1971.
26. An important ambiguity in pluralism is the interpenetration of descriptive and prescriptive doctrines. For many writers, pluralism has represented primarily a social *ideal,* posed in explicit contrast to existing social institutions. Thus Guild Socialists such as Cole advocated the separate institutional representation of citizens' varying functional roles (as producers, consumers, residents in a specific locality) as against the undivided sovereignty of a parliament elected on a single representative principle. For more recent writers, however, pluralism has tended to represent the idealisation of what already exists; both in political and industrial relations theory, the existence of balance is often asserted as desirable and then, with little attempt at substantiation, regarded as actual.
27. The pluralist perspective often founds such an assumption on a narrow definition of those worker interests which are both legitimate and rational. In practice, the legitimacy of existing authority in industry is unquestioned; hence the legitimacy of any aspiration on the part of workers to overturn the rule and political economy of the present owners and controllers of capital is discounted. Similarly, union democracy — control of union policy and organisation from below by the

critical discussion, adding that this assumption gives pluralism 'a clear resemblance to Parsonian consensus'.

The assumption is being made that while, to be sure, conflicts arise over the terms of economic collaboration, values and norms are not so divergent that workable compromises cannot be achieved. Underlying the cut and thrust of marketplace and organizational encounters, in other words, lies the rock-firm foundation of a stable and agreed social system. Men may disagree about the distribution of the social product and other terms of their collaboration — and it is healthy and desirable that they should — but their disagreements are not so great and so lasting that they seek to destroy the system or even put it under serious hazard. In order to maintain that system they submit to compromise and find themselves able, for this purpose, to share moral beliefs which teach the importance of observing agreements freely and honourably undertaken (1973a: 197-8).

Thus, Fox argues, while pluralism is at first sight a theoretical perspective radically different from the unitary approach, it represents in the final analysis 'no more, or no less, than enlightened managerialism' (1973: 213).[28] Put bluntly, pluralism assumes the

---

rank and file — is rarely treated as an important and serious issue. Hence it may be argued that 'the pluralist frame of reference, while recognising the existence of conflicts of interest, is able to assert their reconcilability in part through a *selective* endorsement of the legitimacy of interest groups and their objectives. Those groups and aspirations which challenge the continuation of a collaborative relationship between representatives of rich and poor, exploiting and exploited, are simply denied legitimacy' (Hyman and Fryer 1974:169).

28. Fox develops this point (1973a 218-20) in an analysis which parallels our own previous argument: 'industrial relations pluralists . . . focus their interest on the substance and methods of rule making and conflict regulation within the existing and given institutions and objectives of work. Their "problem areas" they tend to share with individuals, groups, and agencies who are concerned with the practical application of those forms of economically rational, efficient, and humane management which, directed though they may be to profit-making, are seen as producing such incidental benefits as lower-cost operations, better terms and conditions of employment, and "mutually-satisfactory" procedures of joint regulation and conflict resolution. . . . The interest is in "order" — not an imposed order but an order negotiated with representatives of participant interests. . . .

'[But] this negotiation of order within the enterprise takes place only at the margins. Management and the [employee] interests do not jointly build their collaborative structure from the ground floor up. Power and social conditioning cause the employee interests to accept management's shaping of the main structure long before they reach the negotiating table. Thus the discussion may be about marginal adjustments in hierarchical rewards, but not the principle of hierarchical rewards; about certain practical issues connected with the prevailing extreme sub-division of labour, but not the principle of extreme sub-division of labour; about financial (extrinsic) rewards for greater efficiency, but not about the possibility of other types of (intrinsic) reward with some sacrifice of efficiency; about measures which may achieve company expansion and growth, but not about the benefits and costs of company expansion and growth; about how the participant interests can protect and

existence of sufficient convergence of interest to provide a practical basis for moral integration; it endorses the notion of a common 'national interest', even though this position is reached from a different route.

Such perspectives may be identified in the writings of many of the recognised authorities in industrial relations. For example Roberts (1966), in his evidence to the Donovan Commission, explicitly embraces 'the assumption that workers and managers, unions and employers have a common interest'; the idea that there may exist an opposition of interests is dismissed as a 'legacy of the past'. Given this harmonistic premise, Roberts's simplistic use of the concept of 'society' follows naturally: as in his insistence that the right to strike should be removed 'if the costs exceed the benefits to society'. This overt adoption of the 'unitary' stereotype of industrial relations is admittedly untypical of most academic analysts. Thus Kahn-Freund has emphasised (1972: 18-19) that 'any approach to the relations between management and labour is fruitless unless the divergency of their interests is plainly recognised and articulated . . . . It is . . . sheer utopia to postulate a common interest in the substance of labour relations.'

Yet despite this clear commitment to pluralism, Kahn-Freund's orientation to strikes has surprising affinities in both tone and content with that of Roberts. 'Industrial stoppages cause losses to the economy, and hardship to men and women. Everyone, except those on the lunatic fringe, wants to reduce their number and magnitude' (p. 223). The economic impact of strikes is the subject of considerable controversy;[29] but the hardship caused, at least by the small, short strikes characteristic of post-war British industrial relations, is presumably limited. Against this, some strikes (the proportion is, again, a subject of dispute) do yield important gains to those involved. Yet to refer simply to 'losses to the economy' is to

---

advance themselves within the structure operated by management to pursue its basic objectives, but not about the nature of those basic objectives.

'By accepting this definition of "problems", pluralists implicitly accept what might be called the "master" institutions, principles, and assumptions of the *status quo* as non-problematical. In doing so they add their professional status, personal prestige, and influential involvement in public policy making to the factors which lead subordinate groups to continue seeing the *status quo* as legitimate, inevitable, unchangeable, "only to be expected", subject only to changes at the margin.'

29. See for example Turner 1969; Hyman 1972b.

divert attention from the fact that some gain while others lose; moreover, the use of such epithets as 'the lunatic fringe' is hardly calculated to encourage dispassionate analysis of this sensitive issue.

Some similarities may be discerned in what was perhaps the most influential evidence to the Donovan Commission: Flanders's essay 'Collective Bargaining: Prescription for Change' (1970: 155-211). As in the Commission's own terms of reference, such phrases as 'economic growth and social advance' and 'the interests of society at large' recur, without any discussion of the problems inherent in the use of such value-laden concepts. Just as Roberts contrasts the sectional concerns of unions and employers with 'the public interest' (1962: 11), so Flanders refers to a 'conflict between sectional and national interests' (p. 162). Either formulation invites Wedderburn's rejoinder (1971: 405): 'the "public interest" is no unitary third element at the bargaining table; it is a congeries of competing interests'. Hence not surprisingly it 'has a curious habit of coinciding with the interests to which the speaker owes allegiance' (Wedderburn 1965: 287).

The objection to such concepts is not, however, merely that they are open to conflicting subjective interpretations. It is that the interpretation is itself structured by the relationships prevailing within the existing social and economic system. This is, indeed, one of the crucial implications of the analysis which we develop in the following chapter. It is relevant to consider Marx's response to the assertion of 'the bourgeois and their economists' that the 'interests of the capitalist and those of the worker . . . are one and the same' ('Wage Labour and Capital' in Marx and Engels 1958: I, 92-3). The core of truth in this argument is that *within* an economy based on wage-labour and the private ownership of capital, workers and employers are necessarily interdependent. If companies go bankrupt, their employees as well as their owners suffer. Hence, apparently, it is in the interests of workers to limit their economic demands, their aspirations for congenial work conditions, or their wishes for an element of control over the production process, where their employment might otherwise be jeopardized. Yet at a different level of analysis, the *perpetuation* of a system of ownership and control of industry which renders the worker's position so precarious and compels such unpalatable choices might be taken as the focus of a glaring and unbridgeable opposition of interest. This was indeed Marx's argument (p. 93): 'To say that the interests of capital and those of the workers are one and the same is only to say that capital and wage labour are two sides of one and the same relation . . . . As long as the wage-worker is a wage-worker his lot depends upon capital. That is the much-vaunted community of interests between worker and capitalist.' By implication, clearly, as soon as the *necessity* of this economic relation is questioned then the underlying conflict of interests is apparent.

The failure of most writing in industrial relations to raise this question is thus of the utmost importance. Kahn-Freund's description of the 'expectations of labour and management' is extremely revealing:

> It follows from what I have said before that the legitimate expectations of labour and of management belong to those which are inevitably in conflict. Management can legitimately expect that labour will be available at a price which permits a reasonable margin for investment, and labour can equally legitimately expect that the level of real wages will not only be maintained but steadily increased. Management can claim a legitimate interest in obtaining for each job the most qualified worker available; labour can claim a legitimate interest in obtaining a job for each worker who is unemployed. Management can and must always expect that the arrangements of society (through law or otherwise) ensure that labour is as mobile as possible in the geographical as well as in the occupational sense; labour must always insist that workers enjoy a reasonable measure of job security so as to be able to plan their own and their families' lives. Management expects to plan the production and distribution of goods or supply of services on a basis of calculated costs and calculated risks, and requires society to guarantee the feasibility of such planning by protecting it against interruption of these processes; labour well realises that without the power to stop work collectively it is impotent, and expects to be able to interrupt the economic process if this is necessary in order to exercise the necessary pressure. Management's interest in planning production and in being protected against its interruption is the exact equivalent to the worker's interest in planning his and his family's life and in being protected against an interruption in his mode of existence, either through a fall of his real income or through the loss of his job. All this is palpably obvious, except for a person blinded by class hatred either way (1972: 52-3).

The equivocal nature of pluralism could not be more clearly demonstrated. Management and workers have conflicting interests: but the interests of both are *legitimate.* This assertion of legitimacy is, presumably, intended as more than an expression of personal moral judgment: it represents the prevailing *social* evaluation. Yet this merely means that within a capitalist economy, certain rights form part of the 'rules of the game'. To challenge, for example, the right of workers to sell their labour in the dearest market or of employers to buy it in the cheapest is to challenge the ground rules of a 'free market for labour'.[30] Yet if Kahn-Freund's purpose is

30. Marx's ironical comment (1959:176) is justifiably famous: 'This sphere . . . within

merely to state the commonly agreed prerogatives of either side of industry within a capitalist economy, his emotive final sentence would appear to go much further. The seeming implication is that the 'rules of the game' are unchallengeable by men of goodwill; only those 'blinded by class hatred' would consider questioning the desirability of capitalist economic relationships. Hence radical challenge to the *status quo* is denied legitimacy.[31]

---

whose boundaries the sale and purchase of labour-power goes on, is in fact a very Eden of the innate rights of man. There alone rule Freedom, Equality, Property and Bentham. Freedom, because both buyer and seller of a commodity, say of labour-power, are constrained only by their own free will. They contract as free agents, and the agreement they come to, is but the form in which they give legal expression to their common will. Equality, because each enters into relation with the other, as with a simple owner of commodities, and they exchange equivalent for equivalent. Property, because each disposes only of what is his own. And Bentham, because each looks only to himself. The only force that brings them together and puts them in relation with each other, is the selfishness, the gain and the private interests of each. Each looks to himself only, and no one troubles himself about the rest, and just because they do so, do they all, in accordance with the pre-established harmony of things, or under the auspices of an all-shrewd providence, work together to their mutual advantage, for the common weal and in the interests of all.'

31. Kahn-Freund thus articulates explicitly the perspective which, we argued earlier (fn. 27), is normally implicit in the pluralist approach to industrial relations: the selective endorsement of the legitimacy of interest groups and their objectives. The parallel with political pluralism is again significant: writers such as Lipset commonly define as 'authoritarian' and 'undemocratic' any political movement which challenges a system based on minority ownership and control of industry. See for example the critique by Jacobs 1968. It is interesting that the Industrial Relations Act — which Kahn-Freund has sharply criticised — incorporates notions of what is fair and reasonable which bear remarkable similarities to his own. The Act's differentiation between 'fair' and 'unfair' dismissal (ss. 22-32) is based on so firm an endorsement of the 'legitimate expectations of management' that the circumstances in which a dismissed employee can successfully claim redress are defined in a manner which is 'unduly restrictive', while 'the remedies are rather weak' and provide 'relatively meagre' compensation (Anderman 1972: 4-7). Rather than enhancing security of employment, the net effect may well be to reduce the likelihood of strike action resulting from a dismissal, and hence to increase the confidence with which managements pursue their 'legitimate interests' by removing troublesome employees. The Act's specification of 'unfair industrial practices' (especially ss. 96-8) similarly reflects an endorsement of 'management's interest in planning production and in being protected against its interruption': hence the situations in which workers may legitimately apply collective sanctions are extremely narrowly circumscribed. The notions of fairness expressed in the judgments on the Employment Secretary's application against the railway unions in 1972 are also of relevance. Thus the chairman of the NIRC asserted a 'fundamental obligation of every employee to behave fairly to his employer and to do a fair day's work' (*Weekly Law Reports*, 1972, p. 1381); while in the Court of Appeal, Buckley L.J. declared 'that within the terms of the contract

This need not imply that pluralism is to be simply equated with conservatism: most industrial relations pluralists advocate certain changes and reforms. But such reforms do not extend to the basic structure of power and inequality in industry: to propose changes of this order would be to imply a denial of the pluralist premise that existing social institutions and relationships incorporate a reasonable reciprocity and balance of interests. Hence it is natural that the 'legitimate expectations of labour' should be defined extremely modestly and narrowly: 'a reasonable measure of job security', 'steadily' increasing real wages, and the right to strike 'if this is necessary'. Like the Donovan Commission (of which he was a member) Kahn-Freund adopts so restricted a view of worker interests that their 'reconciliation' with management interests is regarded as the natural outcome of a process of 'give and take' (1972: 53-5).

In his emphasis on the purely *market* aspects of the worker's role, Kahn-Freund is in fact untypical of industrial relations pluralism; Fox (1966a), as has been seen, stressed the importance for the worker of *managerial* relations, and Flanders has developed this argument in detail. The effects of union action, he insists, 'extend beyond the securing of material gains to the establishment of *rights* in industry' (1970: 223-5). Attempts to limit managerial control over the work process, and to counterpose more humane values to the impersonal dictates of capitalist economic 'efficiency', constitute 'far more intractable sources of industrial conflict' than the more routine concerns of collective bargaining (p. 230). Yet in their more practically orientated writings, industrial relations pluralists seemingly deny that this conflict is intractable. In an earlier discussion, Flanders notes the 'dilemma . . . of reconciling planning and democracy . . . . The rationality implicit in planning appears to be an enemy of the sectional pressures unleashed by democracy.' But he goes on to insist that 'only the extremists on either side deny that a reconciliation of the two is possible' (p. 114). In this somewhat

[of employment] the employee must serve the employer faithfully with a view to promoting those commercial interests for which he is employed' (*ibid.*, p. 1396). The logic of such legalistic approaches, which threaten the basic principles of trade union organisation and activity, can be effectively countered only from a perspective which recognises that the conflict between the expectations of employers and workers is far more fundamental than pluralists assume. This in turn requires an explicit denial of the legitimacy of managerial expectations and of the political economy which supports them.

abstracted discussion of the opposition between 'planning' and 'democracy', the use of such value-laden terminology as 'rationality', 'sectional pressures', and 'extremists' implies a perspective similar to that of Kahn-Freund. Namely, that the 'planners', at the level of management and the state, somehow transcend sectional pressures; and that the principles which underlie their planning are naturally superior to the vulgar prejudices of those subject to their decisions. This necessarily ignores the fact that the decisions of the planners are rational only within the framework of a set of objectives structured by the prevailing economic system and reflecting the interests of those with economic and social power within that system.[32]

Here is further support for Fox's view (1973a: 219) that, for the pluralist, the 'negotiation of order within the enterprise takes place only at the margins'. The conception of 'democracy' counterposed to the 'planning' necessary within a technologically sophisticated capitalism is a highly diluted version. The pluralist viewpoint on this

32. 'Rationality' is of course a highly dangerous concept within the social studies. As Weber emphasised, there is a considerable difference between appraising the rationality of an action as a means to a given end (a more or less 'scientific' task) and evaluating the rationality of the end itself (a more or less 'pure' value-judgment). Yet writers commonly confound the two senses of rationality, or express purely evaluative judgments of rationality as statements of objective fact. Thus economists commonly assume that *only* actions explicable within the paradigm of capitalist market maximisation may be regarded as rational. Sociologists in the human relations tradition, superficially antagonistic to the assumptions of classical economics, have contrasted the 'logic of efficiency' characteristic of the capitalist enterprise with the 'logic of sentiment' underlying workers' actions — thus depreciating the rationality of the latter. In industrial relations, Barbash (1964) has contrasted the 'enterprise rationality' of the capitalist employer with the 'human non-rationality' of the worker. Similar problems apply to the concept of 'efficiency', also common within industrial relations writing. An action, object or process is efficient or inefficient only in relation to a specific end. Drinking whisky is an efficient means of getting drunk but an inefficient means of staying sober. Often, however, the term 'efficient' is employed without further specification as a simple form of commendation, the implicit end being the maximisation of company profitability. Yet a change which increases profitability at the cost of redundancy for some workers and more oppressive work conditions for others might be highly inefficient in terms of *their* objectives, in contrast to those of management. The same argument applies to the notion of 'restrictive practices': a practice which restricts the ability of employers to achieve their objectives may be an indispensable defence of workers' interests. Again, it is significant that the conventional usage of the term, embraced by most industrial relations academics, involves the unquestioned acceptance of the managerial goals of profitability. For a particularly naive example, see Lincoln 1967.

question is influentially argued by Clegg (1963: 119): 'Industrial democracy must for the most part confine itself to protecting rights and interests.' Far from implying control and initiative on the part of the workers, a radical restructuring of decision-making and hence a transformation of the whole political economy, industrial democracy is interpreted as a process of defensive reaction to management decision *within* the structure of capitalism — in other words, the normally accepted activities of trade unionism. And even the degree with which the 'protection of rights and interests' is deemed appropriate is shaped by notions of moderation and reasonableness. Thus 'most trade union leaders, . . . being reasonable men, acknowledge that redundancies must occur' (Clegg 1965: 9).[33] Yet if it is unreasonable for unions to resist redundancy as such, debate can take place only on such eminently negotiable issues as who should be made redundant, in what circumstances, and with what compensation. The conflict between management's concern with 'planning' and 'efficiency' and workers' interest in job security is thus resoluble by the simple expedient of restricting the degree of security to which workers may reasonably aspire. Where similar criteria of 'reasonableness' are applied to al the objectives of trade unionism, it is hardly surprising that the conflict between 'planning' and 'democracy' loses its intractable character.

A final example of the convergence of the pluralist and managerial perspectives may be noted: the use of the concept of order. The unitary approach, with its denial of the existence of conflicting interests, carries with it a natural predisposition towards 'law and order' in industrial relations: in place of strife, the evident need is to 'get more harmony, positive co-operation and unity of purpose into our industrial life' (Conservative Party 1968: 9). The clearest academic exposition of this approach is provided by Roberts's attack on the decentralisation and informality of British industrial relations (1962: 11).

The present situation is far from satisfactory since it encourages guerilla warfare

33. Roberts states the premise bluntly: 'redundancy is inevitable' (1966: 1408). A similarly 'practical' approach is manifested by Turner and his associates (1967: 339): after discussing such worker aspirations as 'job property rights' they conclude that 'the point is not so much whether or not these ideas are in principle reasonable, as how far they are negotiable'. For an important critique of the manner in which 'practical' discussion of redundancy inevitably accepts the validity of capitalist relations of production, see Fryer 1973.

instead of an orderly system of negotiations.[34] It produces agreements that are shaped by tactics designed to secure concessions, to take advantage of a temporary situation, rather than to develop a comprehensive long-term strategy of collective bargaining that would result in a more organic pattern of industrial relations.

The sheer anarchy and the lack of constructive purpose which pervades so much of collective bargaining today, and the outrageous contempt which both sides of industry so frequently display towards the public interest, must eventually provoke a reaction that will compel the adoption of a more orderly system of industrial relations.

Yet this argument has many parallels with the analysis of the 'challenge from below' presented by Flanders (1970: 108-13) in his essay 'Industrial Relations: What is Wrong With the System?' and developed further in his evidence to the Donovan Commission. Workplace bargaining in Britain, Flanders argues (p. 169), 'is largely informal, largely fragmented and largely autonomous'. 'The case for a radical reconstruction of workplace relations is', he insists (p. 196), 'an overwhelmingly strong one on the immediate, practical grounds that their present state is causing serious damage to the national economy and to the fabric of our industrial relations system.' Despite his emphasis that 'order and peace . . . are not the only ends of industrial relations' (p. 210) the implication is nevertheless that they are highly valued objectives; and this same position was adopted by the Donovan Commission in its *Report.* Its basic diagnosis was that two systems of industrial relations, formal and informal, operated in Britain, and that the conflict between those systems generated anarchy and disorder. As Flanders commented (*The Times,* 14 June 1968): 'Disorder is . . . the cardinal consequence of the informal system's mode of growth, and the word appears time and again in the Commission's report.' 'Consequently', the Commission argued (1968: 40), 'the remedy must seek to introduce greater order into factory and workshop relations.'

Much discussion of 'orderly industrial relations', including that by academic authorities, simply takes for granted that this is a desirable objective. Among attempts to examine in detail the theoretical implications of order and disorder, the most sophisticated is that by Fox and Flanders (1969). Central to their analysis is Durkheim's concept of *anomie,* which they translate as 'a state of normlessness resulting from a breakdown in social regulation'. The importance they attribute to orderly normative

34. The diagnosis of 'guerilla warfare' need not in itself, of course, imply a managerial perspective: cf. Beynon 1973. What is at issue is the causes to which industrial conflict is attributed, and the remedies which are proposed.

regulation is stated as follows (p. 158):

> Although order in itself may not be the highest social good and certainly no normative system can be regarded as sacrosanct, society cannot exist without normative regulation for the maintenance of social order; it depends on such regulation for the integration and predictability of expectations and behaviour. To the extent that necessary normative regulation is lacking or is weakened and threatened with collapse, disorder becomes manifest in unpatterned behaviour leading to an undermining of integration and predictability in social action and events. In more specific terms, disorder emerges as dislocation, disruption and a variety of other symptoms . . . .

In industrial relations the rules and standards prevailing at any time are viewed as the outcome of the power and normative aspirations of the respective parties. Potential conflict over these rules and standards is most effectively contained where collective bargaining operates — both because of the resulting flexibility, and because the joint involvement of employer and worker representatives 'makes for a readier acceptance and observance' of the agreed rules. Yet in contemporary Britain collective bargaining has ceased to perform this stabilising role; for it has failed to adjust to a shift in power towards the shop floor (a result of relatively full employment) and the growth of new and more ambitious worker aspirations. The consequence has been a 'fragmentation of normative systems' and a 'breakdown of normative order'. This, the authors insist, constitutes 'a major problem of social regulation' (p. 174):

> What is at stake is whether the whole normative framework governing the production and distribution of wealth becomes further fragmented and splintered in a manner which threatens cumulative disorder, or whether we are still capable of reconstructing larger areas of agreement upon which larger units of regulation can rest. The answer to this question has great significance . . . for political values. Failure could force us into responses which would be tantamount to a decision that Britain could no longer support its present extreme degree of pluralism, and that a measure of authoritarian state regulation must take over from an anarchic drift resulting from fragmenting regulation.

It is noteworthy that the most influential theoretical commentary on the Donovan analysis should rest so heavily on the arguments of Durkheim; for it is his writings (or at least their Parsonian interpretation) which form the basis of the modern sociological emphasis on shared values as the basis of social order. The sense of moral outrage associated with many academic descriptions of 'disorderly' industrial relations[35] would seem to reflect a profound

35. Thus Kahn-Freund (1972: 74-5) emphasises the Donovan Commission's characterisation of fragmented bargaining as 'the principal evil of industrial relations in this country' and adds that such fragmentation is 'a deplorable fact.'

conviction that once shared values lose their hold, the whole social fabric is liable to crumble. It is clear that this represents a one-sided perspective on social order: a neglect of its *structural* foundations, and in particular the distribution of social power. As already argued, this is in line with the normal tendency of industrial relations pluralism to emphasise the process of regulation *within* the industrial relations system while ignoring the broader societal influences which structure the parameters of decision-making.

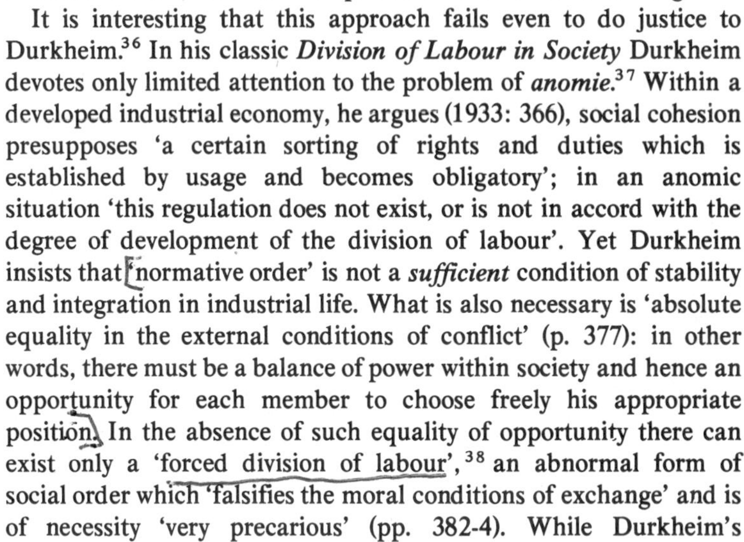

It is interesting that this approach fails even to do justice to Durkheim.[36] In his classic *Division of Labour in Society* Durkheim devotes only limited attention to the problem of *anomie.*[37] Within a developed industrial economy, he argues (1933: 366), social cohesion presupposes 'a certain sorting of rights and duties which is established by usage and becomes obligatory'; in an anomic situation 'this regulation does not exist, or is not in accord with the degree of development of the division of labour'. Yet Durkheim insists that 'normative order' is not a *sufficient* condition of stability and integration in industrial life. What is also necessary is 'absolute equality in the external conditions of conflict' (p. 377): in other words, there must be a balance of power within society and hence an opportunity for each member to choose freely his appropriate position. In the absence of such equality of opportunity there can exist only a 'forced division of labour',[38] an abnormal form of social order which 'falsifies the moral conditions of exchange' and is of necessity 'very precarious' (pp. 382-4). While Durkheim's

---

Roberts has argued that it is 'morally improper' that 'shop stewards think of agreements negotiated by their unions at national level as no more than jumping-off points to be improved upon whenever possible by their own pressures'; such 'irresponsible activities of stewards' reflect 'the unsatisfactory situation' that the steward's 'first loyalty is to the men who have elected him' (1962: 10-11; 1966: 1401).

36. There are many commentaries on Durkheim which emphasise those aspects of his writings often neglected by 'vulgar Durkheimians'. Giddens (1971) has provided a general discussion while Eldridge (1971: 73-91, 112-19) has offered a valuable demonstration of the relevance of the more 'radical' aspects of Durkheim's theories to industrial relations.
37. He treats it as one of several forms of the 'abnormal division of labour', devoting only half a dozen pages specifically to its analysis. Further attention is devoted to anomie in Durkheim's Preface to the second edition. The concept receives most extensive discussion in *Suicide,* but in a far broader context than that of norms regulating *economic* relations.
38. 'There cannot be rich and poor at birth without there being unjust contracts" (1933:384).

treatment is equivocal, the 'forced division of labour' might well be regarded as the *normal* situation within a capitalist society, for the inequalities which Durkheim castigates are integral to capitalist market relations.[39]

For Durkheim, then, 'normative disorder' may represent a predictable and indeed legitimate reaction by the underprivileged to material and political inequality. By contrast, the proposals of industrial relations pluralists for a reconstruction of normative order without any alteration in the broader structure of inequality have profoundly repressive implications. As Goldthorpe has argued (1969: 195), 'Fox and Flanders do not follow Durkheim in relating the problem of anomie to the problem of inequality.' Goldthorpe's point deserves quoting at greater length:

39. In the preface to the second edition, Durkheim writes as follows (1933: 2-3): 'In the economic order, occupational ethics exist only in the most rudimentary state. There is a professional ethic of the lawyer and the judge, the soldier and the priest, etc. But if one attempted to fix in a little more precise language the current ideas on what ought to be the relations of employer and employee, of worker and manager, of tradesmen in competition, to themselves or to the public, what indecisive formulas would be obtained! Some generalizations, without point, about the faithfulness and devotion workers of all sorts owe to those who employ them, about the moderation with which employers must use their economic advantages, a certain reprobation of all competition too openly dishonest, for all untempered exploitation of the consumer; that is about all the moral conscience of these trades contains. Moreover, most of these precepts are devoid of all juridical character, they are sanctioned only by opinion, not by law; and it is well known how indulgent opinion is concerning the manner in which these vague obligations are fulfilled. The most blameworthy acts are so often absolved by success that the boundary between what is permitted and what is prohibited, what is just and what is unjust, has nothing fixed about it, but seems susceptible to almost arbitrary change by individuals. An ethic so unprecise and inconsistent cannot constitute a discipline . . . . It is this anomic state that is the cause . . . of the incessantly recurrent conflicts, and the multifarious disorders of which the economic world exhibits so sad a spectacle. For, as nothing restrains the active forces and assigns them limits they are bound to respect, they tend to develop haphazardly, and come into collision with one another, battling and weakening themselves. To be sure, the strongest succeed in completely demolishing the weakest, or in subordinating them. But if the conquered, for a time, must suffer subordination under compulsion, they do not consent to it, and consequently this cannot constitute a stable equilibrium. Truces, arrived at after violence, are never anything but provisional, and satisfy no one. Human passions stop only before a moral power they respect. If all authority of this kind is wanting, the law of the strongest prevails, and latent or active, the state of war is necessarily chronic.' Fox and Flanders quote from this passage to illustrate the 'normative disorder' which they consider uniquely characteristic of recent British industrial relations. Yet for Durkheim this was the inevitable condition of capitalist economic relations except where there prevailed the quasi-mediaeval 'corporative organisation' which he advocated.

> To follow Durkheim's argument closely here, one has to insist that in so far as the normative order in economic life is not based upon consensus, but is rather founded upon coercion or expediency, then the threat of anomie and of chronic malintegration remains — no matter what degree of internal logic or coherence normative systems may be given. For as Durkheim stresses, unless in modern society the regulation of economic life — and, crucially, the regulation of inequality — does have some accepted moral basis, then it is unlikely to be effective in any continuing way. To the extent that the normative order is imposed by superior power, fundamental discontent and unrest persist if only in latent form: to the extent that it results from the calculation of advantage under given (non-moral) constraints, it is likely to be called into question as soon as these constraints vary.
>
> Thus, while proposals for reform of the kind that Fox and Flanders put forward might well endow collective bargaining institutions and procedures with a good deal more formal rationality than they at present possess, I find it difficult to believe that such measures could go very far towards ensuring stable normative systems, of either a substantive or a procedural kind, at any level of industrial relations. The absence of an accepted moral basis for economic life as a whole in our kind of society must always render precarious the norms which at any time prevail in any specific area — a plant, company, industry, etc . . . . Within a society in which inequality exists as brute fact — largely without moral legitimation — 'disorderly' industrial relations cannot, I think, be understood as a particular pathological development which will yield to particular remedies: rather, to maintain a Durkheimian perspective, this disorder must be seen as 'normal' — as a generalized characteristic of societies of the type in question (pp. 196-7).

Not only is it true that 'disorder' is inherent in a capitalist economy; but in addition, it cannot be assumed that this disorder is equally a problem for all members of the society. Again, this point has been cogently argued by Goldthorpe (1972: 212-13): 'Order looks rather different, depending as it were on which end of it one happens to be . . . . Order in work-place relations is clearly desirable from the point of view of most managements . . . . But is there a problem of disorder from the point of view of the workers and their shop stewards . . .?' On the contrary, as Eldridge (1973: 165) has aptly remarked, the situation might 'be analysed in terms of encroaching control — a response to inequalities no longer regarded and accepted as legitimate or inevitable'. This argument can be related to Fox's own more recent analysis of industrial relations pluralism, and in particular his suggestion that its appeal to most academics lies in

> its appropriateness as a set of 'working assumptions' for those interested in the formulation and application of public policy. Irrespective of personal philosophy, a working acceptance of the basic structure, objectives, and principles which characterize industry is usually a condition of being able to exert influence towards reform (1973a: 227).

Such reform, necessarily, involves only marginal adjustments to a structure the basic elements of which are unquestioned. To this extent academic orthodoxy in industrial relations, despite its peripheral liberalism, has a predominantly conservative orientation.

Pluralism and Inequality

This general orientation is apparent in the specific context of the analysis of incomes. While the natural focus in industrial relations is on *procedures* of collective bargaining rather than on their substantive outcome, there has been considerable recent attention to pay structures, stimulated in particular by the development of government incomes policies in the past decade. What is notable is the convergence between the pragmatism of public policy in this area (discussed in Chapter 4), and the analyses and prescriptions of academic experts.

As was seen previously, since the election of the Labour government in 1964 it has been conventional to include some reference to 'social justice' in the rationale for incomes policy; yet this objective, itself imprecise, has in practice been subordinated to the goal of economic stabilisation. Hence no significant alteration in income inequalities has resulted. A similar order of priorities underlies the preponderance of academic literature: the main problems are defined as the conflict and disorder in domestic pay structures associated with fragmented sectional bargaining, and the inflationary pressures attributed to the unconstrained and uncoordinated use of trade union bargaining power in a context of relatively full employment. If poverty and inequality enter the analysis at all, it is typically in a subsidiary role, as problems of lesser urgency and importance.

Hence much influential discussion of incomes policy, even in recent years, simply ignores non-economic considerations. Thus Guillebaud's statement of 'the need to have an incomes policy' (1967: 71-6) is related solely to the objectives of economic growth and price stability. The Donovan *Report* (1968: 38-9, 52-3) cited these same two reasons for incomes policy, adding as a third its potential contribution to 'a more ordered system of industrial relations' — its notion of order being of course conceived within the framework of assumptions discussed earlier. From such a perspective, then, the use of incomes policy as a means of reforming income *structure* forms no part of the argument. As Crossley has suggested (1966: 184), 'The objective of a national wages policy is to reduce the rate of increase of the general level of money wages in such a way as to disturb other things as little as possible, including, in the present context, the structure of wages.'

The opposing perspective — exemplified by Corina (1966: 50-52) — is exceptional in academic discussion.

> Incomes policy cannot avoid the posing of questions about 'fairness' and 'justice', however vague the ethical content in such concepts. Is it *just* that the chairman of a large printing corporation should receive over £250,000 a year, whilst the chairman of the Coal Board receives very much less? Is it *just* that doctors should earn more than clergymen? Is it *just* that dustmen should receive smaller pay-packets than engineering labourers? All these are meaningful questions to pose, especially when the advantages and disadvantages of comparable occupations are taken into account . . . . From a purely functional viewpoint (whether one agrees or disagrees with equality on value grounds), 'egalitarianism' as a *total* concept undoubtedly widens the area of debate. It stimulates a comprehensive view of incomes policy, in which tax policy is seen as a complement to the adjustment of incomes at source. It envisages wage policy as one component of a policy concerned with the whole complex of incomes. It presents the idea that 'fairness' (whatever its precise definition) should be given more influence in governing the distribution of income between the rich and poor, between the socially secure and the socially deprived, between profit recipients and wage earners, between managers and workers, between wage earners and salary earners, between the wage earning population as a whole, between the skilled, semi-skilled and unskilled, between men and women, adults and juveniles, etc.

Not only is such a plea for greater equality as a central and immediate objective of incomes policy wholly untypical of most analysts of the subject; even in this context, the impact of the prevailing standards of 'appropriate' pay comparisons is evident. Although Corina refers in general terms to inequality between occupational strata, the examples which he cites of 'inequitable' pay relationships all involve comparisons *within* strata. The extreme of inequality between dustman and company chairman is not explicitly posed as a problem to be overcome by incomes policy.

A third approach to the issue of 'equity' is to regard this, though not a central purpose of incomes policy, as a problem of which an effective policy must take account. Thus Clegg (1971: ch. 4) treats equity as grounds for 'exceptional treatment' in the context of a general norm on wage and salary increases which otherwise freezes the existing incomes structure. Normative considerations are seen as important primarily because of their indirect implications: they may motivate trade unionists, whose co-operation is a precondition of a successful policy. Elsewhere, Clegg spells out the implications of this perspective (*Observer,* 30 July 1972):

> The real worry is not that miners care about the pay of High Court judges, but that they get very upset if certain other groups — it might be car workers or dockers — who they feel ought to be just behind them or level with them, seem to be going ahead

of them. This worries them far more. So the objective of an incomes policy, at any rate in the short run, is much more to cope with these rather more marginal problems than the hierarchical pay structure of our country.

The burden of this argument is that the key task of incomes policy is to rationalise those pay relationships which are *already salient* for organised workers, and hence represent potential foci of conflict. The question of equity is significant because of its bearing on the acceptability of a policy, even if the latter's purpose is primarily to facilitate the management of an economy the basic principles of which are not in question. This in turn entails that the definitions of equity prevailing within the society at the time are alone of immediate relevance to incomes policy.

This pragmatic approach to equity, which is probably the predominant orientation within academic industrial relations, is thus sharply differentiated from the conception of incomes policy as a *direct* instrument of social justice. In so far as the latter aims to alter the overall structure of economic inequality, it requires to question and subvert the narrow orbits of conventional pay comparison and their implicit acceptance of the broader incomes hierarchy. For the pragmatist, by contrast, restricted pay comparisons are not a problem: on the contrary, they set the limits of incomes policy's main problematic. Thus it is interesting that while most industrial relations academics strongly favour the 'rationalisation' of the internal pay structures of manual workers at plant or industry level, more radical and ambitious proposals to rationalise the overall national structure of incomes are typically regarded with scepticism. Again the reasoning is pragmatic: the overall incomes structure is not a major source of contention and hence does not constitute a major policy problem; whereas any attempt to reorganise incomes generally on explicit and systematic principles would inevitably generate serious conflict. Many writers have indeed assumed that the limited 'rationalisation' of initial essays into incomes policy might be progressively extended, perhaps leading *eventually* to some form of national job evaluation. Yet it is typically assumed that the main consequence of such an extension would be to systematise and hence underwrite existing inequalities of income, rather than achieving any substantial reduction in income differentials.[40] As was seen in the previous chapter, there is

40. Some writers (e.g. Wootton 1962; Walker 1965) assume that any scheme of national job evaluation would have revolutionary implications. It would be

a marked tendency for writers on income differentials to assume that these reflect the inevitable operation of forces of supply and demand; thus from this perspective, incomes policy can merely remove those marginal inadequacies in the structure of incomes which reflect market imperfections.[41]

It is necessary to recognise, finally, the possibility that some variants of industrial relations pluralism may combine a pragmatic

---

difficult, they argue, to devise any formula — however ingenious — which could plausibly justify the existing structure of incomes; and the attempt would make transparent the inequities which currently receive little attention from most wage-earners: 'the arbitrary elements involved in weighting the major characteristics of widely different employments must become much more obtrusive' (Wootton 1962: 147). While this might conceivably be the *consequence* of such an exercise, it is important to note that the *purpose* of job content comparison is typically to legitimise rather than to alter existing pay relationships; 'rationalisation' may entail minor changes in the position of individual jobs, but takes place *within the context* of the general hierarchy prevailing. The literature commonly makes explicit that an 'acceptable' job evaluation is one which causes the minimum of disturbance to established relationships while conferring on them a 'scientific' rationale which inhibits competitive sectional pressure for increases; to this end, factors and weights are often judiciously manipulated. (This exemplifies two of our previous remarks: that the concepts of 'rationality' and 'rationalisation' are necessarily value-laden ; and that the 'reconstruction of normative order' in industrial relations typically implies the provision of a new basis of legitimation for a structure of inequality which has lost some of its traditional acceptability.) A similar purpose would appear to underlie many proposals for national job evaluation. The tendency for students of industrial relations to criticise such proposals (e.g. Clegg 1961 : 213; Roberts 1958 : 172) normally reflects doubts as to the practicality of the means rather than disagreement with this fundamental objective.

41. The argument that at most limited equalisation of incomes is possible is often associated with a reification of economic processes. Thus the Prices and Incomes Board (NBPI 1971 : 16) asserted that 'pay differentials have a great capacity to reassert themselves'. Similarly, Corina (1968: 259), in arguing that 'policy design has . . . to be socially appropriate in not depending too much upon sudden and radical departures', refers to 'the economy's commitment to a specific set of economic objectives'. In this way, questions relating specifically to human agency are avoided: *who* re-asserts traditional differentials? *who* is committed to a specific set of economic objectives? Likewise, to refer simply to 'economic needs' begs the question: *whose* economic needs? It can be assumed that the economic needs of rich and poor, employers and employed, are one and the same only on the pre-supposition of a unique 'national interest'. Even to employ without qualification the concept of 'the economy' is to evade the fact that what is in question is a specific economy geared to a specific set of priorities — which are not necessarily unalterable. To paraphrase Marx (1959: 737): 'The advance of capitalist production develops a school of economic analysis, which by education, tradition, habit, looks upon the conditions of that mode of production as self-evident laws of Nature.'

approach to considerations of equity or social justice as a short-run strategy with a commitment to more radical restructuring of incomes in the longer run. This approach implies an acceptance that existing differentials are excessive, but insistence that only gradual equalisation is possible. Thus it may be argued that a substantial increase in the earnings of the lower paid would be inflationary, and might provoke an attempt by the higher paid to restore traditional differentials. On the other hand, forcible restraint on the earnings of the higher paid would itself be regarded as unfair and hence objectionable. This argument has been developed by Clegg (1971: 70-71): 'existing pay distribution is unfair', and hence an incomes policy should discriminate against certain higher-paid groups. (He specifies dockers, car workers and newspaper employees — the highest-paid manual groups; but of the far *higher*-earning, non-manual sector, only doctors and university professors.)

> At this point, however, we need to take into account a characteristic of the British people, if not of mankind generally. We like to see justice done, but not too harshly. Otherwise we tend to sympathize with the culprit as a victim of oppression, like train robbers with thirty-year sentences. Except for the car workers themselves, we should all like to see car workers held back — but not too severely. My suggestion is that this can be covered by the rule that everyone is to receive at least the equivalent of the increase in the price level. This means that no one's real income will be cut, but the fruits of economic growth will be used only for those with a good claim upon them.[42]

The problem inherent in such an approach is the danger that — as with the experience of the Labour incomes policy of 1964-70 — long-term equity may be the perpetual hostage of short-term pragmatism. The interpretation which we develop in the following chapter is that the political economy which incomes policy is designed to sustain and stabilise *itself* necessarily generates and perpetuates those inequalities which reforming pluralists aspire to temper. The most fundamental criticism to be made of industrial relations pluralism is not its failure to accept this interpretation — which, as with any theoretical formulation, is not susceptible of definitive proof or disproof; it is that the whole analysis of the

42. It is worth noting that, in public policy, so neat a blend of justice and mercy is not always apparent. Thus the Devlin Report, in proposing an equalisation of dockers' work and earnings, took for granted that 'this evening-out of earnings means that men who are now enjoying preferential treatment will be faced with a reduction in their pay packets. It is they and not their employers who will pay the cost of work-sharing. To meet the general desire for equalisation of earnings it is inevitable that the man with the big pay packet will have to sacrifice something' (1965: 117).

structural implications of the political economy is external to the problematic of the academic analysis of industrial relations.

Conclusions

The typical social-psychological approach to the analysis of pay comparisons takes the specification of employee reference groups as the *end* of enquiry rather than as its starting point; the social-structural sources of comparisons and aspirations are not normally explored at all, let alone systematically analysed. Where reference group theory is allied to a broader sociological frame of reference, it is common to adopt the functionalist approach with its assumption of the necessity of inequality and a natural tendency to value-consensus. Thus the absence of extensive and coherent criticism of the prevailing economic hierarchy is not treated as a problem which requires explanation.

The pragmatism of institutional industrial relations displays similar failings. The structure of power and ideology which forms the context of collective bargaining is not explicitly scrutinised as a crucial influence on processes of job regulation; and this narrow focus encourages the widespread but illegitimate assumption that the pluralist ideal actually describes the reality of industrial relations. Industrial relations pluralism is often associated with the advocacy of institutional reforms, particularly in the context of wage determination; yet such reforms do not challenge — indeed they rationalise and thus reinforce — the socio-economic structure which underlies inequality. In the following chapter we turn to the analysis of this structure.

Chapter 7

Power, Inequality and Ideology

The concept of ideology, the subject of passing reference in previous chapters, now represents a central focus of our analysis. How far do the prevailing notions of fairness in industrial relations reflect a more generalised network of beliefs and values in society, the creation and perpetuation of which entail identifiable social processes? How far, indeed, do the academic perspectives already discussed derive from and in turn reinforce what might be termed a dominant value or meaning system? The answer to these specific questions involves issues fundamental to the more general theoretical problem of the relationship of power and values in social life.

Power and Social Values

In the previous chapter we considered the structural-functional approach to social order as the product of a common value system. Within this perspective, inequalities of power are not regarded as of major sociological significance: rather, they are treated as a natural reflection of the societal division of labour, a differentiation of responsibility for the attainment of consensually defined goals. This approach, we argued, provides an inadequate account of the *origins* of unequal power. But equally unsatisfactory is the neglect of its *consequences.* Even if it were accepted that the powerful derive their positions, in the first instance, from a societal consensus, the very fact of their power would render precarious the harmonistic basis of social order. It can happen (even though it may not always be the case) that 'power corrupts'. Precisely because power is, among other things, *power over other people,* those in positions of power may use this to further personal or sectional, rather than 'societal' goals. Hence even in the absence of an initial structured conflict of interests within society, unequal power may itself create such a conflict. As Gouldner (1970: 243) has put it, using Parsonian terminology: 'this potentiality for system-disruption is inherent in the nature of such a power difference'.

This is to expose a fatal contradiction in the structural-functional model. If it is accepted that, even out of initial harmony, a structurally based conflict of interests may develop, it can no longer be taken for granted that power stems necessarily from the common needs and interests of powerful and powerless. As Rex has argued (1961: 111-12),

> If there is an actual conflict of ends, the behaviour of actors towards one another may not be determined by shared norms but by the success which each has in compelling the other to act in accordance with his interests. Power then becomes a crucial variable in the study of social systems . . . .
>
> Thus even if it is admitted that social integration is in part dependent upon value systems, there is also a substructure to social order which is determined by the struggle for power and the balance of power. Any complete account of a social system must describe the nature of this power.

This is not to argue that social order is to be explained solely as the outcome of overt coercion on the part of those with power in economic, political and social relations generally. It is indeed possible to suggest that, in specific social situations and in given historical circumstances, overtly coercive processes and institutions have been of central importance in maintaining the existing structure of social relations. Yet no serious social theorist has made such instances the basis of a *general* theory of society. In simple terms: those in subordinate positions in an openly coercive relationship comply only with reluctance.[1] In such circumstances the relationship itself is somewhat precarious, for the subordinates may be expected to resist as soon as the opportunity arises.

Hence stable power relations normally require at least an element

1. Etzioni (1964: 60) has made a similar point, in contrasting what he terms 'coercive' power (based on the use or threat of physical sanctions), 'utilitarian' power (based on material inducements), and 'normative' power (based on the manipulation of symbols): 'All other things being equal, at least in most cultures, the use of coercive power is more alienating to those subject to it than is the use of utilitarian power, and the use of utilitarian power is more alienating than the use of normative power. Or, to put it the other way around, normative power tends to generate more commitment than utilitarian, and utilitarian more than coercive.'

of 'voluntary' [2] compliance. This was an important element in Weber's theory of political control: 'a criterion of every true relation of imperative control . . . is a certain minimum of voluntary submission; thus an interest (based on ulterior motives or genuine acceptance) in obedience' (1947: 324). Weber laid particular emphasis on the concept of legitimacy (discussed previously in the context of Parsons's model): every system of control, he argued, 'attempts to establish and to cultivate the belief in its "legitimacy" ' (p. 325). Similarly, the notion that norms and values may exert significant influence in underpinning a structure of power relations and hence social cohesion in general has always figured prominently in Marxist social analysis: witness the use of the concept of ideology in the writings of Marx and Lenin, or of 'hegemony' in those of Gramsci.

The central theoretical issue is therefore not *whether* normative agreement is of sociological significance, but whether it should be assigned *primacy* as an explanation of social order. As Giddens insists (1968: 269-70),

> The main theoretical differences which separate integration and conflict theory do not concern the theoretical significance of 'common value systems', but centre upon the processes which *give rise* to such systems, and the social mechanisms whereby systems of values and ideas are *linked with other structures of society*. That is, the real problems which have to be tackled, and which lie at the root of much of the debate, concern *how legitimation is mediated in its operation in systems of power*. Whereas coercion theorists argue that value-consensus is determined by a combination of coercion and ideological manipulation, integration theory begins from the assumption that consensus derives from natural identity of interest served by some kind of cooperative action. The fundamental questions dividing the two concern *how groups acquire power*, what strategies they use to hold on to power, and how far these are consistent with the ideological basis of their power; the conditions under which those in subordinate groups come to question the legitimacy of those in power, and the channels which they adopt to seek changes in the power system.[3]

What this argument clearly indicates is that the crucial need is to explain how specific norms and values, together with the whole framework of generally prevailing ideas and beliefs, themselves

2. The term 'voluntary' is used here simply as an antonyn to 'overtly coercive'; whether 'voluntary' compliance has covert coercive underpinning will be considered later. A weakness of many sociological analyses of power — as, for example, that of Etzioni — is the narrow identification of coercive control as direct physical compulsion. We argue below the need to take account of more subtle and indirect forms of coercion, and the interdependence of different types of control.
3. For an analysis in some ways parallel, see Lockwood 1964.

derive from a given social structure. This is to require what is conventionally termed a sociology of knowledge.

Sociology of Knowledge and of Values

The sociology of knowledge[4] has its first coherent formulation in *The German Ideology* of Marx and Engels, which though written in 1845-6 was first published (in German) only in 1932. They took as their starting point the dictum that 'consciousness is from the very beginning a social product'.

> In direct contrast to German philosophy which descends from heaven to earth, here we ascend from earth to heaven. That is to say, we do not set out from what men say, imagine, conceive, nor from men as narrated, thought of, imagined, conceived, in order to arrive at men in the flesh. We set out from real, active men, and on the basis of their real life-process we demonstrate the development of the ideological reflexes and echoes of this life-process (1970: 47).

Two particular aspects of their analysis, developed in the more recent literature on the sociology of knowledge, may be noted: that knowledge is socially produced on the basis of particular structures of economic relationships, and that ideology typically reflects particular constellations of class interests. A third aspect, the ideological character of intellectual theories of society, is discussed in the next section.

Marx summarised his theory of the social production of knowledge in his Preface to *The Critique of Political Economy* (Marx and Engels 1958: I, 363): 'The mode of production of material life conditions the social, political and intellectual life process in general. It is not the consciousness of men that determines their being, but, on the contrary, their social being that determines their consciousness.' The most notable example of this argument that economic relationships structure social consciousness is provided by the Marxian analysis of 'commodity fetishism': the argument that social relations geared to commodity production generate a reified conception of social processes. We have discussed this question in Chapter 5 and need not repeat it here.

This leads to the second important element of the sociology of

4. There is a growing literature on the sociology of knowledge. Important discussions are included in Mannheim 1936; Merton 1968; Berger and Luckmann 1967; Goldmann 1969; and Lukacs 1971.

knowledge, as previously noted: while reflecting a pattern of economic and social relations which are *general* within a society, a given ideology may also support the interests of a specific section of that society. In a famous passage in *The German Ideology*, (1970: 64), Marx and Engels argue:

> The ideas of the ruling class are in every epoch the ruling ideas, i.e. the class which is the ruling *material* force of society, is at the same time its ruling *intellectual* force. The class which has the means of material production at its disposal, has control at the same time over the means of mental production, so that thereby, generally speaking, the ideas of those who lack the means of mental production are subject to it. The ruling ideas are nothing more than the ideal expression of the dominant material relationships, the dominant material relationships grasped as ideas; hence of the relationships which make the one class the ruling one, therefore, the ideas of its dominance.

Hence the beliefs that there is an overriding 'national interest' which transcends any sectional conflicts of interest within society; that economic life represents a system of free exchange between equal individuals; that the function of the state is to protect the weak and powerless just as much as the strong and powerful — all serve the interests of those in positions of economic and social control by legitimating their own power. By diverting attention from fundamental conflicts of interest within a capitalist society, such ideological assumptions obstruct the development of any conscious and concerted challenge to the existing structure of power relations.

The notion of ideology as the manifestation of class interests involves many complex issues which need not be pursued here.[5] It may, but need not, imply that a particular set of beliefs and values is deliberately inculcated in order to ensure the acquiescence of those in positions of subordination and deprivation. Marx argued in *The Eighteenth Brumaire of Louis Bonaparte* (in Marx and Engels 1958: I, 275) that 'one must not form the narrow-minded notion that the petty bourgeoisie, on principle, wishes to enforce an egoistic class interest'. In the situation being analysed, a particular section of society genuinely believed that its own special interests reflected the general interests of society. Yet at other times, a particular ideology may be utilised in a more or less cynical and manipulative manner.[6] The point at issue here is not the subjective sincerity of those in positions of social dominance who uphold a particular set of values and beliefs; it is the objective consequences of the acceptance of such

5. For two contrasting discussions, see Lukacs 1971 and Plamenatz 1970.
6. See the reference by Lukacs (1971: 65) to 'mendacious consciousness'.

values and beliefs by those beneath them.

The implication of the classic Marxian analysis for our own discussion is that the beliefs and values which legitimate an unequal distribution of power and an inegalitarian structure of rewards and deprivations are themselves socially produced; and, moreover, that those who benefit in political and economic terms may exert major influence on the formulation and perpetuation of these beliefs and values. Legitimations of inequality would thus both derive from, and in turn reinforce, the unequal distribution of power and privilege.

Given such a dialectic between structure and consciousness, any simple categorisation of forms of control is necessarily misleading. Thus Etzioni's analysis of 'coercive', 'utilitarian' and 'normative' power fails to explore the interdependence of all three. It is true that, within a market economy, a wide range of social relations are mediated by pecuniary transactions. Hence, as we saw in Chapter 5, the model of society as a system of exchange has proved attractive not only to classical utilitarians but also to more recent social theorists. Yet to define the power exercised in market relations in purely utilitarian terms is to accept at face value the ideologically distorted conception of market exchanges as characterised by freedom and equality. The dominant conception of economic exchange, which such theories endorse, neglects the unequal ownership of scarce material resources (or control over access to these resources) and the consequential inequalities in the ability to offer material inducements: or in other words, in economic power. To explain the sources of unequal ownership and control of property, and the processes which perpetuate this inequality, it is necessary to refer to other than utilitarian bases of power.

Clearly relevant is the fact that when prevailing norms relating to the sanctity of (unequally distributed) property are violated, institutionalised coercion normally ensues. Ownership, as Gouldner has noted (1970: 307),

> seems to have some very remarkable attributes, which are not at all common to other social roles. In particular, it has an ease of access to legal enforceability. The inviolability of property rights is more closely monitored and protected by the legal and state apparatus, in the normal course of events, than any other 'rights' except that of protection from bodily harm.[7] The use of the state's force to protect property is

7. It is indeed debatable whether the operation of the law accords protection of the person a consistently higher priority than protection of property; sentencing policy might appear to indicate the contrary. In particular, where *workers* suffer death or injury, or their health is put at risk, through unsafe working conditions,

not at all an instrument of 'last resort', but a *routine* method of enforcement. Normally, one does not bargain, negotiate, remonstrate, or appeal to a thief; one calls the police. This implies something about the priorities that the state assigns to the protection of property rights; but, more than that, it implies something about the nature of the state itself.

It is important to recognise that the use of force to protect property rights does not reflect the physical power of the individual property-owner; nor, indeed, simply of property-owners collectively. What is significant about overtly coercive power in modern societies is the extent to which its use has become institutionalised — has become predominantly the monopoly of the state and its various agencies. The force which guarantees the unequal distribution of control over access to material resources thus derives from a *structure of coercive institutions* whose routine agents may be motivated by material and normative, rather than physical, inducements.

In similar fashion, it follows from the preceding analysis that 'normative' power may rest on utilitarian or coercive foundations. As Mills has argued (1959: 40-41), 'we cannot assume today that men must in the last resort be governed by their own consent. Among the means of power that now prevail is the power to manage and manipulate the consent of men.' Hence there is no clear boundary between 'authority (power justified by the beliefs of the voluntarily obedient) and manipulation (power wielded unbeknown to the powerless'.

This interdependent structure of coercive and utilitarian, economic and political power may best be viewed as dialectically related to the prevailing norms and values of the society. Power relations at one and the same time underlie the production and reproduction of the dominant world-view and value system, and derive legitimacy and reinforcement from them. As Mills (1959: 37) has noted, what Parsons and similar sociologists 'call "value-orientation" and "normative structure" has mainly to do with master symbols of legitimation.' Whether through a sincere identification of sectional with collective interests, or through a more cynical process of ideological manipulation, might can *make* right (Gouldner 1970: 293) by generating the beliefs and values which provide its own legitimation. In either case the consequence is the

---

their employers commonly escape with impunity or incur only derisory penalties (cf. Kinnersly 1973).

same: those in positions of power are less dependent on overtly coercive control.

It would be wrong, however, to regard the mutual reinforcement of power and values as wholly unproblematic. One issue arising is the *primacy* of power and values within this dialectic. To argue that might (through its ability to manufacture legitimacy) is able to make right, is to assert that common values are in the last analysis secondary or derivative and that the power structure itself is fundamental. Such an assertion involves a high level of abstraction, and as with all high-level theoretical generalisation does not admit of any simple empirical proof or disproof. It is nevertheless possible to offer empirical justification for preferring a theory which assigns primacy to the structure of power relations to one which centres on value consensus.

An obviously relevant fact is the extent to which the efficacy of ideologies legitimating the power structure depends on their continual reproduction or reaffirmation through identifiable social processes and institutions. We explore this question in a later section of this chapter.

The primacy of the material (economic and coercive) basis of power as against the common value system is also demonstrated in situations where the two are in conflict. Thus in Britain it is possible to note the coexistence of more or less egalitarian values (at times expressed in the election of Labour governments) with the perpetuation of the massive inequalities of wealth and income which provide the focus of our study. It can be convincingly argued that it is precisely the concentration of economic power within a small section of society which frustrates any serious attempt to redress inequalities which offend against prevailing values.[8] Ironically, Parsons himself (1960: 247) has provided a corroborating analysis from the USA: 'The role of the economy in American society and of the business element in it is such that political leadership without prominent business participation is doomed to ineffectiveness and to the perpetuation of dangerous internal conflict. It is not possible to lead the American people *against* the leaders of the business world.'

8. For the detailed argument see Worsley 1964; Westergaard 1965; Miliband 1969. As Worsley puts it (pp. 22-3): 'The uninterrupted, albeit modified dominance of the property-owning classes, in a society which has long been the most highly "proletarianized" in the world, is surely one of the most striking phenomena of modern times.'

It can only follow that should the bulk of the American people espouse values hostile to the interests of the economically powerful, the impotence of moral values — and of 'political authority' itself — in the face of unequal power would be brutally manifest.

There are two main reasons why material power, in critical instances, tends to prevail over normative standards. First, moral values which are endorsed in the abstract may be less acceptable when they involve important conflicts with self-interest. Whether morality outweighs expediency in such circumstances may well depend on whether it is backed by sanctions. As Gouldner (1970: 296) has argued, the powerless are far more easily subject to sanctions than the powerful; for the structure of power in society necessarily affects the interpretation and application of normative standards. 'The possession of power itself enables some to *default* on their moral obligations'; while 'the lack of power constrains others to accept less than they might legitimately claim'. (In the old adage, some hang for stealing the goose from the commons, while others steal the commons with impunity.)

The customary mediation of morality by power is facilitated by the abstract and generalised character of moral values. Such values, as Becker has remarked (1963: 130-32), are for this reason poor guides to action.

> The standards of selection they embody are general, telling us which of several alternative lines of action would be preferable, all other things being equal. But all other things are seldom equal in the concrete situations of everyday life. We find it difficult to relate the generalities of a value statement to the complex and specific details of everyday situations . . . . Just because values are ambiguous and general, we can interpret them in various ways and deduce many kinds of rules from them. A rule may be consistent with a given value, but widely differing rules might also have been deduced from the same value. Furthermore, rules will not be deduced from values unless a problematic situation prompts someone to make the deduction. We may find that certain rules which seem to us to flow logically from a widely held value have not even been thought of by the people who hold the value, either because situations and problems calling for the rule have not arisen or because they are unaware that a problem exists. Again, a specific rule, if deduced from the general value, might conflict with other rules deduced from other values. The conflict, whether consciously known or only recognized implicitly, may inhibit the creation of a particular rule. Rules do not flow automatically from values.

Simply because moral values are typically abstract, ambiguous, and even contradictory, they are open to interpretations which equate morality with expediency. Religious ideologies, for example, may be so flexible as to be utilised *both* in support of radical attacks on inequality *and* as a means of endorsement of the existing social and economic order.[9] The rich and powerful may thus select an interpretation which permits them to cling to wealth and power with good conscience — and persuades others of their moral integrity. Thus the distribution of power and resources in a society is likely to ensure that the prevailing interpretation of moral values is conservative in character; or at least that any radical implications bear only marginally on the fundamental structure of the social order.

Ideology in Intellectual Life

It has already been argued in Chapter 5 that, despite widespread pretensions to 'objectivity', academic analysis cannot escape the implications of value-attachment. The growth of attention to the sociology of knowledge has resulted in the application of some of its insights to sociology itself: an openness to self-criticism which is in principle healthy.[10] For where the social influences on the conceptual and theoretical foundations of academic analysis are unrecognised, it is particularly likely that these will merely incorporate the taken-for-granted perspectives of the beliefs and values prevailing in the society. As with other aspects of the sociology of knowledge, awareness of the ideological implications of social theory can be found in *The German Ideology*. In particular, Marx and Engels assert a tendency for the intelligentsia to act as the theorists of those with material dominance in society.

> The division of labour, which we already saw above as one of the chief forces of history up till now, manifests itself also in the ruling class as the division of mental and material labour, so that inside this class one part appears as the thinkers of the class (its active, conceptive ideologists, who make the perfecting of the illusion of the class about itself their chief source of livelihood), while the others' attitude to these ideas and illusions is more passive and receptive, because they are in reality the active members of this class and have less time to make up illusions and ideas about themselves. Within this class this cleavage can even develop into a certain opposition and hostility between the two parts, which, however, in the case of a practical collision, in which the class itself is endangered, automatically comes to nothing . . . (p. 65).

In our discussion of economic theory we have noted that the

9. For an important analysis of the normally conservative uses of religious ideology, see Miliband 1969: 198-205.
10. Though the sociology of sociology can degenerate into a narrow and arid form of academic introspection; see Friedrichs 1970.

Marxian critique of Bentham and his fellow utilitarians emphasised the social origins of their writings. Despite the contrast in levels of abstraction, Marx argued, their analysis was clearly rooted in the social world-view of the capitalist entrepreneur and merchant: utilitarian political and economic theory both *reflect* the assumptions and orientations of the rising bourgeoisie, and provide a *justification* for the latter's social and economic power. Despite the many refinements, qualifications and embellishments since the time of Bentham, as we argued in Chapter 5, modern economic orthodoxy remains founded on the paradigmatic utilitarian assumptions of economic man as a desocialised 'rational calculator' and of commodity exchange as the measure of all social activity. Thus economic theory continues to suppress attention to disparities of *power* in economic life. The ideological implications of conventional economics are obvious: in so far as its formulations are influential, the power of the socially dominant disappears from view, while their material privileges are justified as the rewards of special qualifications and contributions.

We have also seen the extent to which ideologically loaded concepts and perspectives are current in sociology. To take just two examples: the concept of 'function', as conventionally employed in sociology, involves an assumption that society forms an integrated whole and that existing institutions have advantageous and even indispensable consequences. The concept of 'role' is normally used in a manner which presupposes that the rights and obligations of those in different positions in society are unambiguously and uncontroversially defined; that there is, in other words, a 'democratic' consensus on the validity of the existing social structure. That the various forms of functionalist orthodoxy provide uncritical legitimations of prevailing social relations is, by now, surely a commonplace.[11]

In the previous chapter, the ideological implications of conventional approaches to industrial relations likewise received emphasis. We saw that most studies of employee attitudes to pay, and of the processes of wage determination, have been conducted within one of two perspectives. The first approach is that of

11. It is less immediately obvious, but may be validly argued, that even sociologists whose purpose is explicitly *critical* often fail to escape this tendency; insofar as their criticisms bear on the margins of the social order rather than its basic structure, they underwrite by default what they do not criticise: cf. Nicolaus 1972.

reference group theory, normally interpreted within a social-psychological frame of reference. The central concern is typically *how* workers compare the net advantages of their own employment with those of other individuals or groups; the question *why* particular orbits of comparison are selected rarely receives much attention. The other approach is that of students of industrial relations institutions who, despite occasional reference to the notion of an 'industrial relations system' in which economic, technological, political and ideological influences interpenetrate, are usually content to leave consideration of the social-structural context of collective bargaining to other disciplines. Hence the existence of a *political economy* of industrial relations is not a focus of enquiry; and from a restricted analytical perspective stems a pragmatism in which the formulation of industrial relations 'problems', and the presuppositions underlying the proposed solutions, accord closely with the perspectives of those in positions of economic and political domination.

This may be regarded as one aspect of a more general ideological problem: the *disciplinary segmentation* of respectable intellectual endeavour. The division of labour within the economy — the existence of 'rationalisation' within each segment of the production process, in the absence of rational overall control in the total economic system — is replicated in the production of knowledge. Traditional political economy has become fragmented into a series of academic specialisms each jealous of its own area of demarcation; and as Lukacs has noted (1971: 103), 'the specialisation of skills leads to the destruction of every image of the whole'. Thus economics is studied with minimal attention to political institutions; politics with a total neglect of the system of production; while sociology is commonly conceived as a residual discipline, merely cultivating a set of 'problem areas' to which no other discipline has staked a claim. Yet this entails that it is the normal practice for academic disciplines to take for granted the overall structure of society, to accept it as the unquestioned framework for analysis. It follows that where conflicts are diagnosed these are related not to possible contradictions in the overall structure but to 'strains', 'maladjustments', 'recalcitrance' or 'irrationality' at the level of specific institutions or individuals. This point is particularly relevant to the study of industrial relations. Aron (himself no radical) has noted (1967: 24) that students of the subject often 'at the outset brush aside questions concerning the ownership of the firm or the structure of society'. He goes on: 'Not to ask these questions (which are called ideological or political) is really to ask them in a particular way.' It is to endorse, by default, the unquestioned structure of power and control; and hence to define the orientations of study as the accommodation to this structure of the institutions and processes of industrial relations. It is to embrace what Mills (1959: 95-9) has termed the strategy of 'illiberal practicality'. In this respect the study of industrial relations exhibits in its clearest form the practical implications of the absence from modern social studies of an analysis of the total society.

Awareness of the distorting consequences of disciplinary segmentation points to a possible escape from the incorrigible relativism inherent in some formulations of the sociology of knowledge. If all social thought is the product of a specific social context and is thus (given the definition which we employ) ideological, can any social theory — including the sociology of knowledge itself — escape ideological distortion? And can the superiority of any one theory or interpretation over any other be rationally demonstrated, if the criteria of truth and validity are themselves defined according to specific theoretical presuppositions? Such questions are over-simplistic. What is involved in the social production of knowledge is not properly conceived as a mere process of distortion; for to expose the social sources of a theory or *Weltanschauung* is not, in itself, to demonstrate its falsity. Two separate issues are in fact raised. Where it is argued that ideology bears the character of 'false consciousness', different types of distortion may be involved permitting different degrees of corrigibility. And the adequacy of a theory may be related to the interests of a specific social group in a specific historical context, without any necessary argument that this historicity implies fundamental theoretical and epistemological flaws.[12]

Four distinct sources of distortion commonly subsumed under the label 'false consciousness' have been specified by Miller (1973: 442-4). The first is conceptual inadequacy, manifest when

12. To these remarks might be added the argument of Berger and Luckman (1967), that the sociology of knowledge often incorporates questions which are both social and epistemological in nature. While the two types of question necessarily interpenetrate, they cannot readily be resolved within the same problematic.

'phenomena are co-classified on the basis of superficial resemblance, and without regard to their underlying structure'. Secondly, phenomena may be considered and analysed in isolation from their context. Thirdly, institutions or relations which are conventional or historically contingent may be treated as naturally fixed and inevitable. Finally, social relations may be reified and attention to human agency in social life suppressed.

Without venturing into highly complex epistemological issues, we would point out that the social determinations underlying such distortions are multi-dimensional. Reification, as we argued in a previous chapter, is not *merely* an ideological distortion of reality: it reflects a context in which social institutions are *genuinely* remote from conscious human control, and thus exercise an externally dominating influence on all members of society.[13] Hence a theoretical transcendence of reified consciousness cannot be dissociated from a *practical* transcendence of reified social relations. The distorting effects of reified consciousness can however be minimised by an awareness of the historically specific and contingent character of a given, externally coercive pattern of social relations. The application of a critical-historical perspective is thus a strategy which bears alike on the third and fourth sources of ideological distortion.[14] The problem of reification also relates to that of the segmentation of social analysis: the failure to locate the investigation of specific institutions or segments of society within their structural context. 'The trouble is that the statistics, measurements, and field studies of empirical sociology and political science are not rational enough,' Marcuse has argued (1968: 153). 'They become mystifying to the extent to which they are isolated from the truly concrete context which makes the facts and determines their function. This context is larger and other than that of the plants and shops investigated, of the towns and cities studied . . .

13. It is worth emphasising that while Marx laid great stress on the power disparities within capitalist society, he insisted that *all* were subject to the external constraint of reified social relations. 'The propertied class and the class of the proletariat present the same human self-alienation. But the former class finds in this self-alienation its confirmation and its good, *its own power*: it has in it a *semblance* of human existence. The class of the proletariat feels annihilated in its self-alienation: it sees in it its own powerlessness and the reality of an inhuman existence' (Marx and Engels 1957: 51). The subjection even of the powerful to 'external coercive laws' was of course a key argument in *Capital.*
14. The absence of a serious historical dimension is one of the major weaknesses in the otherwise fertile and sophisticated analysis of Berger and Luckman.

And it is also more real in that it creates and determines the facts investigated . . . . This real context in which the particular subjects obtain their real significance is definable only within a *theory* of society.' The maxim 'only connect' points to part of a solution: 'a truly human science like a truly human society must give full cognitive status to the whole man which a reified reality fragments and hides; it must give cognitive status to consciously active men who strive to transcend their determination by things' (Horton 1971: 177). Again, fragmentation may be regarded as a real social, not merely an analytical, distortion: the division of labour in intellectual production replicates that in material production. Yet if an adequate theoretical orientation to the problem of totality is unattainable without a *practical* solution to the problem of the division of labour in society, nevertheless the awareness of the problem of totality *as a problem* is a crucial step towards reducing the distorting consequences of fragmentation.

The problem of conceptual adequacy is in several respects different in character: at this point the specific problem of relativism is of particular import. To repeat our argument in Chapter 5: social (and indeed material) reality does not fall naturally into categories; these must be *imposed* as part of the cognitive process. The adequacy of a conceptual framework is therefore not a simple question of objective truth or falsity; the appropriateness of a system of categorisation cannot be meaningfully assessed without reference to the purposes and interests of those who employ it, for these necessarily structure what aspects of reality are *relevant for them*. The critique of a particular conceptual framework as ideologically distorting must therefore refer to its inadequacy in respect of *specific human goals and purposes*. Thus it may be argued that, within a society in which a fundamental conflict of interests is structurally generated, the appropriateness of a conceptual framework, paradigm or *Weltanschauung* will necessarily differ according to group or class interests. Where an ideology which reflects the objectives of a particular social group is embraced by others with conflicting interests, it may reasonably be argued that for the latter this ideology contains an element of 'false consciousness'. If it can be shown that, even for the former group, the ideology is in some respects inadequate or inappropriate, the same diagnosis is legitimate.

Hence while the evaluation of any theory or system of ideas

necessarily involves an area of relativism, this relativism is by no means incorrigible. What our argument does imply is that the interpenetration of consciousness and interests creates a radical epistemological conflict resoluble not through the detached ratiocinative activities of a 'free-floating intelligentsia' — for such activities are themselves socially and historically structured — but through real social transformation which reduces structured social antagonisms from a fundamental to a marginal feature of societal relations.[15] In the last analysis, as Marx argued in the Theses on Feuerbach, 'the question whether human thought can achieve objective truth is not a question of theory but a *practical* question'.

Inequality and Domination: Processes of Ideological Production

The concept of 'hegemony' is commonly applied to a situation in which a structure of power relations is fully legitimised and reinforced by an integrated system of cultural and normative assumptions. This notion is particularly associated with the writings of Gramsci, who defined hegemony in terms of the ' "spontaneous" consent given by the great masses of the population to the general direction imposed on social life by the dominant fundamental group' (1971: 12). If at first sight such a characterisation bears a marked resemblance to value-consensus, three key features necessitate a clear differentiation. First, cultural and ideological hegemony is never absolute: a fact which we explore in a later section. Second, the historical origins of a particular situation of hegemony may be traced to the *material* domination of a specific social group. And third, as we noted earlier (and as Gramsci's use of inverted commas indicates), normative endorsement of a particular social order does not occur 'spontaneously' but must be continually produced and reproduced.

The various mechanisms of ideological production have been analysed in detail by Miliband (1969). Hegemony, he insists (p. 181), 'is not simply something which happens, as a mere superstructural derivative of economic and social predominance. It is, in very large part, the result of a permanent and pervasive *effort,* conducted through a multitude of agencies.' Important examples are the press

15. For a more detailed consideration of these questions, see Gramsci 1971: Part III.

and other media of communication and persuasion, educational institutions and religious organisations. The control of certain of these agencies is the virtual prerogative of those with economic power, which can enable their use in an unambiguously propagandist manner. Other agencies are relatively immune from direct manipulation by those with economic and social power; yet more subtle constraints ensure that their overall effect is to provide solid support for the established order (support which their apparent 'independence' may render the more effective).[16]

Generalised processes of ideological formation are of obvious relevance in explaining the attitudes and orientations discussed in the first part of this study. The various agencies we have mentioned play an important part in the creation and maintenance of those norms of work performance which provide essential cultural support for the social relations of production in modern capitalist industry. Historically, the development of a working class susceptible to the moral appeal of managerial authority necessitated a deliberate and sustained process of ideological indoctrination, often as part of a broader process of 'religious terrorism'. As Andrew Ure, the most notable pioneer of managerial science, insisted in 1835:

> It is . . . the interest of every mill-owner to organise his moral machinery on equally sound principles with his mechanical, for otherwise he will never command the steady hands, watchful eyes, and prompt co-operation, essential to excellence of product. . . . [Religion] excites to obedience; it purchases strength for obedience; it makes obedience practicable; it makes it acceptable; it makes it in a manner unavoidable, for it constrains to it; it is, finally, not only the motive to obedience, but the pattern of it.[17]

The introduction of elementary education in Britain was in part designed to the same end: 'to gentle the masses was [an] explicit purpose' (Glass 1961: 395). Today, the typical worker commences his occupational career having already spent a decade within a hierarchical institution in which subordination and obedience are systematically enforced and inculcated. As Fox has indicated (1971: 45-6), this is merely one aspect of a broad process of early socialisation inflicted on prospective workers:

> As children we are urged to obey parents, teachers, policemen, and public officials

16. For a more detailed analysis and documentation of the role of such 'socialising agencies', see Miliband: chs. 7-8. See also Parkin 1971: ch. 2; Hyman 1972b: ch. 6.
17. *The Philosophy of Manufactures,* quoted in Thompson 1968: 397-8. For other discussions of the inculcation of a work ethic, see Bendix 1963; Pollard 1965.

simply *because* they are parents, teachers, policemen and public officials .... We also learn that if punished for transgression we are receiving no less than our just desert. These are lessons in the behaviours appropriate to subordination. The importance of the family, the group, the school, the community, the society at large, in shaping our perceptions of legitimacy is therefore crucial. In the case of any particular individual, of course, socializing influences brought to bear may or may not conform to the predominant pattern. So far as the majority are concerned, however, by the time they take up employment they are trained to accept that they must work for a living, that this normally involves employment in a privately or publicly owned organization, and that they there come under a generalized expectation that they will accept the orders of persons appointed to govern them. This generalized expectation is likely to be supported, in the case of private industry, with certain propositions about the 'rights' of 'ownership', and in the case of the public sector, the 'right' of public officials. These expectations and their supporting propositions are likely, for many people, to be only vaguely conceived, and to have the status of traditional rather than rationally evaluated behaviours. Their effect is nevertheless crucial, for they ensure that the employer or manager receives an employee who is already socialized and trained in obedience.

In similar fashion, generalised ideological assumptions underlie prevailing notions of fair pay. The dominant cultural perspective, persistently inculcated by the various agencies of social indoctrination, is that high material advantages are the rewards for personal ability, effort or initiative, a prize potentially open to all.[18] Unearned incomes are a consequence of the rights of property, the preservation of which cannot reasonably be questioned (for within this perspective, the same issue of property rights is involved in the private ownership of a corner grocery shop, a pair of trousers, or a chemical industry). Inherited wealth is likewise of obvious legitimacy, since it follows naturally from the sanctity of familial relations that what parents have legitimately accumulated should be transmissible to their children. Popularly inculcated attitudes may indeed castigate *some* gains as ill-gotten — as a reflection of 'the unpleasant and unacceptable face of capitalism'; but such criticism, by virtue of its exceptional character, reinforces the presumption that the *normal* processes of income distribution generate 'fair' rewards and 'honest' profits. The prevailing cultural assumptions thus systematically suppress any consciousness that power and exploitation might be intrinsic to the production and distribution of wealth.

It would be wrong to suggest that extremes of inequality are uncompromisingly legitimated within the prevailing value system.

18. This doctrine in its extreme form is particularly influential in the United States: 'the American dream'; but in some form it serves to legitimate every inegalitarian industrialised society.

On the contrary, notions of 'social justice' set limits to conceptions of acceptable inequalities; in particular, there is a widespread assumption that living standards below a certain minimum are socially intolerable. In consequence, prevailing attitudes often display a contradictory character, and different aspects may be emphasised by members of different social groups. Thus according to a survey by Behrend (1971), those in the highest socio-economic strata — who both benefit most from an inegalitarian income structure, and have the greatest influence on the production of the dominant ideology — are most likely to approve the level of incomes received in their own type of occupations and the consequential large differentials above those in manual occupations. Yet endorsement of their own privileged position is tempered by a certain sensitivity to the situation of the underprivileged. Among those in lower-status occupations the tensions in the dominant ideology are further developed, for conceptions of legitimate differentials are considerably narrower.

Among no social group, however, does the basic *principle* of substantial inequalities receive serious criticism; competing moral notions merely qualify, but do not undermine, the dominant norm of inegalitarianism. And in explaining the strength of this norm, the previous discussion of ideology is of obvious relevance: what is at issue is, as Parkin (1971: 95) puts it, 'the relationship between class power and the moral framework of inequality'. The various socialising agencies to which we have called attention help inculcate a *Weltanschauung* through which the underprivileged regard their situation as natural and inevitable. The same processes which lead the majority of school leavers to frame 'realistic' (that is, restricted) aspirations in respect of job entry (Carter 1966) also structure their expectations in respect of pay and the other social and material accompaniments of employment: in both cases a position in the lower levels of a hierarchy is regarded as normal.[19] These general

19. There is no *inevitability* in the acceptance of an inegalitarian income structure. Thus Walker (1965: 126) cites the case of the islanders from Tristan da Cunha, accustomed to equal pay in their local employment, who complained at the unfairness of differential payment when employed in British factories. In Schutz's terms (1964), whether or not individuals are thought to deserve equal treatment in any specific respect depends on the 'domain of relevances' which is taken for granted within their society. Schutz fails to add that the *structure of economic relations* is likely to exert a powerful influence on such taken-for-granted social assumptions. In Tristan da Cunha, wage-labour (in the island's fish-canning factory) did not play any central role in the structure of property

pressures often receive reinforcement from the media of communication: for example, Behrend *et al.* (1967: 41-2) report that the occupations widely believed to deserve pay increases 'are those which have been in the news and where publicity seems to have resulted in the creation of stereotyped views'. It is possible, then, to draw a close parallel with the analysis of Fox (1971: 45-6) quoted earlier: just as 'the employer or manager receives an employee who is already socialized and trained in obedience', so he receives an employee whose normal pay horizons do not extend far beyond those in kindred occupations.

Such general ideological pressures are of crucial significance in explaining the phenomena of pay comparisons described in Chapter 3. Given the preceding analysis, it would not be difficult to predict that most employees would not explicitly challenge the fundamental principles of the political economy and the basic structure of incomes deriving from this. It could be assumed that their choice of reference groups would be structured by prevailing norms of the 'proper' rewards and status of different socio-economic groups; and that being modest rather than ambitious, these would tend to limit relative deprivation. Because of the contradictions in the dominant assumptions, mentioned above, attitudes to particular aspects of the pay hierarchy do of course involve many complexities; we consider the whole question in more detail below.

A number of specific concepts and formulations mediate between the generalised ideological perspectives inculcated within society and concrete social relations within industry. In this respect it could be argued that the 'unitary frame of reference' described in the previous chapter, with its black-and-white interpretations of industrial relations and industrial conflict, reflects the dominant ideology in its purest form. The stereotypes of the media and the stark formulations of 'issue politics' typically assume (or explicitly assert) a natural harmony of interests within industry, such that conflict is explicable only through a demonology of militant trade unionists and wildcat shop stewards (together, in more sophisticated

---

and production relations; thus norms of equality prevailing in local fishing and agricultural (as well as other social) activities were carried over into factory employment. In a predominantly capitalist economy, by contrast, where inequality of property and hence income from property is a fundamental principle, it is natural that inequality of employment incomes should be taken for granted.

analyses, with 'maverick' employers). Within the perspective which is most extensively propagated, the nature of industrial relations 'problems' is unproblematic: these include all activities or institutions which obstruct the exercise of managerial control within the enterprise or at the level of overall economic management.

This definition of problems meshes neatly with the profoundly ideological notion of 'national interest', through which the interests of the dominant social groupings are sanctified as the interests of all. In so far as those with predominant social and economic power exert disproportionate influence on the content of the prevailing values, it is natural that *their* interests should be assigned universal value. Conversely, 'one of the penalties which the subordinate classes pay for their subordination — indeed what almost defines them as subordinate classes — is that *their* demands can be made to appear . . . injurious to the 'national interest', especially when members of these classes take it into their heads to press their demands with a vigour which is necessarily and by definition disruptive' (Miliband 1969: 207). In industrial relations this problem is particularly acute. By organising to further their interests as sellers of labour power and subordinates in a control hierarchy, wage- and salary-earners articulate the conflict of interests between themselves and those for whom labour is a cost of production and a resource to be manipulated. By demanding improved wages and conditions, or by attempting to restrict management's right to control, trade unionists threaten profit margins and hence the interests of those whose incomes derive from profits. Where such demands are pursued by strike action the challenge to entrenched interests is particularly overt. Hence the mobilisation of such ideological formulae as 'national interest' has major implications for industrial relations.

Miliband has noted how the dominant ideological framework provides a hostile basis for press reaction to trade union activity.

> Not, it should be said, that newspapers in general oppose trade unions as such. Not at all. They only oppose trade unions, in the all too familiar jargon, which, in disregard of the country's welfare and of their members' own interests, greedily and irresponsibly seek to achieve short-term gains which are blindly self-defeating. In other words, newspapers love trade unions so long as they do badly the job for which they exist. Like governments and employers, newspapers profoundly deplore strikes, and the larger the strike the greater the hostility: woe to trade union leaders who encourage or fail to prevent such manifestly unsocial, irresponsible and *obsolete* forms of behaviour (1969: 222).

Such a perspective would appear to underlie recent extensions of legal intervention in British industrial relations. Government spokesmen, in moving the second reading of the Industrial Relations Bill in December 1970, referred repeatedly to the objective of 'discipline and order in industry' as being necessary for 'the health of our society'. It was taken as self-evident that there exists a common 'national interest'; that strikes constitute a 'disease' in an otherwise healthy society; and that 'responsible management and responsible trades union leadership' would alike welcome 'a more orderly and disciplined system'. Only 'the wildcat strike leader and the Communist agitator' would suffer.[20]

A very similar view of industrial relations would seem to underlie the succession of judicial decisions adverse to trade unionism in the decade preceding the Conservative legislation, and in the subsequent operation of the Industrial Relations Act. Judges, as Dicey noted 'are for the most part men of a conservative disposition'. An unusually frank and perspicacious High Court judge has recognised that 'the habits you are trained in, the people with whom you mix, lead to your having a certain class of ideas of such a nature that, when you have to deal with other ideas, you do not give as round and accurate judgments as you would wish. This is one of the great difficulties at present with labour .... It is very difficult sometimes to be sure that you have put yourself into a thoroughly impartial position between two disputants, one of your own class and one not of your class' (quotations from Miliband 1969: 139-41). As Wedderburn has indicated, in his survey of judicial policy in the application of labour law (1971: 23-30), the majority of judges have shown no such self-awareness. In general their *Weltanschauung* reflects closely the unitary frame of reference within which the existence of a national interest is unproblematic, the activities of trade unions are somewhat suspect, and the occurrence of industrial

20. See the speeches by R. Carr, D. Smith and E. Heath, *H.C.Deb.*, Vol. 808, cols. 961-87, 1065-76, 1129-43. The one significant shift by government spokesmen to a more realistic characterisation of the Bill was provided by Heath (cols. 1134-5) in describing it as 'an essential part of a long-term industrial strategy.... The competitive pressures inherent in the existing system of collective bargaining and the consequences of industrial disputes, as other forms of industrial disruption, have pushed up money incomes beyond what is possible in a productive economy.' In other words, some sections of the community — organised workers — actually *gain* from industrial militancy, and the government's aim was to strengthen the power of employers at their expense. The everyday stereotypes through which industrial conflict and trade union action are interpreted and denounced bear a close resemblance to what Young (1971), in a different context, has termed 'the absolutist monolith'.

conflict is naturally deplorable.[21]

The perspectives of academic analysts of industrial relations, as we saw in the previous chapter, cannot be simply identified with such simplistic formulations as dominate public discussion. The more sophisticated conception of industrial conflict within the pluralistic approach might indeed be taken as exemplifying Marx's comment, cited earlier, that the 'active conceptive ideologists' may well generate theories which contradict the assumptions of those directly engaged in controlling society. But it must be added that outside relatively intellectual circles, pluralism has had only limited impact on public debate on industrial relations. Moreover, as we argued previously, the unitary and pluralistic perspectives run in parallel in many of their basic presuppositions: the assumption of at least a broad convergence of interests, the definition of industrial relations problems, the emphasis on the need for order. It could indeed be argued that the controversy around the issues which divide the two perspectives — especially in the period since the Donovan *Report* — diverts critical attention from those assumptions on which both are agreed.

There can be little doubt that such presuppositions do indeed exert an influence on actual practice in industrial relations. A range of studies indicate that the majority of employees endorse at least partially the ideology of 'national interest' and the associated 'teamwork' model of the industrial enterprise.[22] This entails that workers generally mediate their employment experiences through a frame of reference which is at least conducive to the adoption of an internalised work ethic. These experiences may indeed induce limitations and qualifications to this generalised ideological framework: nevertheless it defines the *point of departure* for their perceptions of work. Moreover, this framework may represent the only available source of what Gerth and Mills (1954: 116-18) term 'acceptable justifications' or 'vocabularies of motive'.

> Along with the conduct patterns appropriate for various occasions, we learn their appropriate motives, and these are the motives we will use in dealing with others and with ourselves. The motives we use to justify or to criticize an act thus link our conduct with that of significant others, and line up our conduct with the standardized expectations, often backed up by sanctions, that we call norms. Such words may function as directives and incentives: they are the judgments of others as anticipated

21. See also fn. 31 in the previous chapter.
22. For a comprehensive survey, see Bulmer 1973.

> by the actor . . . . Conceived in this way, motives are acceptable justifications for present, future, or past programmes of conduct. But to call them 'justification' is not to deny their efficacy; it is merely to indicate their function in conduct. Only by narrowing our view to the point where we see the isolated individual as a closed system, can we treat verbalized motives as 'mere justifications'. By examining the *social* function of motives, we are able to grasp just what role motives may perform in the social conduct of individuals. We know that even in purely rational calculations acceptable justifications may play a rather large role. Thus, we may reason, 'If I did this, what could I say? And what would they then say or do?' Decisions to perform or not to perform a given act may be wholly or in part set by the socially available answers to such queries.

The manifest absence of socially available justifications for uncompromisingly oppositional behaviour by workers — which would be dismissed as 'sheer bloody-mindedness' and hence irrational — is clearly an inhibiting factor against uncompromising resistance to managerial priorities in the course of the negotiation of order at workplace level. And similarly, the general modesty of wage aspirations is in part attributable to the absence of any vocabulary of motives which could provide a manual worker, for example, with a plausible rationale for demanding a level of income or the associated material advantages conventionally regarded as the prerogative of higher-status groups. Indeed, aspirations which from this perspective are remarkedly limited may still be denounced as 'irresponsible' and 'excessive' (Fox 1973b: iii) — with almost inevitably inhibiting results.[23]

The Limits of Hegemony

We have already emphasised the danger of exaggerating the coherence and stability of the prevailing values; moral values are on the contrary typically abstract, ambiguous and even contradictory, and thus permit the powerful to espouse interpretations which justify their own situation and any default on their apparent obligations. Yet by the same token the flexibility of moral values may attenuate their impact on the underprivileged. For even if the prevailing generalised values are accepted, together with the associated interpretations and evaluations of the social order, this may have little direct effect in determining the actions of those in subordinate social positions. Mann (1970) in his survey of studies of

23. For a more detailed discussion of the role of vocabularies of motive in trade union action, see Hyman and Fryer 1974.

working-class attitudes has emphasised repeated findings of *inconsistencies* in workers' ideologies. The predominant pattern is a failure to question the dominant generalised philosophies of society, conjoined with a cynical attitude towards those in positions of power and a readiness to engage in actions (going on strike, for example) deprecated by other sections of society.

Parkin (1971) has taken this analysis a stage further, with his classification of dominant, subordinate and radical meaning-systems or ideologies. What he terms subordinate values are, he suggests (pp. 92-5), characteristic of the working class. 'Members of the underclass', he argues, 'are continually exposed to the influence of dominant values by way of the educational system, newspapers, radio and television, and the like. By virtue of the powerful institutional backing they receive these values are not readily negated by those lacking other sources of knowledge and information.' Yet in so far as such values reflect the situation and interests of powerful and privileged groups, they are of questionable 'appropriateness' for subordinate groups. Thus while the latter do not reject the dominant values, neither do they wholly accept them: they are 'constrained to accept the dominant moral framework as an abstract and perhaps somewhat idealized version of reality, although their life conditions tend to weaken its binding force in the actual conduct of affairs.' The 'subordinate value system' which emerges is 'a negotiated form of the dominant values'; the subordinate groups 'negotiate or modify them in the light of their own existential conditions'.

It is therefore somewhat misleading to speak of the 'legitimacy' of the structure of power and inequality in society, if this is meant to imply an unambiguous moral commitment to the social order on the part of the working class. Indeed, as Harris (1971: 230) has pointed out, 'even the term "accept" is suspect, since most men do not consider government one of the factors they can change. It is rather like the weather, and one can neither accept nor reject it for it is not subject to our wills.' Or as Mann (1970: 425) has put it, 'normative acceptance' must be distinguished from 'pragmatic acceptance, where the individual complies because he perceives no realistic alternative'. A particular system of society can appear natural, inevitable, hence legitimate, simply because it is there. Lukacs captured this fact succinctly when he wrote (1971: 260): 'Every system of state and law, and the capitalist system above all, exists in the last analysis because its survival, and the validity of its statutes, are simply accepted as unproblematic.'

The predominately passive nature of working-class commitment to the social order has the consequence that workers often act in ways deemed illegitimate by the custodians of the moral order. But conversely, the restricted and ambiguously articulated nature of working-class deviance has the normal consequence that no explicit or co-ordinated challenge to the social order is posed. There is a world of difference, in Parkin's terms, between 'subordinate' and 'radical' value systems — the latter implying a generalised critique of the existing structure of society and a vision of an alternative social order.[24] Here is manifest the potency of the dominant ideology even in its most passive form. 'If the proletariat finds the economic inhumanity to which it is subjected easier to understand than the political, and the political easier than the cultural, then all these separations point to the extent of the still unconquered power of capitalist forms of life in the proletariat itself' (Lukacs 1971: 76-7).

Yet, again, it is necessary to emphasise the dangers of an overdetermined model of the efficacy of the dominant values in underpinning social order. Ideological and social stability is in fact doubly precarious. In the first place, normative stability depends on the continuance of radical inconsistencies within the subordinate value system. Yet a minority of workers (and in specific historical situations a far larger proportion) *do* relate their concrete everyday experiences to their images of the overall social system, developing a consistently radical (or in terms of the dominant ideology, deviant) value system. It is true that a lack of transparency in the structure of economic and political power makes it natural for the majority to hold contradictory images of their immediate *milieu* and the wider society. But the different levels of consciousness do not form hermetically sealed compartments; and the connections which some succeed in making may potentially be made by others.

This potential is perhaps enhanced by the *practical* consequences of the inconsistencies in the subordinate value system. For example: the cumulative effect of workers striking for substantial wage increases may in certain circumstances be a wholly ***unintended***

24. Parkin's categories derive from, though they might be said to oversimplify and vulgarise, Lenin's classic distinction between 'trade-union' and 'social-democratic' (i.e. revolutionary socialist) consciousness.

threat to economic stability. To meet this threat, those in positions of social control may feel obliged to respond coercively; yet such a response may increase the transparency of the power structure and encourage the development of consistently radical interpretations of society. Hence may ensue a cumulative devaluation of legitimacy.[25]

At a more mundane level, the existence of inconsistencies in the subordinate value system entails that social situations are often indeterminate: a specific outcome of the interaction of power and values cannot be confidently predicted. This fact is of particular importance for a study of the role of values in industrial relations. While we have argued that there is a substantial measure of agreement in the presuppositions underlying public pronouncements by managers, politicians, public commentators, academic analysts, and the judiciary, it is problematic how far the dominant normative assumptions determine what actually occurs in industrial relations. Indeed the preceding discussion points to the probability that such abstract and generalised assumptions will be modified and re-interpreted in the actual practice of trade unionists (and subordinate employees generally).

To give one example: while the legitimacy of managerial authority is strongly endorsed by the prevailing system of values, the effect of this ideological reinforcement of the structure of control in industry is weakened in at least four separate ways. First, though the virtue of 'respect for authority' is inculcated by a variety of socialising agencies, our culture also embraces such values as 'freedom' and 'democracy'. Hence management is conventionally conceived as a *technical function*; its coercive aspect, as control *over other people*, is rarely confronted explicitly and is only weakly legitimated. Second, and partly in consequence, the prevailing values give little precise guidance on the extent of managerial authority and thus the limits of worker obedience. To assume that workers surrender their autonomy absolutely during working hours would contradict too blatantly what are important elements of the dominant culture — would imply that workers are indeed 'wage slaves'. Thus there exists scope for employees to argue that *specific* applications of managerial authority are unreasonable and that in such cases obedience is not

25. Fox (1971: 38) has indicated an analogous process which may occur at the level of the individual company: 'finding its authority failing, management falls back on the coercive sanctions of power, only to find that this further undermines its legitimacy, which in turn prompts the intensified use of power'.

incumbent. Third, employees may accord particular salience to those elements in the dominant value system which qualify the legitimacy of managerial authority and justify the exercise of their autonomous judgment. Finally, the *practical* implications of managerial prerogative in its impact on employees' immediate experiences may provoke discontent and resentment even among those who in the abstract do not question its legitimacy.

Hence it follows that, as was clear from the first part of this study, workers' normative integration into an inegalitarian hierarchy of rewards and deprivations is by no means unproblematic. In consequence, as we showed in Chapter 4, the mediation of the various *institutions* of the labour movement may be of key importance in determining the specific outcome of normative ambiguity or conflict. We have also suggested that while the manifest functions of trade union action are oppositional, challenging managerial decision-making autonomy over earnings and conditions of employment, such action tends to have the general effect of reinforcing the legitimacy of managerial authority and of inegalitarian rewards and deprivations. This is not to say that such a consequence is typically *intended* by those involved in the labour movement. An important question therefore arises: in what ways do the activities of labour organisations relate on the one hand to their officially expressed beliefs and objectives, and on the other to those assumptions which are dominant within the society?

The Dominant Values and the Labour Movement

We have so far suggested that because the influence of those in positions of economic and social power extends to the processes and institutions of socialisation and communication, the dominant interpretation of social reality is normally the only coherent world-view to be extensively accepted. At the same time, working-class commitment to the social order is often relatively passive; while failure to challenge the abstract and generalised formulations of the dominant ideology does not preclude the possibility of conflicting or 'deviant' attitudes and actions on specific concrete issues. The persistence of conflict between the generalised value system and particular experiences and actions opens the possibility of a radicalisation of ideology.

It is within the sphere of employment that such conflict is probably most obvious. As was emphasised previously, the organisation of wage- and salary-earners into trade unions reflects a radical conflict of interests within society. Collective action for improved wages and conditions, greater security of employment, and a measure of control over the work process, runs counter to the employer's 'legitimate interest' in treating labour as a simple factor of production to be bought in the cheapest market and applied with maximum intensity. It is thus a practical contradiction of the notion that there exists an over-arching 'national interest', that the 'social and economic advance' of one section of the community will necessarily prove advantageous to all.

Yet the development of this practical contradiction of the dominant value system into an ideological rejection requires, as Parkin has argued, the intervention of an organised labour movement committed to a 'radical value system'. 'The subordinate value system restricts man's consciousness to the immediacy of a *localized* setting; and the dominant value system encourages consciousness of a *national* identity; but the radical value system encourages consciousness of *class*' (1971: 97). Britain does, of course, possess a particularly long-established labour movement — represented, since the turn of the century, by its own political party. Yet the mere existence of such working-class organisation is no guarantee of the generation of an oppositional ideology. A labour political party may be created as the embodiment of a subordinate value system, designed to further the special cause of labour within the framework of a social order which is itself regarded as legitimate.[26] Or a party initially committed to a class-conscious socialist ideology may, through achieving an established position within the existing structure of political institutions, experience integrating pressures which induce 'a long-term trend towards de-radicalization' (Parkin 1971: 98).

It is a commonplace that the British Labour Party has never been in more than the most tenuous sense a vehicle of oppositional ideology. It originated as a defensive pressure group, designed to protect the traditional prerogatives of trade unionism against the threats of judicial repression and employer consolidation. Initially it lacked a general political programme, let alone a distinctive political

26. This would represent what Anderson (1965), following Gramsci, has termed 'corporate' class consciousness.

theory; given the rationale of its founders to appeal to the mass of workers who accepted the ideology of the dominant parties, it was indeed thought essential that it should in no way challenge the established system of political assumptions. In particular, explicit identification with socialism was strongly resisted; hence even when an independent identity as a party was asserted, and a broader set of policies gradually developed, Labour remained only partially differentiated from traditional Liberalism.[27] Only in 1918, with the disintegration of Liberalism, did the Party adopt a comprehensive programme (*Labour and the New Social Order*) which could be seriously proclaimed as socialist. Yet its 'socialism' derived directly from Fabianism, an eclectic doctrine which incorporated the utilitarianism of nineteenth-century British capitalism, and involved a primary commitment to the piecemeal reform of the existing social structure through the established institutions of political administration and control.[28] As Miliband has argued (1964: 62),

> the new programme was much less the manifesto of a new social order, altogether different, economically and socially, from the old one, than an explicit affirmation by the Labour Party of its belief that piecemeal collectivism, within a predominantly capitalist society, was the key to more welfare, higher efficiency, and greater social justice. Shorn of its rhetoric *Labour and the New Social Order* was a Fabian blueprint for a more advanced, more regulated form of capitalism, which had been in the making over the past decades and whose image had been given more definite shape by the war.

One paradox of the status of Fabianism as the ideology of the Labour Party is its commitment to a theory *which denies the importance of theory.* 'Indifference towards all theory is one of the main reasons why the English working-class movement crawls along so slowly in spite of the splendid organization of the individual unions,' wrote Engels in 1874 (Marx and Engels 1958: I, 652). Tawney expressed the same point in eloquent fashion (1961: 9).

> It is a commonplace that the characteristic virtue of Englishmen is the power of sustained practical activity, and their characteristic vice a reluctance to test the quality of that activity by reference to principles. They are incurious as to theory, take

27. Anderson (1965: 39) has noted the implication of the title Labour, rather than Socialist Party: 'The name designates, not an ideal society . . . but simply an existent interest.'
28. Fabianism thus neatly articulates the traditional political perspectives of British trade unionism, which inspired Lenin's comment that 'trade unionist politics of the working class is precisely *bourgeois politics* of the working class'. As their historian has commented, 'the Fabians supplied a doctrine which could enable a churchwarden, or an English trade unionist, to call himself a Socialist' (McBriar 1962: 348).

> fundamentals for granted, and are more interested in the state of the roads than in their place on the map . . . . Most generations, it might be said, walk in a path which they neither make nor discover, but accept; the main thing is that they should march. The blinkers worn by Englishmen enable them to trot all the more steadily along the beaten road, without being disturbed by curiosity as to their destination.

By entailing a refusal to develop any *systematic* critique of prevailing social institutions and ideology, pragmatism makes its advocates prisoners of both. As Foot (1968: 332) has commented, 'pragmatism is not neutral. It accepts the existing structure and values of society. Social reforms offered pragmatically, which seek to alter that structure, can, when they conflict with that structure and those values, be pragmatically abandoned.'

This pragmatism has always been intimately associated with a fervent commitment to the constitutional proprieties of the established order. As Miliband insists (1964: 13),

> Of political parties claiming socialism to be their aim, the Labour Party has always been one of the most dogmatic — not about socialism, but about the parliamentary system. Empirical and flexible about all else, its leaders have always made devotion to that system their fixed point of reference and the conditioning factor of their political behaviour. This is not simply to say that the Labour Party has never been a party of revolution: such parties have normally been quite willing to use the opportunities the parliamentary system offered as one means of furthering their aims. It is rather that the leaders of the Labour Party have always rejected any kind of political action (such as industrial action for political purposes) which fell, or which appeared to them to fall, outside the framework and conventions of the parliamentary system. The Labour Party has not only been a parliamentary party: it has been a party deeply imbued by parliamentarism. And in this respect, there is no distinction to be made between Labour's political and its industrial leaders. Both have been equally determined that the Labour Party should not stray from the narrow path of parliamentary politics.

Just as pressure through constitutional channels was the party's original rationale, so — once the limited perspectives of a pressure group had given way to the possibility of governmental office — its later ambition was to meet the accepted criteria of 'fitness to govern'. This involved an explicit endorsement of the 'inevitability of gradualness': a Labour government would accept as its starting point social and economic relations *as they existed*; its implicit (or even explicit) priority would be the maintenance of social stability and 'efficient' economic management; social reform would be subject to the dual conditions of not threatening these prior objectives and being attainable through legislative and administrative machinery itself devised to suit the prevailing political economy.

One criterion of 'fitness to govern', it is commonly argued, is the ability of a party to present itself as representative of the 'national' rather than merely class or sectional interest. This has presented considerable problems for the Labour leadership. For while it has never been an aggressively class-oriented party, its trade union origins and traditional working-class base have made Labour necessarily a class-related party, while it has long been associated with policies (greater equality, social reform, welfare provision, public ownership) with obvious class implications. Yet as if to compensate for this 'unfortunate' class image, the party's leaders 'have always sought to escape from the implications of its class character by pursuing what they deemed to be "national" policies: these policies have regularly turned to the detriment of the working classes and to the advantage of Conservatism. Nor can it be otherwise in a society whose essential characteristic remains class division' (Miliband 1964: 348). Efforts to abandon the 'cloth cap image, were particularly strongly pursued in the 1950s, in the aftermath of electoral defeat; while the retreat into classlessness further accelerated in the early 1960s. In the 1964 election, 'the "fundamental inspiration" to make Britain "up-to-date, dynamic, vigorous" had replaced the "central theme" of the 1959 election — to close the gap between rich and poor. The accent had switched from reform to efficiency' (Foot 1968: 148).

Yet in subordinating even the traditionally muted appeal to equality and social welfare to the rhetoric of economic dynamism and the technological revolution, in embracing 'the — essentially Conservative — doctrine that the efficient management of the economy is the key to electoral success' (Goldthorpe *et al.* 1969: 193), Labour adopted a strategy which was not indeed classless but was implicitly hostile to workers' interests. As Foot has argued (1968: 325), the party's economic priorities in the context of the private ownership and control of major sectors of the economy necessitated an orientation towards increased profits, restraint on earnings, greater 'flexibility' (i.e. insecurity) of employment, and attacks on customary shop-floor controls over labour utilisation. Given acute problems of external trade and capital movements, moreover, and a stubborn commitment to the 'defence of the pound', these same priorities entailed that even the traditional Labour objectives of improved social services and welfare provisions were brutally circumscribed.[29]

29. It is too early for us to evaluate the significance of the 'left turn' which the Party,

Hence the tendency in recent years has been for the Labour Party to differentiate itself from its chief rival in terms less of a commitment to social reform than of the efficiency with which it can administer the *status quo*. Rather than justifying class politics as a natural and necessary response to a class society, it has posed as the most worthy representative of the 'national interest', thus adding its endorsement to the dominant ideological assumption that such a phenomenon does indeed exist. 'Official Labour doctrine and language', as Fox has shown (1973b: vi), preclude any serious analysis and critique of the *structural* sources of those social evils which Labour has traditionally deplored; hence effective reform is effectively prevented. This means that, far from offering an alternative value system which might articulate the specific experiences and discontents of wage and salary-earners, Labour has sought integration within a 'consensus' whose boundaries are set by the dominant value system.[30]

If the political institutions of the Labour movement fail to provide the rudiments of an oppositional value system, it is scarcely likely that this will be generated by its industrial institutions: the trade unions. For the essence of normal trade union action involves negotiation around the terms and conditions of workers' employment: negotiation that presupposes as unproblematic the existence of capitalist employment relations. Even a union representative who questioned the very institution of wage-labour, the subordination of employee to employer, would have to operate in his routine activities *as if* capitalism were permanent: would have to 'fight the battles for improvement and reform according to the nature of the terrain, which is that of "realistic" calculation in a capitalist economy and a capitalist state' (Hobsbawm 1964: 339). Such tendencies are accentuated by what Allen (1966: 24-35) has termed 'the disarming consequences of the socialisation process'. Union officials are particularly exposed to ideological pressures antipathetic to effective union action, and this often increases their

---

in opposition, has exhibited in the early 1970s. But historical experience suggests that such radicalisation of policy proves rhetorical rather than real, once Labour regains office.

30. This process has occurred at the level of local as well as national party politics; see Hindess 1971. One consequence, he suggests (p. 150), is 'an estrangement from politics' within the working class. A somewhat similar analysis has been presented by Goldthorpe *et al.* 1969.

reluctance to become committed to ambitious demands or militant action. The conventional definitions and assumptions discussed in the previous sections can thus have serious inhibiting effects on trade unionists. Indeed, they exert a very powerful influence on the manner in which the very *purpose* of trade unionism is conceived.[31] Yet precisely because trade unions represent a defence and protest against the practical consequences of the worker's role within the political economy of capitalism they cannot be effectively integrated within the dominant value system. Hence the ambivalence noted by Parkin (1971: 91-2): 'an uneasy compromise between rejection and full endorsement of the dominant order'. Unions do pursue an *improvement* in the material conditions of their members; yet the strategies they adopt in collective bargaining 'imply a general acceptance of the rules governing distribution'. Pressure for increased wages and salaries forms part of 'an accommodative response to inequality . . . . Collective bargaining does not call into question the values underlying the existing reward structure, nor does it pose any threat to the institutions which support this structure. Trade unionism could in fact be said to stabilize the modern capitalist order by legitimizing further the rules and procedures which govern the allocation of resources.' Arguably, the established social position achieved by British unions and their leaders during the past century reflects the fact that their activities pose no serious threat to the structure of power and inequality.

The very existence and everyday activities of trade unions, it was suggested earlier, contradict the notion of a 'national interest' uniting every section of society. At times this is recognised explicitly, as in the evidence of the Trades Union Congress to the Donovan Commission (1966: 61-2).

> The behaviour of individuals and groups can be most readily explained by reference to their interests . . . . Trade union leaders are usually much more candid than others in recognising that their primary responsibility is to their members. It can plausibly be argued that trade union leaders should disguise the truth of this proposition and talk about 'the national interest' as frequently as everybody else. The alternative, of course, is for leaders of other groups to show the same integrity as trade unionists in recognising publicly the reason why they themselves do not pursue policies other than those based on self-interest.
>
> The interests of different individuals and groups diverge in many respects. Where this is so, some groups clearly think it is effective propaganda to claim that their

31. The impact of the dominant ideology, and of the intervention of those with economic and social power, on the definition of the 'proper' objectives of trade unionism is discussed by Hyman and Fryer 1974.

policy corresponds to, or reflects, the national interest and that other groups ought likewise to take account of the national interest. However successful in the propaganda battle such advocacy might be, it is almost invariably based on myths, and a few moments' consideration would convince the disinterested observer, if such could be found, that this was so. Trade unionists therefore take a somewhat jaundiced view of those whose interests are different to their own lecturing them on their social responsibilities, with the real intention of producing a result which is favourable to their own interests. The argument from the national interest is but one of a rich repertoire employed by those whose interests are different to those of trade unionists.

Yet the forthrightness of this comparatively academic formulation of the TUC perspective contrasts strangely with the more popularly oriented utterances of its leaders. 'This Movement is as conscious of the national interest as the Government is and much more so than most of our critics,' declared its General Secretary in 1969.[32] 'Neither the Government nor the employers can solve the country's problems without the co-operation of the TUC and the workers,' he insisted four years later (*Coventry Evening Telegraph,* 17 Jan. 1973). Possibly such statements are deliberate attempts to 'disguise the truth of the proposition' that the 'national interest' is a myth and that the 'problems' of government and employers are not necessarily those of the TUC and the workers. Yet by endorsing the assumption that one can meaningfully speak of 'the national interest' and 'the country's problems', the TUC participates in the propaganda battle on its opponents' terms.

An illustration of the limitations of this approach is provided by the experience of incomes policy in the 1960s. In 1961 the TUC deplored the Conservative government's pay pause, insisting that it rejected the notion of wage restraint. This attitude was reiterated at subsequent Congresses, and the TUC therefore refused to co-operate with the National Incomes Commission (NIC). Yet at the same time, TUC spokesmen insisted that their attitude was not merely negative: the main tenor of objections at Congress was to restraint on wages and salaries *alone,* and to restraint in the context of *deflationary* economic strategy. Hence the majority reaction in 1962 was to welcome the decision to create the National Economic Development Council (NEDC) — a decision which appeared to mark the government's conversion to economic planning and expansion. The main reservation was that the General Council 'would not agree to joining if the NEDC was to be responsible for administering a policy of wage restraint to which it would be committed' (Lovell and

32. Special Trades Union Congress, 5 June 1969.

Roberts 1968: 170). The government obliged by hiving off the administration of incomes policy to a separate body, the NIC. Yet institutional separation did not alter the fact that the two bodies were elements in a single economic strategy. This was made explicit by the NEDC in one of its first reports (1963: 51) : it envisaged an annual increase of 3¼ per cent in output per head, and went on to argue that 'money incomes per head would have to rise at approximately this rate . . . . There will thus be a need for policies to ensure that money incomes (wages, salaries, profits) as a whole rise substantially less rapidly than in the past'. In the absence of any suggestion to the contrary, the implication of the report (endorsed by the TUC representatives on the NEDC) was that wage restraint would indeed be accepted as part of a general policy of restraint, without any provision for *redistribution* of incomes.

The equivocal nature of the TUC position was further demonstrated when the Labour Party made economic planning the centrepiece of its election strategy and specified as parts of this programme 'an incomes policy to include salaries, wages, dividends, and profits'. Endorsing these proposals, Cousins insisted that they involved 'a planned growth of wages, not wage restraint' (Labour Party Conference Report, 1963). Yet a policy of tying general movements in wage and salary levels to the rate of increase in national production guaranteed a planned growth of incomes *only* if economic expansion was indeed achieved. And even then, such a policy implied restraint on any aspirations for a more equitable distribution of national income. Only a year previously a distinguished commentator had considered this point and had concluded that 'no trade union leader in his senses would publicly commit himself to support what is, in effect, a proposal to maintain the existing national income distribution and to abandon the claim for a redistribution in favour of labour' (Smith 1962: 40-41). Yet by the 1964 election most union leaders had come close to just such a position.

Both before and after participating in the Joint Statement of Intent the TUC did, it is true, repeatedly emphasise that its support for incomes policy presupposed the control of prices and profits as well as wages and salaries, and that the policy was regarded as a basis for economic expansion and rising real incomes, and for special attention to the low paid as part of a strategy for 'social justice'. But in practice, support was not *conditional* on these latter points. According to Woodcock, 'I am prepared to say that an incomes policy would be justifiable to the trade union Movement if it were concerned only to avoid price increases and to avoid British industries being priced out of export markets by increased costs' (Conference of Executives, 30 April 1965). Hence the *principle* of incomes policy was accepted on simple grounds of government economic strategy (grounds basically the same as those underlying the Conservative policy of 1961-2); the social objectives were in effect pressed as adjustments of detail to a structure in itself acceptable. In 1966, when the government imposed its standstill, the General Council 'reached the conclusion that the interests both of trade unionists and of the nation as a whole in the current critical situation compelled them to acquiesce in the Government's proposal' (TUC Report, 1966: 326). Even when the logic of the economic criteria underlying the policy was reflected in a *decline* in the real net earnings of many workers, and particular discrimination against the low paid,[33] the withdrawal of TUC support was gradual, tentative and partial. In particular, opposition and criticism focused on questions of machinery and detail (whether the policy should be voluntary or legally enforced, how rigid or flexible should be the criteria for increases),[34] rather than on the principle of incomes policy and the analysis underlying its introduction. In this context, Hughes's remarks (1972: 162) are of interest: 'all the official "norms" of pay increase throughout the whole period represented in *real* terms a reduction in pay . . . . In retrospect what is surprising is that the trade unions co-operated for as long as they did, and tried for as long as they did to develop a constructive dialogue with the

33. For a discussion and documentation of these tendencies, see Jackson *et al.* 1972: 76-81, 89-95.
34. From 1967 resolutions were carried at Congress opposing legislative enforcement of incomes policy; these culminated in 1969 in the adoption, by a narrow majority and against the General Council's recommendation, of a resolution calling for the repeal of both parts of the Prices and Incomes Act, 1966. On criteria for increases, Congress adopted in 1966 a demand for 'effective measures to assist lower paid workers, particularly those whose earnings are close to modern conceptions of subsistence levels'; this was applied by the Incomes Policy Committee of the General Council in its scrutiny of union wage claims. In the following year a series of resolutions were adopted, calling for a £15 minimum wage, equal pay for work of equal value, the maintenance of 'proper differentials for skill and responsibility', and the acceptance of comparability and the cost of living as criteria for increases. The General Council itself, however, refused to endorse the full implications of these resolutions in its *Economic Review* for 1968.

Government about both growth and income distribution.'

In consequence, the TUC largely underwrote the dominant assumption that restraint on wage increases was in the 'national interest' and represented an inevitable response to 'economic needs'. Little serious attention was paid to the argument that radically different economic priorities and economic relations might better serve the interests of trade unionists and the majority of the population. In the last resort, TUC spokesmen employed the argument of *force majeure*: the power of capital, which set the framework of government economic strategy, could not be resisted by trade unionists. Hence Woodcock insisted that if the TUC did not provide 'full co-operation' with incomes policy, the government would either create unemployment or else would legislate 'to circumscribe free collective bargaining and . . . to limit the right to strike'.[35]

This argument neatly encapsulates the perspectives of trade union consciousness: an overriding commitment to the goal of *accommodation* with the priorities of those in positions of economic and political control. Where government policies have threatened employee interests, both the form and content of union opposition have typically been modest and restrained. Radical criticism of capitalist economic priorities, and active mobilisation of trade unionists' industrial strength, would alike jeopardise the goal of stable bargaining relationships with employers and the government. A predisposition to acquiescence is exemplified by the TUC response to Labour proposals, in 1965 and 1969, to legislate to curb wage increases and to control strikes; in both cases, Congress agreed to establish its *own* machinery to achieve the same objectives. Even during the subsequent Conservative administration — despite much talk of 'confrontation' — the TUC strove to square its opposition to the Industrial Relations Act with constitutional proprieties and (as we have seen) did not challenge the basic rationale of post-1972 income controls.[36]

35. Conference of Executives, 30 April 1965. Ironically, little more than a year later the government had legislated to curb trade union action, and unemployment was rising towards a record post-war level — *despite* 'full co-operation' on the part of the TUC.
36. In our brief sketch of the perspectives of the TUC we necessarily neglect the greater radicalism of the policies embraced by certain British unions. The recent growth of such radicalism is a development of immense significance; but it is typically ambivalently articulated and in no case amounts to a *comprehensive*

Thus it is evident that conflict over prevailing norms of fairness in industrial relations is not primarily the outcome of a clash of opposing ideologies: for no clear counter-ideology to the prevailing values is purveyed by the main institutions of the labour movement, and those organisations which do propound a radical or revolutionary perspective are as yet of only limited influence. 'As a consequence of the policies, behaviour, and ideology that those active in the Labour Movement have adopted, for reasons good and bad, in their conduct of the institutions through which we handle political and industrial conflict, the essential structural bases of that conflict are allowed to remain in the shadowy background, not merely unstressed but usually unmentioned. As a consequence, the realities of the conflict remain muffled' (Fox 1973b: i). This means that where conflict does occur, it is likely to reflect the outcome of highly specific industrial situations, aspirations and experiences. At the same time, both the form and content of such conflict are likely to be influenced by the ideological factors that have been discussed.

The characteristic feature of the subordinate value system, we have seen, is that pragmatic considerations of restricted power, together with possible normative considerations of legitimacy, inhibit those in subordinate occupational positions from posing any general and explicit challenge to the prevailing social and economic hierarchy. Thus the basic principles of a highly inegalitarian income structure are not seriously and extensively questioned: discontent focuses on more parochial grievances. The pressures towards a restricted frame of reference in evaluating incomes are both reflected in and reinforced by the official institutions of the labour movement — as is to be expected from the above analysis. As Hindess has argued (1971: 40-41), the narrow reference groups reported by many sociologists must be viewed in a context in which 'none of the major political organizations offer any hope of changing the overall pattern of income distribution . . . . In the absence of political organizations dedicated to large-scale changes, when in other words there appears to be no prospect of anything but minor changes here and there, it is hardly surprising that people indulge in such limited comparisons.' In the absence of a serious *political* challenge to the structure of incomes (in itself as much a political as

critique of the traditional perspectives of trade unionism. For a more detailed discussion of the nature and limits of trade union radicalism, see Hyman 1974.

an economic issue), it is natural that the bargaining activities of trade unions should be 'closely linked to what is immediately realizable' (Allen 1966: 29). The application of comparisons in a manner which is primarily conservative in terms of endorsing the broad structure of established relativities, and a commitment to the institutionalised processes of 'realistic' compromise and accommodation, are central to the normal dimensions of trade union wage policy. The 'management of discontent' is thus a process manifest not only in the controlled resolution of specific grievances and conflicts but also in the articulation and reinforcement of a generalised *ideology* of industrial relations; and the immediate perceptions and aspirations of trade unionists cannot fail to bear the imprint of these conventional assumptions. It is only from this perspective that the phenomena discussed in the first part of our study become fully comprehensible.

Power, Ideology and the Incomes Hierarchy

We conclude this chapter by seeking to relate the preceding analysis of power and ideology to the interpretation of the incomes hierarchy. In Chapter 5 we concluded that despite the limitations inherent in the economic paradigm, market forces clearly do exert some influence on wage structure and wage movements. Yet we insisted that any analysis is incomplete which fails to recognise that the market is itself both a medium of power and a reflection of the distribution of power in society. Tawney's comments are particularly apposite: 'Economic laws . . . indicate the manner in which, given certain historical conditions, and a certain form of social organization, and certain juristic institutions, production tends to be conducted and wealth to be distributed.' This *institutional context* of market relations, Tawney insisted, 'is determined, not by immutable economic laws, but by the values, preferences, interests and ideals which rule at any moment in a given society' (1964: 53-4). It might be added that this *socially contingent* character of market forces, evident even in the context of a *laissez faire* economy, is particularly manifest in an era of monopoly capitalism when economic power carries with it the ability deliberately to manipulate the market.

Where economic analysis excludes this perspective it treats the incomes hierarchy in a reified manner; ideologically it carries the implication that existing inequalities are in large measure inevitable.

Those theorists who, by contrast, emphasise the role of social values in determining relative incomes often fall victim to an idealist bias; while ideologically they imply that existing inequalities are consensual. Here too, it is essential to consider the system of class structuration and the distribution of social power in explaining the structure of occupational prestige and the criteria of rank which this incorporates. Lockwood has made this point succinctly: 'A dominant class has never existed which did not seek to make its position legitimate by placing the highest value on those qualities and activities which came closest to its own' (1958: 209). It is very evident that the dominant legitimations of high income — which are reflected and systematised in formal schemes of job evaluation — accord comfortably with the actual situation of those in elite positions. Two criteria in particular are assigned supremacy. The first is formal educational qualifications: access to which, as educational sociologists have emphasised, is powerfully influenced by class origins; and which in turn provide a crucial medium of career advancement to positions of high prestige and material reward. The second is responsibility, a concept which in a hierarchical and undemocratic structure of industrial governance is primarily a euphemism for domination.

The latter criterion is particularly relevant as a legitimation of the salaries of industrial management. It is presumably not wholly coincidental that the upper managerial strata both receive the highest levels of 'earned' income of any occupational group, and also possess the unique power to determine their own remuneration. The candid discussion of this question by Marris is of great interest. Where individual managerial salaries are increased, he notes, 'the change is often legitimised by some real or simulated increase in responsibility'. The key ideological importance of this criterion 'may explain the relative downgrading of otherwise worthy persons who are notably free of responsibility'. Hence Marris concludes that 'managers have developed a system of incentives reflecting their own perception of their role'; they act 'within a system of rules developed from their own functional needs and based on their own norms' (1964: 90, 93). Precisely because of their managerial role, it must be added, they have the rare capacity to ensure that their self-conceptions of importance are both ideologically influential and practically effective.[37] The equation of responsibility and domina-

37. Pen (1971: 358) has developed a similar analysis.

tion thus brings power, ideology and income into happy equilibrium.

Both of the socially dominant criteria of occupational prestige are highly relevant in the case of the traditional professions. The 'merging of skill and money' is in this context in part at least culturally based: the rationale of professional status and its material accoutrements is closely related to the esoteric and awe-inspiring character of professional knowledge and techniques. Yet as sociologists of occupations have increasingly argued, there is only limited *practical* justification for the conventionally sharp status demarcation between professional and non-professional groups;[38] hence as Johnson (1972: 42-3) makes clear, the achievement of professional status represents a successful *imposition* of a definition — or more appropriately, perhaps, a 'mystification' — of occupational worth.

Unlike top managers, most members of the learned professions lack the direct and immediate power to determine unilaterally the social and market valuations of their capacities. However, professional institutions of occupational control, by ensuring monopoly of a defined area of practice for a restricted body of practitioners, enhance their members' economic power and also contribute to the mystique of professionalism. The legally privileged position of these institutions reflects the fact that the resources of power at the disposal of the group 'are articulated with other and wider bases of social power'. As Johnson insists, a group is only likely to impose the exalted professional definition of its own status when it 'shares, by virtue of its membership of a dominant caste or class, wider resources of power'. More specifically, what is involved is the mutual influence of class and state power.[39] Parkin (1971: 27-8) has indicated that 'the state plays an important role in preserving the structure of class inequality by giving powerful institutional and legal backing to the rules and procedures which decide the distribution of advantages and the process of recruitment to different positions . . . . By giving legal and institutional backing to the 'laws' of supply and demand, the state effectively buttresses existing inequalities of reward in favour of the non-manual or

38. See for example Hughes 1958; Wilensky 1964. The former points to important similarities in occupational activities and strategies between doctors and plumbers, prostitutes and psychiatrists.
39. For an elaboration of this inter-relationship, see Miliband 1969.

dominant class.'[40] The experience of incomes policy demonstrates that direct governmental interference with the labour market is oriented towards the containment of certain marginal contradictions associated with its 'free' operation rather than its more fundamental inegalitarian tendencies. What is particularly significant in the case of the professions, however, is the *transparency* with which state power is used to support the prestige and privileges of an elite occupational group.

More complex theoretical issues are raised by the position in the incomes hierarchy of the generality of white-collar occupations. Their earnings are on average significantly above those of manual workers, and they enjoy systematic advantages in terms of working conditions and 'fringe' benefits, even though they do not themselves have access to noticeably greater social power. The problems of accommodating the distinctive characteristics of white-collar employment to the Marxian categories of class are of course notorious. For most contemporary sociologists, Weber's theory of class (1948: ch. 7) — with its differentiation between property and income as determinants of class situation — is considered of greater utility. In Weber's terms, 'the kind of services that can be offered in the market' distinguish white-collar from manual employees, and help explain both their material advantages and their much-vaunted lack of proletarian class-consciousness.

It is important to emphasise, however, that the Weberian perspective typically involves an exaggeration of the autonomy of the market. The previous argument must be repeated: the labour market reflects the valuations imposed by the distribution of societal power, and in these valuations the dimensions of social class and social prestige interpenetrate with far greater intimacy than Weber himself admitted. In effect, routine white-collar employees benefit from a diffuse association with those in positions of genuine power. They enjoy the advantages of a partial and contingent parallel in work tasks and qualifications — as well as in some cases a place, however modest, in the same hierarchy of control — with those in elite and dominant occupational roles.

40. Parkin's discussion is unfortunately weakened by the facile assumption of a 'class boundary' differentiating white-collar employees as a whole from manual workers. He thus ignores the radical contrast between top managerial and professional groups, and routine white-collar employees, in terms of income, authority, congeniality of employment, social status, political influence, etc.

The implication is thus that the social prestige and material privileges enjoyed even by menial white-collar employees by comparison with the generality of manual workers do not derive primarily from a *practical* economic rationale: for the necessary qualifications in terms of literacy, for example, hardly possess important scarcity value.[41] Nevertheless, it is arguable that such advantages are *required* if the integrity of the dominant cultural norms of occupational prestige is to be preserved. By the same token, the claim of skilled manual workers for special status and rewards — however dubious the technical basis of the assertion of exceptional qualifications and expertise may sometimes be —[42] is more readily conceded in the market valuation because it represents a diluted version of the ideology of professionalism.[43]

Conclusions

In this chapter we have argued that any adequate explanation of the structure of inequality in industrial relations and of attitudes towards this inequality must give the necessary weight to the distribution of power in society; the analysis of power must therefore be integrated with the various theoretical perspectives the limitations of which we have criticised in previous chapters. Thus while 'social values' undoubtedly play an important role in stabilising inequality, it is necessary to explore inegalitarian values as a specific example of ideological processes in society. This entails that an adequate understanding of pay aspirations and negotiations must take account of the complex interrelationship between the

41. For a discussion of this point, see Lockwood 1958.
42. See the discussion of the meaning of skill and the extent to which definitions of skill are socially imposed, in Turner 1962: 111.
43. The Webbs (1920: 218) cite the explicit comparison with professional status by the main nineteenth-century union of engineering craftsmen: 'The youth who has the good fortune and inclination for preparing himself as a useful member of society by the study of physic, and who studies that profession with success so as to obtain his diploma from the Surgeons' Hall or College of Surgeons, naturally expects, in some measure, that he is entitled to privileges to which the pretending quack can lay no claim; and if in the practice of that useful profession he finds himself injured by such a pretender, he has the power of instituting a course of law against him. Such are the benefits connected with the learned professions. But the mechanic, though he may expend nearly an equal fortune and sacrifice an equal proportion of his life in becoming acquainted with the different branches of useful mechanism, has no law to protect his privileges.'

structure of inequality, the prevailing standards of occupational worth and hence the dominant legitimations of this structure, and the institutions of class power and political control. Likewise, the role of the institutions of the labour movement in mediating the dominant ideology and in modifying and absorbing conflict can be fully comprehended only within a similarly broad perspective.

Against the consensual perspectives of functionalist sociology, we have however rejected any assumption that legitimation of an inegalitarian hierarchy of power, rewards and deprivations is absolute and unproblematic. Social values are in general imprecise, ambiguous and even contradictory, and this is certainly the case in respect of attitudes to inequality. Moreover, prevailing beliefs and values, even though profoundly influential in shaping working-class consciousness, are modified and re-interpreted in the light of the objective situation and experiences of employees. Hence our analysis does not underestimate the scope for normative and material conflict and instability: rather we suggest that *contradictory* social processes underlie the impact of normative values in industrial relations. In the concluding chapter we focus on this point, examining the relative significance of pressures towards conflict and change, stability and acquiescence in respect of inequality in employment and in society.

Chapter 8

Industrial Relations: The Dynamics of Inegalitarianism

Conflict and change are central to the processes involved in industrial relations. It is the fundamental opposition of interests between employers and employees, together with the less radical but nevertheless pervasive divergences of specific group interests, which necessitate the existence of institutions and procedures generating the accommodations and understandings without which industrial activity would be impossible. These accommodations and understandings are in turn typically *ad hoc* and provisional; in any case they require adjustment in the face of changes in the technical and economic context or the power relationship of the respective parties; while the interpretation and application of agreements can represent a source of conflict. Hence the essential dynamism of industrial relations.

Yet there are many modalities of change. It can be gradual or sudden, peaceful or violent. It can create a basis for stable relationships or a source of continuing and increasing instability. It can occur solely within the industrial relations sector, having no significant implications for general economic and political relations in the broader society; or its impact can extend beyond the specific institutions of employer-employee relations to the whole social structure. The focus of this concluding chapter is on the interrelationship between values in industrial relations and the more general factor of stability and instability in society.

Values and Social Stability

The preceding chapters have presented considerable evidence that social values may serve to moderate and contain conflict. It would seem that the prevailing beliefs and values of a society, in their most basic and general form, tend naturally to reinforce the material dominance of those with economic power; and that there exist a range of institutions through which values conducive to social stability can be inculcated. Within the context of industrial relations, the main burden of our analysis has been that the dominant framework of normative assumptions serves to legitimise a political economy based on the private ownership of the means of production and the associated forms of massive social inequality. Finally, we have devoted considerable attention to the stabilising implications of the language of fairness — the basis of Marx's insistence that 'a fair day's wage for a fair day's work' was at root a 'conservative motto'.

In brief, notions of a 'fair day's work' can be regarded as a crucial support for any economic system based on wage-labour, in particular where a relatively high level of technological development has been reached. For the degree and consistency of application required of the employee cannot be guaranteed by overtly coercive managerial control; this may indeed prove counter-productive. Hence what is required, if economic organisations are to operate effectively, is that the employee should at least partially endorse *normative* standards of work obligation. Durkheim's notion of 'organic solidarity' is of obvious relevance here: in a society characterised by an elaborate division of labour and hence a high degree of interdependence among individuals and groups, stable relations require normative agreement on the rights and obligations of each.

Norms of fairness in relations to levels of income have equally conservative implications. As was emphasised in Chapters 3 and 4, conceptions of 'fair comparisons' are interpreted primarily in the light of custom and convention. According to the Webbs (1897: 693-4, 332), 'over a large part of the industrial field, the wage-earners cling with stubborn obstinacy to certain customary standards of expenditure'. So powerful was this commitment to traditional standards and relationships, they asserted, that

> the actual earnings of any class of workers are largely determined by its Standard of Comfort, that is to say, the kind and amount of food, clothing, and other commodities to which the class has become firmly accustomed. It would not be easy to persuade an English engineer to work at his trade for thirteen shillings a week, however excessive might be the supply of engineers. Rather than do such violence to his own self-respect, he would work as a labourer, or even sweep a crossing. On the other hand, however

much in request a Dorsetshire labourer might find himself it would not enter into his head to ask for two pounds a week for his work. There is, in fact, the Trade Unionist asserts, in each occupation a customary standard of livelihood, which is, within a specific range of variation, tacitly recognised by both employers and employed. Upon this customary standard of weekly earnings, the piecework or hour rates are, more or less consciously, always based. [1]

According to Phelps Brown (1959: 273-4), the typical employer shared these perspectives: 'his judgment of what was a fair wage would be formed by what had customarily been paid and what other reputable employers were paying now. Thereby an element of self-perpetuation and self-justification entered into the wage structure.' Hence 'forces of convention and equity' could prove stronger than the pressures of the labour market. At times this could maintain wages above the level of economic 'normalcy'; yet it could also, by constraining workers' aspirations, keep them below the level of the economically possible. [2]

The implications of a conception of equity so heavily influenced by custom and convention have been eloquently asserted by Wootton (1962: 162).

The weight of social influences involved falls overwhelmingly on the side of conservatism. That every wage bargain must be 'fair' or 'reasonable' now goes without saying. Also unspoken — though for a different reason — is the rubric by which the fair and the reasonable are defined; nobody knows in this context what justice is, and no Socrates walks the streets pestering us to find out. That is where conservatism comes to the rescue. Change — always, everywhere, in everything — requires justification: the strength of conservatism is that it is held to justify itself. It is not therefore surprising that the maintenance of standards, absolute or comparative, should be woven as warp and woof into the texture of wage discussions; or, to change the metaphor, that history should be summoned to fill the void when moral actions must be performed without moral principles to guide them.

Even where notions of *equality* intrude in wage determination, these may incur a conservative transmutation: 'equalizing tendencies in collective bargaining are directed toward equalization of adjustments as often as equalization of rates' (Ross 1948: 46). The incorporation of such notions into the machinery of pay determination thus helps stabilise the income hierarchy. As Turner and Jackson have commented (1969: 5), 'these institutional mechanisms act as vehicles for concepts of "equity", "wage

1. Marx had previously recognised that normative convention could underlie levels of wages in general and wage differentials in particular: see for example 1959: 171, 197-8; 1962: 837.
2. This was of course a central element in Weber's discussion of traditionalism, to which we referred in Chapter 3.

solidarity", "fair comparison", "customary differentials". . . . The main burden of these concepts or conventions is conservative, so the resultant pressures strongly reinforce the economic pressures at work in a reasonably efficient labour market in maintaining the constancy of the relative wage structure.' [3]

Thus ideas of fairness operate through the institutions of wage determination to stabilise an inegalitarian income hierarchy: they also serve to give direct ideological legitimation to this hierarchy. We have previously cited the argument of Lupton and Hamilton that there exists a status hierarchy of occupations which is the subject of a broad degree of normative agreement, such that inequality receives an important measure of legitimation. Attitudes towards this hierarchy, they claim (1970: 268), possess 'considerable historical inertia which will give it endurance in the cultural tradition over time'. In consequence, the prevailing acceptance of the hierarchy 'may legitimise now a social status gained by illegitimate power in the past; and it legitimises the use of economic power in the present'.

Whilst we have strongly criticised the exaggeration by Lupton and Hamilton of the coherence and consensual character of social attitudes towards inequality, and also their failure to relate these attitudes to an analysis of processes of ideological formation, their argument possesses a core of validity. Because massive inequalities in the rewards and deprivations associated with work are conventionally regarded as natural and inevitable, major disparities between and within classes are not a serious and persistent source of discontent. Hence, in the opinion of Livernash (1953:431), 'there is a strong conservative tendency among workers to accept the status quo in wage differentials regardless of its origin and merits. . . . For the individual, the most significant rate relationships are those within his small work group.'

This predominant concern with parochial relativities of pay would appear to exert a further stabilising influence. For the resultant sectionalism of workers' collective aspirations necessarily inhibits united action on a broad front. One consequence is to limit the objectives of trade unionism: 'if workers' economic aspirations are shaped by an exclusive concern with relativities, then the share of

3. It is a further revealing indication of prevailing academic value-orientations that one index of a 'reasonably efficient' labour market is apparently the perpetuation of major inequalities of income.

production accruing to profits remains unchallenged; workers ignore the fact that their earnings fall considerably short of the value of their labour' (Hyman 1972b:134). Another is to weaken the collective power of labour: as Simmel recognised (1950: 160), 'conflicts among workmen gravely undermine their position toward the entrepreneur'. More fundamentally, it can be argued, a multiplicity of sectional conflicts inhibits the articulation of a more fundamental cleavage within society (Simmel 1955; Coser 1956). Hence a conception of fairness which emphasises the maintenance of traditional relativities *within* the working class may be said to obstruct any serious challenge to the political economy of capitalism. This in turn helps explain why those in positions of privilege and control diligently perpetuate an ideology within which conventional notions of fairness occupy a central place.

Values and Instability

Thus the most *general* effect of the prevailing values in industrial relations is to contribute towards order and stability. Yet to emphasise this tendency alone would be to present a one-sided and distorted picture. For there are tendencies in the reverse direction which derive from at least four separate though related sources. First, the centrality of custom as a basis of legitimacy gives normative stability a precarious character. Second, industrial relations ideologies contain ambiguities and inconsistencies. Third, traditionally accepted beliefs and values may become a source of instability when objective circumstances alter. And fourth, changes which disturb relationships customarily accepted as fair may well provoke conflict.

That custom is a precarious rationale for a system of social relations is an insight inherent in Weber's classic analysis of the basis of legitimacy.

> In Weber's view beliefs in the legitimacy of a system of domination are not merely philosophical matters. They can contribute to the stability of an authority relationship, and they indicate very real differences between systems of domination. Like all others who enjoy advantages over their fellows, men in power want to see their position as 'legitimate' and their advantages as 'deserved' and to interpret the subordination of the many as the 'just fate' of those upon whom it falls. All rulers therefore develop some myth of their natural superiority, which usually is accepted by the people under stable conditions but may become the object of passionate hatred when some crisis makes the established order appear questionable (Bendix 1966: 294).

As Bendix remarks (p.418), 'every such belief is in a sense question-begging. For example, charismatic authority depends upon a belief in the sanctity or exemplary character of an individual person, but this person loses his authority as soon as those subject to it no longer believe in his extraordinary powers.' Yet, arguably, custom is a *particularly* precarious rationale since it is less a justification for a pattern of behaviour or relations than a reason why such a pattern is unquestioned: "it is very often a matter of almost automatic reaction to habitual stimuli which guide behaviour in a course which has been repeatedly followed' (Weber 1947:116). If individuals *should* question what has previously been taken for granted, a simple appeal to custom is unlikely to satisfy them. Custom, Weber argued, may be regarded as mid-way between pure expediency and a rationally based sense of legitimacy, and its binding force is correspondingly weak.

> An order which is adhered to from motives of pure expediency is generally much less stable than one upheld on a purely customary basis through the fact that the corresponding behaviour has become habitual. The latter is much the most common type of subjective attitude. But even this type of order is in turn much less stable than an order which enjoys the prestige of being considered binding, or as it may be expressed, of 'legitimacy' (p. 125).

In the context of industrial relations, it has been argued that workers' acceptance of a particular notion of work obligation and a particular structure of relative incomes is primarily attributable to custom and convention. Yet this is to imply that this acceptance is as much pragmatic as normative, is based on the absence of an obviously available alternative rather than on a strong moral commitment. Weber's reference to 'motives of pure expendiency' is echoed in the recent arguments of Goldthorpe and his associates. 'The generally positive attitudes towards their firms revealed by the majority of our affluent workers [should] be seen as deriving not so much from a moral but rather from a largely successful *calculative* involvement with the organisations in question. . . . The affluent worker, as he emerges from our research, is far indeed from being any kind of "organisation man", bound to a firm by a sense of personal commitment and long-term career expectations. On the contrary, rather than regarding his firm as being to some extent a moral community, he would appear to accept it as an essentially economic form of association, within which his hopes for the future must largely rest on the price that he and his fellow workers can collectively obtain for the labour they provide' (1968:80; 1969:81-2). Westergaard's comments (1970:120) have already been mentioned: 'If the . . . worker is tied to his work only by the size, security and potential growth of his wage packet — if his commitment to the job and to everyday cooperation with foremen and managers depends essentially on the fulfilment of such monetary conditions — his commitment clearly is a brittle one. He may be willing to accept the lack of other interests and satisfactions in the job, for the sake of money. But should the amount and dependability of the money be threatened, his resigned toleration of the lack of discretion, control and "meaning" attached to the job could no longer be guaranteed . . . The single-stranded character of the "cash orientation" implies a latent instability of workers' commitments.' If, by extension, workers' habitual acceptance of a structure of incomes and work obligations which has no inherent rationale rests on a similarly narrow pragmatism, this instability has even more fundamental implications. Tawney's argument (1961:40-41) is particularly apposite:

> Since the income available for distribution is limited, and since, therefore, when certain limits have been passed, what one group gains another group must lose, it is evident that if the relative incomes of different groups are not to be determined by their functions, there is no method other than mutual self-assertion which is left to determine them. Self-interest, indeed, may cause them to refrain from using their full strength to enforce their claims, and, in so far as this happens, peace is secured in industry, as men have attempted to secure it in international affairs, by a balance of power. But the maintenance of such a peace is contingent upon the estimate of the parties to it that they have more to lose than to gain by an overt struggle, and is not the result of their acceptance of any standard of remuneration as an equitable settlement of their claims. Hence it is precarious, insincere and short.

If this is so, relatively arbitrary shifts in consciousness may serve 'to break down the power of these false standards, of the enslaving and demoralizing notion of "fairness" within an unfair system' (Coates 1967:83). A dramatic example is the Pilkington strike of 1970. A trivial dispute over errors in a few workers' pay packets escalated into a 7-week stoppage by 10,000 workers demanding a £10 increase; and in the process a tradition of submissive loyalty to employer and union alike was overthrown (Lane and Roberts 1971).

The possibility of such shifts in consciousness, and a consequential heightening of aspirations, is created by the inconsistencies and ambiguities in industrial relations ideologies, the existence of which has been emphasised at several points in the preceding chapters. Fox (1971:125) has argued that 'on neither the management nor the collectivity side does the ideology take the form of a consistent and related body of ideas and values. Rather does it consist of a ragbag of assorted notions fashioned to suit varying exigencies, sometimes quite incompatible with each other.' Thus we have seen that inconsistent frames of reference may be applied in judging incomes, and reference groups may at times be fluid and tenuous. Moreover, it is highly significant that the general standards of morality (and hence the specific notions of fairness) which normally apply in industry often diverge from those commonly deemed appropriate in other areas of interpersonal relations. Hence 'varying and competing vocabularies of motives operate co-terminally and the situations to which they are appropriate are not clearly demarcated' (Mills 1963:449). Were employees to attempt to assert at work the standards of humanity commonly advocated in other areas of social life, the consequences could be dramatic.

In this context, an important factor revealed by survey data is a positive association between social status and ideological coherence; Mann (1970:432-5) reports that 'working-class individuals . . . exhibit less internal consistency in their values than middle-class people,' and suggests as an explanatory hypothesis that 'only those actually sharing in societal power need develop consistent societal values'. Moreover, of course, the generalised social values which are forcefully inculcated at every level of the societal hierarchy may attune most closely with the particular social experience of those in dominant positions, hence entailing that they alone can enjoy a reasonably coherent *Weltanschauung*.

It is thus the inconsistencies in the subordinate value system which are of particular significance. Parkin's characterisation of the subordinate as a 'negotiated version' of the dominant value system has already been cited. It is interesting to compare this analysis with Westergaard's argument (1970:123-4)

> that there exists among the bulk of working class . . . a 'counter-ideology' critical of the present social order. It is a 'quasi-ideology', an ideology at half-cock — not a full-blown radical (let alone revolutionary) ideology — because its elements are contradictory, and lack the coherence implied in classical concepts of working class consciousness; and because, partly for that reason, its political potential is uncertain, ambivalent and to a considerable extent latent. Social criticism co-exists with attitudes that involve a practical, everyday acceptance of established institutions.

From these ideological inconsistencies follow contradictory implications for stability in industrial and social stability. On the one hand, an explicit, coherent and generalised challenge to the prevailing structure of economic and social order is prevented. But conversely, this absence of any generalised ideological challenge to the established order does not preclude particular actions which from the viewpoint of those in positions of social dominance are highly 'deviant' and which pose a serious practical threat to this order. That this contradiction may on occasions give rise to a highly unstable situation has already been emphasised. And in such situations, the presence within a workforce of individuals with a more developed and coherent oppositional ideology — perhaps occupying influential positions within workplace trade unionism — can increase the significance of such practical challenges to the established order.

The present conjuncture of objective processes would appear to increase the prospects of such practical threats to stability and the seriousness of their consequences. Recent trends in the British political economy have made the outcome of 'free collective bargaining' — the virtues of which were for many years largely uncontroversial — far less acceptable than in the past to employers and governments. The escalating costs and complexity of capital equipment and the growing size of productive units have created urgent pressures towards managerial rationalisation and planning; and planning, to be effective, requires predictability and control. Labour costs and labour utilisation, the aspects of companies' economic environment over which they have the greatest direct influence, represent one of the primary targets for rationalisation and control. Yet such a process is inhibited where workers, through their unions, seek to defend their traditional status and their established customs and practices. Hence the growing denunciation in recent years of trade unions as conservative institutions, as vehicles of Luddism,[4] and the insistence that 'we have somehow got to try to alter the social attitudes of the class whose aspirations the unions exist to express' (Shanks 1961:102).

In the context of wage negotiation, similarly, it is of crucial

4. Luddism (1811-13) was the semi-insurrectionary reponse of artisans to the indiscriminate introduction of capitalist production methods in a manner which spelled the degradation of their craft and their personal impoverishment. The form of this response — which received widespread community support — was dictated by the severe legal repression of collective organisation and action in this period. It is indicative of the ideological pressures discussed in the present study that the conventional conception of 'Luddism' as a term of abuse is almost universally shared by trade unionists.

importance that British capital, handicapped by decades of low investment, requires a substantial increase in profitability in order to meet the growing pressures of international competition. The increasing role of the state in economic management is also significant: with an economy characterised by persistent malaise and recurrent crisis, governments have embraced the twin pre-occupations of stimulating investment and holding down labour costs, particularly in export industries. Yet such a strategy — implying the limitation of a rate of increase in earnings which could be regarded as customary and hence 'fair' — is a recipe for conflict. Moreover, it has become recognised that the institutionalisation of the principle of 'fair comparisons' in collective bargaining entails that economic growth leads automatically to price inflation: for wage increases negotiated in sectors of high productivity growth are generalised throughout the economy (Turner 1970; Jackson *et al.* 1972; Jones 1973). This helps explain why prevailing attitudes have been increasingly critical of union power and union wage policy — an antipathy which *antedates* the recent wage and strike 'explosions'.[5]

This leads to a discussion of the fourth source of disturbance: the disruptive implications of changes in customary relationships induced by such external pressures. In the words of Flanders (1958:117), 'outraged custom . . . can be a very dynamic factor'. For traditionalism ensures stability and consensus only when there are no exogeneous sources of change — while dynamism is the normal condition of any capitalist economy.

As one example, any change in socio-technical arrangements or managerial practice is liable to disrupt the prevailing balance between wages and work standards. The 'effort bargain' creates an inevitable worker interest, however tacit, in the sphere of 'managerial prerogatives' — an interest which is no less real even when consciousness of it is suppressed by acceptance of generalised notions of the legitimacy of managerial control. Gouldner's study showed that a management's withdrawal — under external economic pressure — of its traditional 'indulgency pattern' provoked persistent conflict even though workers' expectations that management should act leniently were 'of tenuous legitimacy in an industrial situation' (1954b:24). Phelps Brown (1959:96-7) has made

5. Though these have undoubtedly accentuated hostility to established union goals and activities.

a similar point in relation to the introduction of work study as part of the process of 'scientific management' at the beginning of the present century.

> Time study in fact threatened a breach of the contract between employer and workman. In its essence that contract always has to provide that so much pay shall be given in return for so much effort, but since effort cannot be measured the amount to be put forth cannot be specified in the contract and has to be left to a tacit understanding or convention that defines 'a fair day's work'. The phrase seems empty if we ask, what do you mean by fair? but at any one time and place there was a consensus that defined an acceptable level of exertion, and stigmatized those who gave more and also those who gave less. Since the wage-earner, unlike the sub-contractor, put himself under the employer's direction, he was sensitive to the threat of being hard driven, and the standard of the fair day's work was a vital safeguard to him. The stop-watch threatened to undercut it.

It is noteworthy that Baldamus (1961:ch. 10) has located a major source of conflict and instability in industrial relations in externally generated pressures towards continually increasing productivity, and the resulting disruption of established relationships between pay and effort. A notable historical example of this process was the gradual intensification of work pressure in the British gas industry in the late nineteenth century, culminating in the explosion of militancy and unionisation in 1889-90 (Hobsbawm 1964:163-4). Today, the fight of production-line workers against 'speed-up' can often represent a constant and bitter conflict — as documented, for example, in Beynon's study of the Ford Halewood car assembly plant (1973).

Another significant consequence of technical change is the creation of new categories of occupations whose proper place within the established pay hierarchy constitutes a source of controversy and conflict; while changes in the work content of existing occupations may undermine the traditional rationale of their pay position. Rowe (1928:157-9) argues that developments in British engineering at the beginning of this century were a case in point: 'technical changes began to disturb the old conception of the proper wage diffentials between skilled and unskilled'. Other factors interacted with this process: the spread of egalitarian doctrines; labour market pressures; and the impact of wartime inflation. In consequence, Rowe suggests, 'the last lingering traces of the old idea of "just", meaning customary and therefore fair and proper, wages was completely swept away'. Economic changes may be similarly disruptive; thus in recent years, Phelps Brown has suggested (1973:334), 'expectations and the market environment have changed, and they have changed on to a collision course'.

Economic and technological changes may also have an important effect through their impact on the occupational security of employees. It is significant that in the study in which Goldthorpe and his associates argue the possibility of a calculative accommodation between 'affluent workers' and their employers, over 80 per cent of the car workers surveyed had never experienced unemployment and over 90 per cent considered their existing employment secure (1968:117-18). This contrasts with the consciousness of insecurity which has been cited as a cause of militancy in other car firms. 'There is the sense that, since phases of high demand and output are fleeting, opportunities to extract concessions from managements should be exploited while they are available' (Turner *et al.* 1967:331). Insecurity has often been mentioned as a source of conflict in other industries. In the docks, the Devlin Report argued (1965:8) that 'casual labour produces a casual attitude'; while casualism has also been suggested as an explanation of strike-proneness in the building industry (Knowles 1952:180-81). Insecurity is also a characteristic of another strike-prone industry, shipbuilding and repairing.

It is plausible to assume that insecurity of earnings and employment inhibits the development of stable and acquiescent attitudes towards work and wages. At the very least it may accentuate other grievances; the CIR stated, in its Report on Hoover Ltd (1970:22) that 'the emotions aroused by perceived inequalities in the factory are undoubtedly strengthened by a sense of insecurity'. There may well be more general implications. Leggett's survey of workers in Detroit (1968) has suggested that economic insecurity can provide an important source of militant class consciousness. British studies indicate that the emotional shock of redundancy — an increasingly widespread phenomenon in recent years — may weaken the hold of established frames of reference (Wedderburn 1965; Martin and Fryer 1973). Economic insecurity may also have an indirect influence on worker attitudes by increasing inter-industry and inter-occupational mobility. It seems likely that the higher the proportion of a labour force with other recent employment experience, the greater the tendency for external pay comparisons to be utilised. There is evidence, for example, that the unprecedented recent militancy among manual employees of local authorities and the health service may be associated with the presence of a significant number of workers with an active background in trade unionism in private industry. Similarly, increasing recruitment from outside St Helens was seen by some commentators as an important factor behind the Pilkington strike of 1970, since comparisons were encouraged with higher earnings on Merseyside.

Economic change may also be reflected in changes in company structure which accentuate the potentialities of conflict within established orbits of pay comparison. It was argued in a previous chapter that while the conventions established by collective bargaining tend to institutionalise the salience of particular comparisons they do not necessarily stabilise a pay structure. In shipbuilding, 'action by small groups distinguished from the others by the work they do, for example welders, cranedrivers and so on who, by disturbing relativities, trigger off action by other groups in defence of their relative position, has been a feature of the disputes pattern in the industry' (CIR 1971:91). In engineering, the use of overlapping orbits of coercive comparison — for example, by district and by product group — is commonly regarded as a source of instability and conflict: groups find it 'necessary to run faster and faster to stay in the same place' (Routh 1965:152). This tendency is likely to be exacerbated by the process of company mergers which unites previously distinct bargaining units. Thus the absorption of Briggs Bodies by Ford in 1953, and of Pressed Steel by BMC in 1967, appears to have created a sensitivity to differentials which were not previously salient, stimulating new types of comparability demands. The strike of Leyland workers in 1969, for parity with Midland employees of the newly formed British Leyland combine, is a clear example of the heightening of aspirations stimulated by company reorganisation. Trends towards the formation of multi-product conglomerates may cause even greater disturbance by encouraging comparisons between groups whose pay negotiations have traditionally been wholly separate.

Perhaps the most pervasive of disturbing factors, however, is the deliberate intervention of governments and employers — in response to the pressures described previously — to alter the processes and outcome of pay determination. It is plausible to discern a link between the experience of incomes policy, described in Chapter 4, and the recent turbulence in British industrial relations. An explicit aim of the policy was to reduce the force of comparisons and substitute other influences in collective bargaining — most notably the productivity criterion. Yet the scope for the negotiation of comprehensive productivity agreements was not uniform: the greatest opportunities appeared to exist in large-scale processing and manufacturing establishments. The consequence was that a limited number of (by traditional standards) spectacular wage increases were agreed, the new pay levels receiving far more publicity than the sacrifices in job control and working conditions which often accompanied them.[6]

Yet as Clegg has noted (1971:64),

> The actual negotiation of a productivity agreement involves great strains which may easily cause stoppages, and after a productivity agreement is signed, such strikes as do occur are likely to be bigger than before. Productivity agreements cut down on the opportunity for fragmented sectional bargaining and concentrate attention on general increases throughout the whole of the undertaking. The classic case is coalmining. The 1966 'powerloading' agreement transferred most face-workers from piecework to day work on rates of pay settled in industry-wide negotiations. This agreement has been followed by a rapid decline in the number of strikes, but the negotiations over general increases in 1969 and 1970 have been the occasion for the biggest stoppages the industry has seen since the war, both of them unofficial. [7]

More generally, the introduction of 'rationalised' pay structures in place of fragmented sectional bargaining may cause a heightening of formerly parochial horizons. In shipbuilding, for example, it was found that such developments 'may sharpen and draw attention to competitive elements by comparison with a larger number of sectional groups' (CIR 1971:115). Such unintended consequences of procedural reform have led to the application of the label 'post-Donovan' strikes to the major plant-wide stoppages which have been a growing feature of the last few years (Durcan and McCarthy 1972).

The *external* repercussions of productivity agreements and revised pay structures may be even greater than the internal effects. 'Productivity agreements can lead to large-scale strikes in other companies by means of the targets which they establish for pay increases': this would appear to have been a significant factor behind the series of disputes in car assembly and component factories in 1969-70 (Clegg 1971:64). At the same time, it has already been seen, the use of comparability as an argument for pay increases was strongly discouraged by the NBPI. The conflict which this

6. An important example is the measured day work agreement at Rootes Motors (now Chrysler) in 1969, which established a basic wage for production workers of £35.
7. This was of course followed by the massive official strike of 1972.

provoked was accentuated by the fact that the impact of incomes policy was uneven: it bore most heavily on those who were dependent on formal industry-wide pay settlements, while groups whose earnings could rise through sectional domestic bargaining experienced far less constraint. The restrictions on the principle of 'fair comparisons' which traditionally protected their relative position must form part of the explanation of the growth of official strike action among groups of public employees with a long record of industrial peace. And indeed it is likely that any sense of *relative* deprivation has been accentuated by the impact on *absolute* living standards of rapid price inflation and more onerous taxation policies. After more than a decade of steadily increasing real earnings, the period of Labour incomes policy was one of general stagnation — and for some an actual decline in real disposable income. In consequence, as Turner and Wilkinson comment (1971:310),

> The 1970 wage explosion may well represent, therefore, one of frustrated — but perhaps not altogether unjustified — expectations. Immediately after the 1967 devaluation, the near-freezing of real consumption could be reasonably argued as necessary to release resources for exports. However, the more recent effect of automatically rising state deductions from wages has been to produce enormous national budget surpluses and increased unemployment.
>
> The impact of price increases and state deductions, together, on real wages is now such that most workers clearly have to run as hard as they can, in wage terms, merely to stay where they are in real or relative ones. But if *net* income determines workers' living standards, it is *gross* earnings that determine costs and prices. Public policy on wage taxation may itself be the most potent of current inflationary forces. It also explains our coincidence of accelerated inflation with spreading recession.

A final consequence of incomes policy which deserves particular emphasis is its explicit rejection of custom and convention as a sufficient justification for any given level and relationship of pay: some more 'rational' principle of fair pay is to be required. Yet as previously suggested, once the principle of legitimation by tradition is cogently challenged, its normative content is liable to evaporate. A historical parallel may be drawn with the period of the First World War. Previously, according to Clay (1929:74), 'the abstract and unanswerable general problem, What is a fair wage? never came up; the problem was always the problem of a particular rate for a particular job'. But once this question *was* successfully provoked, the legitimacy of the existing structure of incomes became eroded, while no new principle of income distribution was agreed to provide normative support. The consequence was a period of considerable instability and conflict. In the current situation, this weakening of ideological commitment would appear closely related to the process that Fox and Flanders (1969) have analysed as 'normative disorder'.

All these points have a bearing on the analytical approach outlined in the previous chapter. Our argument was that both material and ideological factors — the influence of supply and demand, and of bargaining power, on the one hand; and of ideologies of occupational worth, on the other — exert an important impact on the structure and dynamics of incomes. Yet at times these factors have *contradictory* implications. 'When the bases of the acquisition and distribution of goods are relatively stable,' wrote Weber (1948:193-4), 'stratification by status is favoured. Every technological repercussion and economic transformation threatens stratification by status and pushes the class situation into the foreground.' Thus during the present century there has occurred a narrowing of differentials between skilled and non-skilled, and clerical and manual groups, which would seem at least in part attributable to diminished scarcity value. This historical accommodation between material and ideological pressures has important contemporary implications. For given the current predicament of both national economic policy and individual company profitability, the importance of labour costs will inevitably increase, generating pressures to reduce further those income advantages which have no obvious economic rationale. Though the top managerial and directional salaries — which, as the prerogatives of a small minority, form an insignificant proportion of total labour costs — will presumably be immune from consequential stringencies, differentials for craft or white-collar groups which appear to owe more to historical than to contemporary reasons of scarce or irreplaceable skills may well be vulnerable. Yet further narrowing would not only generate conflict in its own right; it would diminish the ideological foundations of the more extreme dimensions of income inequality — and, by extension, the even greater inequality of wealth in contemporary Britain.

Pressures on traditional relativities may be upwards as well as downwards. Sex differentials — which probably owe far more to cultural and ideological factors than to market forces [8] — have recently been subject to considerable social and political challenge;

8. See for example Pen 1971.

and any narrowing would probably accord with the demand for female labour in a number of sectors of modern employment. Yet changes in sex differentials would affect established relativities both within and between industries. Fear that altered relativities might generate a chain reaction, as we saw in Chapter 4, has inhibited any attempt to deal seriously with the problem of low pay in the context of incomes policies.

Instability may be greatest where material and ideological pressures interact. We saw in the previous chapter that because the dominant value system is most influential where it is most general and most abstract, its impact on *specific* attitudes and aspirations is limited; and in particular, the constraint it imposes on the parochial activities of subordinate social groups is often problematic. Moreover, social valuations of occupational worth and prestige are insufficiently precise to have much bearing on the finer gradations of the labour force, and hence impose only broad constraints on the bargaining activities of specific occupational groups. Thus through their own collective strength, car assembly workers have in recent decades raised their earnings almost to the top of the manual hierarchy, in the face of intense ideological hostility from those who consider their own relative status threatened. This does not mean that normative factors are of no effect in such cases: exclusion from socially acceptable legitimations typically constrains the pay aspirations of subordinate occupational groups, or inhibits the confidence with which 'deviant' aspirations are pursued, even when strategic power is considerable. Thus even sections of workers who are regularly accused of 'holding the country to ransom' are remarkably modest in their objectives. Car workers have normally demanded parity with earnings in other companies or plants in the same industry; or, in the context of fragmented piecework bargaining, the earnings of the highest-paid sections have provided others with their targets. They have *not* demanded parity with the professional or managerial strata which alone have access to 'legitimate' arguments for the highest income levels.

It is also important to note that because of ambiguities or inconsistencies in the dominant criteria of prestige, or the existence of sub-cultural norms and standards, some manual groups may derive confidence from 'deviant' evaluations of occupational worth. This was clearly exemplified by the miners' pay dispute of 1973-4. After more than a decade of attenuated bargaining power, coalminers' strategic strength was radically enhanced. Their demand for substantially increased wages was supported by reference to the dangerous and unpleasant nature of their work: an argument which was widely regarded as cogent. In the face of changed economic exigencies, the government endorsed these criteria as a means of conceding the claims of a strong and determined group while confining and minimising the alteration. Yet is is doubtful whether the 'exceptional' character of such a concession can be effectively sustained. Miners are anxious to limit the differentials between underground and surface workers (who are often former face-workers compelled by age or injury to change their jobs); yet increases for surface workers would form 'legitimate' targets for railwaymen, power workers, and many others. More generally, workers in other occupations which are both dirty and dangerous (even if in a less extreme form than in coalmining) might be encouraged to press for alterations in their own relative pay: indeed, almost *all* sections of the manual labour force could find at least a measure of personal relevance in the miners' case. Potentially at least, the principle that hazardous and uncongenial working conditions should justify pay advantages challenges the domination of the incomes hierarchy by those whose work is both safe and comparatively pleasant.

All such factors contribute to a chronic 'disorder' in pay relationships and pay movements. Even if no *comprehensive* challenge to the existing hierarchy of income inequality is intended, nevertheless acceptance of the fairness and legitimacy of this hierarchy is weakened, and a rationale is provided for actions the cumulative results of which threaten serious economic disruption. In such a situation — when governments themselves, through their strategies to control incomes, raise the issue of the fairness of customary pay relationship — the *possibility* of a more general and explicit questioning of the structure of rewards and deprivations in industry necessarily arises.

Social Conflicts and System Contradictions

All these factors point to the probability of intensified social conflict over income distribution and other work-related issues. Yet to focus merely on *normative* discontinuities and conflicts, as they interact with the struggles and accommodations of groups wielding varying degrees of power, is to understate the significance of sources of instability. To explore these sources further, and also to consider how far such conflicts contain a potential for major change in social relations, it is necessary to consider — if only briefly — the distinction between social conflicts and system contradictions. The levels of analysis involved have been defined by Lockwood (1964:245) as follows: 'Whereas the problem of social integration focuses attention upon the orderly or conflictful relationships between the *actors*, the problem of system integration focuses on the orderly or conflictful relationships between the *parts*, of a social system.'

The concept of social system calls for some comment at this point. In a previous chapter we criticised the manner in which it is conventionally employed in sociology and industrial relations; yet this does not imply that we reject the very notion of system. On the contrary: without venturing into a detailed discussion of complex issues of sociological theory, we would argue that meaningful social analysis and explanation must be predicated on some idea of system. The concept indicates that social life involves more than the random activities of a multiplicity of individuals; that social action is in large measure patterned and organised by identifiable social *institutions* which tend to persist even though individuals come and go; and that these institutions are in turn interrelated such that social relations exhibit an underlying *structural* regularity. It is these institutional or structural regularities and interrelationships which the notion of social system denotes, and which form the necessary subject-matter of any genuinely sociological analysis. What is illegitimate, however, is the functionalist premise that social systems tend naturally to a double equilibrium, such that the norms and interests of individuals are compatible and harmonious, while the operation of the various social institutions is smoothly and unproblematically integrated.

We have already shown that while the material and ideological domination of the socially powerful tends towards the maintenance of social order, there is nevertheless considerable evidence that individuals and groups do pursue conflicting goals and embrace opposing values. But it is also important to recognise that the interaction of the various social institutions may generate contradictory social forces which represent a radical source of social instability. The argument that capitalism, as a total political economy, is a system beset by fundamental internal contradictions (a proposition 'sociologised' in Lockwood's essay) is central to Marxian analysis: 'capitalist production begets, with the inexorability of a law of Nature, its own negation' (1959:763).[9] 'The *real barrier* of capitalist production is *capital itself.* It is that capital and its self-expansion appear as the starting and closing point, the motive and the purpose of production; that production is only production for *capital* and not vice versa, the means of production are not mere means for a constant expansion of the living process of the *society* or producers.' Hence 'the means — unconditional development of the productive forces of society — comes continually into conflict with the limited purpose, the self-expansion of the existing capital' (1962:245).

This analysis relates closely to Marx's familiar discussion of the conflict between the 'forces of production' and 'social relations of production'. The former concept denotes, roughly, the physical 'hardware' of production and communication (plant, machinery, computers, railways etc.) and also the system of knowledge on which their development and application depend; the latter, the property institutions, work organisation, class structure, and the various other social institutions whereby a given productive system is located within a specific political economy. Within capitalism, Marx argued, the forces of production reach such a high level of development that for the first time in history the potential exists for the conquest of poverty and material deprivation, for the transition from the 'realm of necessity' to the 'realm of freedom' and the construction of a genuinely humane and civilised society. But this potential is thwarted by the social relations of production. Economic activity is harnessed to the overriding goal of profitability; consideration of the human needs of members of society in their role as producers and as consumers is at best marginal. The priorities of the minority who own and control the means of production conflict systematically with the interests of the majority who are exploited as producers and manipulated as consumers. The predominance within economic life of the accumulation of capital (or, in contemporary terminology, 'productivity' and 'economic growth') as an end pursued essentially *for its own sake* is quite literally irrational, involving as it does the abdication of conscious human decision to 'impersonal' economic forces.

9. For a fertile — if at times tortuous — elaboration of the Marxian conception of contradiction see Althusser 1969.

Almost a century ago, Engels (1959:392) identified the central contradiction of capitalist production in the contrast 'between socialized organization in the individual factory and social anarchy in production as a whole'. Despite the technical and managerial sophistication within individual productive units, the productive system as a whole lacked co-ordination; and the consequence was a recurrence of severe economic depression and the accompanying degradation of mass unemployment and impoverishment. Such 'crises of overproduction' occurred, not indeed because members of society were satiated with the products of industry (the opposite was clearly the case), but because the pressure on employers to minimise labour costs entailed that aggregate wages were too low to absorb the value of products available on the market. The economic system was thus inherently unstable.

Recent years have seen developments which have in part contained this central contradiction of capitalist production: but these in turn have generated new contradictions. In the present century, the most potent instrument of relatively full employment has been war or preparation for war, which has served to absorb 'surplus' productive capacity. Yet recent experience has shown that the arms industry can acquire its own dynamic (with the military-industrial complex exerting powerful political influence); the escalating waste of economic resources has serious inflationary implications (quite apart from posing a threat to human survival). The growing internationalisation of capitalism is associated with problems not only of the traditional exercise of *Realpolitik* but also of trade and monetary relations. Yet attempts to rationalise international economic relations through commercial and monetary co-operation (or even union) meet the resistance of old-established nationalist ideologies, and at the same time generate as by-products new social and economic contradictions. (Thus British membership of the European Common Market has entailed, for example, sharp increases in some living costs, accentuation of problems of regional and sectoral stagnation and decline, and increased competitive constraints in some industries with consequential pressure on pay and effort.) The rapid trend towards manipulation of consumer demand through advertising and similar techniques (a virtual substitute for price competition in many oligopolistic industries) has served as an additional stabiliser of aggregate demand; and has provided the poor with new orbits of comparison. It is not implausible to regard this as a contributory factor to the increased labour militancy in most industrialised nations in recent years.

More generally, the search for remedies to the 'social anarchy in production as a whole' has involved the eclipse of *laissez faire* ideology and growing state intervention to curb the 'dysfunctional' consequences of a system of economic relations based on competitive private capital. Yet as Blackburn has insisted (1965:133), such intervention is predicated on the continuing centrality of profit as the fundamental social dynamic, and cannot therefore resolve the contradiction which is basic to the political economy. 'The ultimate goals of capitalism are not changed, but increasingly rational methods are employed to attain these goals — the accumulation of capital and the making of profits. Of course, the ultimate irrationality of these goals continually and endemically contaminates the "rational" means being used to pursue them.'[10] Without a transformation of the structure of class domination, of property ownership and of employment relationships, state intervention and managerial and governmental planning cannot engender a genuinely rational social organisation whereby the system of production and distribution is consciously subordinated to the collective decisions of societal members.[11] Hence current

10. We have previously indicated some of the problems associated with the concept of rationality: what is rational for one social group may not be rational for another group with conflicting interests, and what one group condemns as irrational may be rational to others. Yet the ***general*** irrationality inherent in capitalist production is represented by the fact that 'accumulation for accumulation's sake, production for production's sake' is an 'external coercive law' to which capitalists and workers alike are subject; it does not represent a consciously chosen social goal. In the present context, it is clearly impossible even to attempt a discussion of the irrationality of capitalism and its internal contradictions which does justice to the importance and complexity of the question. Such an analysis was of course central to Marx's whole theory of political economy. For recent discussions see Blackburn 1965; Baran and Sweezy 1968; Kidron 1970.
11. Engels (1959: 384) anticipated this point almost a century ago. 'The transformation, either into joint-stock companies, or into state ownership, does not do away with the capitalistic nature of the productive forces . . . . The modern state . . . is only the organization that bourgeois society takes on in order to support the general external conditions of the capitalist mode of production against the encroachments as well of the workers as of individual capitalists. The modern state, no matter what its form, is essentially a capitalist machine, the state of the capitalists, the ideal personification of the total national capital. The more it proceeds to the taking over of the productive forces, the more does it actually become the national capitalist, the more citizens does it exploit. The capitalist relation is not done away with. It is rather brought to a head.'

strategies and techniques of planning and public policy cannot adequately resolve such problems as the coexistence of stagnant growth and inflation, the social costs and conflicts associated with declining industries and depressed regions, the economic as well as social and aesthetic implications of the wanton spoliation of environmental resources, the unpredictable human responses to the dehumanising and manipulative pressures of the organisation of production and consumption within contemporary capitalism, the windfall gains of speculators and asset strippers so embarrassing to most ideologists of 'free enterprise'.[12]

In the context of industrial relations, such developments create new problems and conflicts. State intervention to control labour costs, and to reduce the ability of autonomous union organisation to obstruct more 'rational' (and more oppressive) managerial control, makes increasingly transparent the interdependence of economic and political power in society. Traditional trade union goals and actions thus acquire a new political dimension; potentially at least, the resulting conflicts become radicalised. Government incomes policies, as we argued above, may provoke a more critical attitude to inequality even as they seek to contain conflict and instability. The 'right to work', in itself by no means a radical slogan, becomes a subversive demand in the face of redundancies and plant closures imposed by national and multi-national conglomerates whose pursuit of profit displays a new degree of single-mindedness. Attempts to increase productivity by intensifying the pressures on the employee, extending the aspects of his work activity which are subject to rigid managerial standards of utilitarianism,[13] can provoke new and often unpredictable outbreaks of resistance and rebellion. The contradictions inherent in modern industrial relations, it is abundantly evident, are irresoluble within the framework of capitalism.

12. So manifest are these contradictions that a few otherwise orthodox economists (e.g. Mishan 1969) have felt compelled to challenge the overriding priority assigned to growth. Such writers treat accumulation as a particular and remediable aspect of economic policy, rather than as a fundamental dynamic of a total political economy.
13. See the interesting discussion by Gouldner 1969.

Conclusions

In response to the question, do notions of fairness in industrial relations represent a source of stability or instability, the paradoxical conclusion must be: *both.* A major consequence of the prevailing values in industrial relations would appear to be to contain disputes within relatively narrow boundaries; but within these confines even intense conflict is not inhibited and may indeed receive a rationale from such ideological notions. The nature and influence of norms of fairness provide part of the explanation why trade unionists exert the power to obstruct, but lack the will to transcend, the political economy which constrains them. It is this centrally *contradictory* character of prevailing ideological standards and assumptions which gives current industrial relations their evident unpredictability and volatility. This helps explain a variety of significant developments in recent years: the vogue for notions of 'job enrichment' and 'participation' in the context of strategies to supplement and hence strengthen workers' predominantly instrumental nexus to their employment; and, at the national level, the notion of a 'new social contract' in which trade unions would accept their own virtual emasculation as the necessary price for a modest humanisation of capitalist social relations. Such proposals represent a redefinition of those aspects of prevailing ideologies the consequences of which have proved unacceptable in terms of managerial goals; the aim is a 'reconstruction of normative order' which avoids serious challenge to a basically exploitative and irrational political economy.

We have argued that the social conflicts which ideologies of fairness mediate and qualify are too intense and too pervasive to be contained by such stratagems. But in any case, the key implication of our discussion of the structural contradictions inherent in the existing political economy is that the effects of *any* normative framework will be uneven and contradictory. Norms of fairness, as this study indicates, even though couched in terms wholly conducive to the stability of the social order and the interests of those in positions of privilege and power, nevertheless can provoke and legitimise actions with quite contrary effects; and this is likely to occur even if the prevailing ideology is internally consistent. The argument, then, is that such consequences reflect not merely 'normative disorder' but far more fundamental societal characteristics. Strategies which rest essentially on the paternalistic manipulative or authoritarian intervention of those in controlling positions in management or government fail to transcend these contradictions. In the last analysis, the practical and the normative problems in industrial relations can be resolved only by the creation of social relations of production whereby economic activity is consciously and collectively controlled by the members of society generally. To achieve such a society, in the face of existing structures of material and ideological domination, is inconceivable except through the activity and struggle of the mass of producers. Where social conflicts and system contradictions interpenetrate, and the oppressive character of the social structure becomes increasingly transparent, the possibility of such a challenge to capitalist social relations is increased. This point evidently raises immense issues which can ultimately be resolved, not by theoretical discussion but by practical action. For the present, though, we may safely conclude that the notion of a 'reconstruction of normative order' in industrial relations which leaves intact the basic structure of the political economy is a singularly futile goal.

Bibliography

B. Abel-Smith and P. Townsend, 1965. *The Poor and the Poorest,* London: Bell.

J.S. Adams, 1963. 'Wage Inequities, Productivity and Work Quality', *Industrial Relations,* 3, pp. 9-16.

J. S. Adams, 1965. 'Inequality in Social Exchange' in L. Berkowitz (ed.), *Advances in Experimental Social Psychology,* Vol. II, New York: Academic Press, pp. 267-99.

M. Albrow, 1968. 'The Study of Organizations: Objectivity or Bias?' in J. Gould (ed.), *Penguin Survey of the Social Sciences 1968,* Harmondsworth: Penguin, pp. 146-67.

K.J.W. Alexander, 1970. 'Equality and Inequality', *Scottish Journal of Political Economy,* 17, pp. 249-65.

V.L. Allen, 1966. *Militant Trade Unionism,* London: Merlin.

L. Althusser, 1969. *For Marx,* Harmondsworth: Penguin.

S.D. Anderman, 1972. *Voluntary Dismissals Procedure and the Industrial Relations Act,* London: Political and Economic Planning.

P. Anderson, 1965. 'Origins of the Present Crisis' in Anderson and Blackburn 1965, pp. 11-52.

P. Anderson and R. Blackburn (eds.), 1965. *Towards Socialism,* London: Fontana.

R. Aron 1967. *Eighteen Lectures on Industrial Society,* London: Weidenfeld and Nicolson.

A.B. Atkinson, 1972. *Unequal Shares: Wealth in Britain,* London: Allen Lane.

A.B. Atkinson (ed.), 1973. *Wealth, Income and Inequality,* Harmondsworth: Penguin.

J. Backman, 1959. *Wage Determination: an Analysis of Wage Criteria,* Princeton: Van Nostrand.

W. Baldamus, 1957. 'The Relationship Between Wage and Effort', *Journal of Industrial Economics,* 6, pp. 192-201.

W. Baldamus, 1961. *Efficiency and Effort,* London: Tavistock.

P.A. Baran and P.M. Sweezy, 1968. *Monopoly Capital,* Harmondsworth: Penguin.

J. Barbash, 1964. 'The Elements of Industrial Relations', *British Journal of Industrial Relations,* 2, pp. 67-78.

F. Barth, 1966. *Models of Social Organization,* London: Royal Anthropological Institute.

E. Batten, 1923. *A Fair Wage,* London: Pitman.

F.J. Bayliss, 1962. *British Wages Councils,* Oxford: Blackwell.

G.S. Becker, 1964. *Human Capital,* New York: National Bureau of Economic Research/Columbia University Press.

H.S. Becker, 1963. *Outsiders,* Glencoe: Free Press.

H. Behrend, 1957. 'The Effort Bargain', *Industrial and Labor Relations Review,* 10, pp. 503-15.

H. Behrend, 1961. 'A Fair Day's Work', *Scottish Journal of Political Economy,* 8, pp. 102-18.

H. Behrend, 1964. 'Price and Income Images and Inflation', *Scottish Journal of Political Economy,* 11, pp. 85-103.

H. Behrend, 1966. 'Price Images, Inflation and National Incomes Policy', *Scottish Journal of Political Economy,* 13, pp. 273-96.

H. Behrend, 1971. 'What is Lower Pay? 1971 Follow Up Survey', *Social Science Research Council Newsletter,* 12, pp. 5-7.

H. Behrend, 1973. 'Frames of Reference for Judging Incomes', Edinburgh University Department of Business Studies (mimeographed). 

H. Behrend, A. Knowles and J. Davies, 1970a. *Views on Pay Increases, Fringe Benefits and Low Pay,* Dublin: Economic and Social Research Institute.

H. Behrend, A. Knowles and J. Davies, 1970b. *Views on Income Differentials and the Economic Situation,* Dublin: Economic and Social Research Institute.

H. Behrend, H. Lynch, H. Thomas and J. Davies, 1967. *Incomes Policy and the Individual,* Edinburgh: Oliver and Boyd.

D. Bell, 1962. 'Work and its Discontents' in *The End of Ideology* (2nd edn), New York: Free Press, pp. 227-72.

R. Bendix, 1963. *Work and Authority in Industry* (2nd edn), New York: Harper and Row.

R. Bendix, 1966. *Max Weber: an Intellectual Portrait,* London:

Methuen.
J. Bentham, 1838. *Works* (ed. J. Bowring), Vol. I, Edinburgh: Tait.
P.L. Berger and T. Luckmann, 1967. *The Social Construction of Reality,* Harmondsworth: Penguin.
W.H. Beveridge, 1944. *Full Employment in a Free Society,* London: Allen and Unwin.
H. Beynon, 1973. *Working for Ford,* Harmondsworth: Penguin.
O.A. Bird, 1967. *The Idea of Justice,* New York: Praeger.
R. Blackburn, 1965. 'The New Capitalism' in Anderson and Blackburn 1965, pp. 114-45.
R. Blackburn, 1967. 'The Unequal Society' in Blackburn and Cockburn 1967, pp. 15-55.
R. Blackburn (ed.), 1972. *Ideology in Social Science,* London: Fontana.
R. Blackburn and A. Cockburn (eds.), 1967. *The Incompatibles: Trade Union Militancy and the Consensus,* Harmondsworth: Penguin.
P.M. Blau, 1964. *Exchange and Power in Social Life,* New York: Wiley.
R. Blauner, 1960. 'Work Satisfaction and Industrial Trends in Modern Society' in W. Galenson and S.M. Lipset (eds.), *Labor and Trade Unionism,* New York: Wiley, pp. 339-60.
N. Bosanquet, 1969. *Pay, Prices and Labour in Power,* London: Fabian Society.
E. Bott, 1957. *Family and Social Network,* London: Tavistock.
R.K. Brown, P. Brannen, J.M. Cousins and M.L. Samphier, 1972. 'The Contours of Solidarity; Social Stratification and Industrial Relations in Shipbuilding', *British Journal of Industrial Relations,* 10, pp. 12-41.
W.A. Brown, 1971. 'Piecework Wage Determination in Coventry', *Scottish Journal of Political Economy,* 18, pp. 1-30.
W.A. Brown, 1972. 'A Consideration of "Custom and Practice" ', *British Journal of Industrial Relations,* 10, pp. 42-61.
W.A. Brown, 1973. *Piecework Bargaining,* London: Heinemann.
W.B.D. Brown, 1963. *Piecework Abandoned,* London: Heinemann.
W.B.D. Brown, 1973. *The Earnings Conflict,* Harmondsworth: Penguin.
M. Bulmer (ed.), 1973. *The Occupational Community of the Traditional Worker,* Durham: Department of Sociology and Social Administration (mimeographed).

E. Burns, 1926. *Wages and the State,* London: King.
E.H. Carr, 1964. *What Is History?* Harmondsworth: Penguin.
M. Carter, 1966. *Into Work,* Harmondsworth: Penguin.
A. M. Carter and R. R. Marshall, 1967. *Labor Economics,* Homewood: Irwin.
F.G. Castles, D.J. Murray and D.C. Potter (eds.), 1971. *Decisions, Organizations and Society,* Harmondsworth: Penguin.
N.W. Chamberlain, F.C. Pierson and T. Wolfson (eds.), 1958. *A Decade of Industrial Relations Research,* New York: Harper.
E. Chamberlin, 1933. *The Theory of Monopolistic Competition,* Cambridge, Mass.: Harvard University Press.
J. Child (ed.), 1973. *Man and Organization,* London: Allen and Unwin.
A.V. Cicourel, 1964. *Method and Measurement in Sociology,* New York: Free Press.
J.B. Clark, 1886. *The Philosophy of Wealth,* Boston: Ginn.
H. Clay, 1929. *The Problem of Industrial Relations,* London: Macmillan.
H.A. Clegg, 1961. 'The Scope of Fair Wage Comparisons', *Journal of Industrial Economics,* 9, pp. 199-214.
H.A. Clegg, 1963. *A New Approach to Industrial Democracy,* Oxford: Blackwell.
H.A. Clegg, 1965. 'Mobility of Labour', *National Provincial Bank Review,* 70, pp. 9-13.
H.A. Clegg, 1971. *How to Run an Incomes Policy and Why We Made Such a Mess of the Last One,* London: Heinemann.
H.A. Clegg, 1972. *The System of Industrial Relations in Great Britain* (2nd edn), Oxford: Blackwell.
T. Cliff, 1970. *The Employers' Offensive,* London: Pluto Press.
K. Coates, 1967. 'Wage Slaves' in Blackburn and Cockburn 1967, pp. 57-92.
K. Coates and R. Silburn, 1973. *Poverty: the Forgotten Englishmen,* Harmondsworth: Penguin.
A. Coddington, 1968. *Theories of the Bargaining Process,* London: Allen and Unwin.
P.S. Cohen, 1968. *Modern Social Theory,* London: Heinemann.
S. Cohen (ed.), 1971. *Images of Deviance,* Harmondsworth: Penguin.
G.D.H. Cole, 1913. *The World of Labour,* London: Bell.
G.D.H. Cole, 1918. *The Payment of Wages,* London: Fabian

Research Department/Allen and Unwin.
G.D.H. Cole, 1957. *The Case for Industrial Partnership,* London: Macmillan.
O. Collins, M. Dalton and D. Roy, 1946. 'Restriction of Output and Social Cleavage in Industry', *Applied Anthropology,* 5, pp. 1-14.
Commission on Industrial Relations, 1970. Report 11, *Hoover Ltd,* London: HMSO, Cmnd. 4537.
Commission on Industrial Relations, 1971. Report 22, *Shipbuilding and Shiprepairing,* London: HMSO, Cmnd. 4756.
Commission on Industrial Relations, 1972. Report 29, *Alcan Smelter Site,* London: HMSO.
J.R. Commons, 1932. *The Legal Foundation of Capitalism,* New York: Macmillan.
Conservative Party, 1968. *Fair Deal at Work,* London: Conservative Political Centre.
J. Corina, 1966. *The Development of Incomes Policy,* London: Institute of Personnel Management.
J. Corina, 1968. 'Can an Incomes Policy be Administered?' in Roberts 1968, pp. 257-91.
J. Corina, 1972. *Labour Market Economics,* London: Heinemann.
L. Coser, 1956. *The Functions of Social Conflict,* London: Routledge and Kegan Paul.
S. Cotgrove, 1967. *The Science of Society.* London: Allen and Unwin.
M.A. Coulson and D.S. Riddell, 1970. *Approaching Sociology,* London: Routledge and Kegan Paul.
J.R. Crossley, 1966. 'Collective Bargaining, Wage Structure and the Labour Market in United Kingdom' in Hugh-Jones 1966, pp. 156-235.
M. Crozier, 1964. *The Bureaucratic Phenomenon,* Chicago: University of Chicago Press.
D.C. Cummings, 1905. *A Historical Survey of the Boilermakers' and Iron and Steel Shipbuilders' Society,* Newcastle: Robinson.
S. Cunnison, 1966. *Wages and Work Allocation,* London: Tavistock.
M. Dalton, 1948. 'The Industrial "Rate-Buster" ': A Characterization', *Applied Anthropology,* 7, pp. 5-18.
M. Dalton, 1950. 'Unofficial Union-Management Relations', *American Sociological Review,* 15, pp. 611-19.
W.W. Daniel, 1970. *Beyond the Wage-Work Bargain,* London: Political and Economic Planning.

W.W. Daniel and N. McIntosh, 1972. *The Right to Manage?*, London: Political and Economic Planning.

K. Davis, 1948. *Human Society,* New York: Macmillan.

K. Davis and W.E. Moore, 1945. 'Some Principles of Stratification', *American Sociological Review,* 10, pp. 242-9.

A. Dawe, 1970. 'The Two Sociologies', *British Journal of Sociology,* 21, pp. 201-18.

N. Dennis, F. Henriques and C. Slaughter, 1957. *Coal in Our Life,* London: Eyre and Spottiswoode.

M. Derber, 1955, *Labor-Management Relations at Plant Level under Industry-Wide Bargaining,* Illinois University: Institute of Labor and Industrial Relations.

M. Derber, 1967. *Research in Labor Problems in the United States,* New York: Random House.

Devlin, Lord, 1965. Chairman, Committee of Inquiry into the Port Transport Industry. *Final Report*, London: HMSO, Cmnd. 2734.

Donovan, Lord, 1967. Chairman, Royal Commission on Trade Unions and Employers' Associations. Research Paper 4 Part 2, *Restrictive Labour Practices,* London: HMSO.

Donovan, Lord, 1968. *Report*, London: HMSO, Cmnd. 3623.

P.H. Douglas, 1934. *The Theory of Wages,* New York: Macmillan.

J.T. Dunlop, 1950. *Wage Determination Under Trade Unions,* Oxford: Blackwell (first published 1944).

J.T. Dunlop, 1957. 'The Task of Contemporary Wage Theory' in Dunlop (ed.) 1957, pp. 3-27.

J.T. Dunlop (ed.), 1957. *The Theory of Wage Determination* London: Macmillan.

J.T. Dunlop, 1958. *Industrial Relations Systems,* New York: Holt.

J.W. Durcan and W.E.J. McCarthy, 1972. 'What is Happening to Strikes?' *New Society,* 22, pp. 267-9.

E. Durkheim, 1933. *The Division of Labour in Society,* London: Macmillan (original publication 1893).

J. Edmonds and G. Radice, 1968. *Low Pay,* London: Fabian Society.

J.E.T. Eldridge, 1971. *Sociology and Industrial Life,* London: Michael Joseph.

J.E.T. Eldridge, 1973. 'Industrial Conflict: Some Problems of Theory and Method' in Child, 1973, pp. 158-84.

F. Engels, 1959. *Anti-Dühring,* Moscow: Foreign Languages Publishing House (original publication 1878).

A. Etzioni 1961. *A Comparative Analysis of Complex Organizations,* New York: Free Press.

A. Etzioni, 1964. *Modern Organizations,* Englewood Cliffs: Prentice-Hall.

A. Fels, 1972. *The British Prices and Incomes Board,* Cambridge: Cambridge University Press.

L. Festinger, 1957. *A Theory of Cognitive Dissonance,* New York: Row, Peterson.

A.G.B. Fisher, 1926. *Some Problems of Wages and their Regulation in Great Britain since 1918,* London: King.

M. R. Fisher, 1971. *The Economic Analysis of Labour,* London: Weidenfeld and Nicolson.

M.R. Fisher, 1973. 'The Human Capital Approach to Occupational Differentials', *International Journal of Social Economics,* 1, pp. 40-62.

A. Flanders, 1950. *A Policy for Wages,* London: Fabian Society.

A. Flanders, 1958. 'Can Britain Have a Wage Policy?' *Scottish Journal of Political Economy,* 5, pp. 114-25.

A. Flanders, 1964. *The Fawley Productivity Agreements,* London: Faber.

A. Flanders, 1970. *Management and Unions,* London: Faber.

M.P. Fogarty, 1961. *The Just Wage,* London: Chapman.

P. Foot, 1968. *The Politics of Harold Wilson,* Harmondsworth: Penguin.

P. Ford, 1964. *The Economics of Collective Bargaining,* Oxford: Blackwell (first published 1958).

A. Fox, 1966a. *Industrial Sociology and Industrial Relations,* London: HMSO.

A. Fox, 1966b. *The Time-Span of Discretion Theory: An Appraisal,* London: Institute of Personnel Management.

A. Fox, 1971. *A Sociology of Work in Industry,* London: Collier-Macmillan.

A. Fox, 1973a. 'Industrial Relations: a Social Critique of Pluralist Ideology' in Child 1973, pp. 185-233.

A. Fox, 1973b. 'Is Equality a Necessity?' *Socialist Commentary,* June 1973, pp. i-viii.

A. Fox, 1974. *Man Mismanagement,* London: Hutchinson.

A. Fox and A. Flanders, 1969. 'The Reform of Collective Bargaining: From Donovan to Durkheim', *British Journal of Industrial Relations,* 7, pp. 151-80.

R.W. Friedrichs, 1970. *A Sociology of Sociology,* New York: Free Press.

R.H. Fryer, 1973. 'Redundancy, Values and Public Policy', *Industrial Relations Journal,* 4, pp. 2-19.

J.K. Galbraith, 1973. 'Power and the Useful Economist', *American Economic Review,* 63, pp. 1-11.

N. Geras, 1972. 'Marx and the Critique of Political Economy' in R. Blackburn 1972, pp. 284-305.

H. Gerth and C.W. Mills, 1954. *Character and Social Structure,* London: Routledge and Kegan Paul.

A. Giddens, 1968. ' "Power" in the Recent Writings of Talcott Parsons', *Sociology,* 2, pp. 257-72.

A. Giddens, 1971. *Capitalism and Modern Social Theory,* Cambridge: Cambridge University Press.

M. Ginsberg, 1965. *On Justice in Society,* Harmondsworth: Penguin.

D.V. Glass, 1961. 'Education and Social Change in Modern England', in A.H. Halsey, J. Floud and C.A. Anderson (eds.), *Education, Economy and Society,* New York: Free Press, pp. 391-413.

A. Glyn and R. Sutcliffe, 1972. *British Capitalism, Workers and the Profits Squeeze,* Harmondsworth: Penguin.

L. Goldmann, 1969. *The Human Sciences and Philosophy,* London: Cape.

J.H. Goldthorpe, 1969. 'Social Inequality and Social Integration in Modern Britain', *Advancement of Science,* 26, pp. 190-202.

J.H. Goldthorpe, 1972. 'Comment on "The Industrial Relations Act in Theory and Practice" ' in *Proceedings of a Seminar: Problems and Prospects of Socio-Legal Research*, Oxford: Nuffield College (mimeographed).

J.H. Goldthorpe, D. Lockwood, F. Bechhofer and J. Platt, 1968. *The Affluent Worker: Industrial Attitudes and Behaviour,* Cambridge: Cambridge University Press.

J.H. Goldthorpe, D. Lockwood, F. Bechhofer and J. Platt, 1969. *The Affluent Worker in the Class Structure,* Cambridge: Cambridge University Press.

P.S. Goodman, 1967. 'An Empirical Examination of Elliott Jaques's Concept of Time Span', *Human Relations,* 20, pp. 155-70.

M.E. Gordon, 1969. 'An Evaluation of Jaques's Studies of Pay in the

Light of Current Compensation Research', *Personnel Psychology*, 22, pp. 369-89.

A.W. Gouldner, 1954a. *Patterns of Industrial Bureaucracy,* New York: Free Press.

A.W. Gouldner, 1954b. *Wildcat Strike,* Yellow Springs: Antioch Press.

A.W. Gouldner, 1957. 'Cosmopolitans and Locals: Toward an Analysis of Latent Social Roles', *Administrative Science Quarterly,* 2, pp. 281-306.

A.W. Gouldner, 1969. 'The Unemployed Self' in R. Fraser (ed.), *Work 2,* Harmondsworth: Penguin, pp. 346-65.

A.W. Gouldner, 1970. *The Coming Crisis of Western Sociology,* London: Heinemann.

Government Social Survey, 1968. *Workplace Industrial Relations,* London: HMSO.

J.J. Gracie, 1949. *A Fair Day's Pay,* London: Management Publications.

A. Gramsci, 1971. *Selections from the Prison Notebooks,* London: Lawrence and Wishart.

C. Grunfeld, 1971. *The Law of Redundancy,* London: Sweet and Maxwell.

C.W. Guillebaud, 1967. *Wage Determination and Wages Policy,* London: Nisbet (first published 1951).

C.W. Guillebaud, 1970. *The Role of the Arbitrator in Industrial Wage Disputes,* London: Nisbet.

P. Halmos (ed.), 1964. *The Development of Industrial Societies,* Sociological Review Monograph 8, Keele: University of Keele.

A.H. Halsey, J. Floud and C.A. Anderson (eds.), 1961. *Education, Economy and Society,* New York: Free Press.

R.S. Hammett, J. Seidman and J. London, 1957. 'The Slowdown as a Union Tactic', *Journal of Political Economy,* 65, pp. 126-34.

N. Harris, 1971. *Beliefs in Society,* Harmondsworth: Penguin.

L. Hazard, 1957. 'Wage Theory: a Management View' in Taylor and Pierson 1957, pp. 32-50.

J.J. Healy, 1966. *The Just Wage,* The Hague: Nijhoff.

R. Herding, 1972. *Job Control and Union Structure,* Rotterdam: Rotterdam University Press.

J.R. Hicks, 1955. 'The Economic Foundations of Wage Policy', *Economic Journal,* 65, pp. 389-404.

J.R. Hicks, 1963. *The Theory of Wages,* London: Macmillan (first published 1932).

D.J. Hickson, 1961. 'Motives of Workpeople who Restrict their Output', *Occupational Psychology,* 35, pp. 11-21.

G.H. Hildebrand, 1963. 'External Influences and the Determination of the Internal Wage Structure' in J.L. Meij (ed.), *Internal Wage Structure,* Amsterdam: North-Holland pp. 260-99.

B. Hindess, 1971. *The Decline of Working Class Politics,* London: MacGibbon and Kee.

J.R. Hinrichs, 1969. 'Correlates of Employee Evaluations of Pay Increases', *Journal of Applied Psychology,* 53, pp. 481-9.

E.J. Hobsbawm, 1964. *Labouring Men: Studies in the History of Labour,* London: Weidenfeld and Nicolson.

G.C. Homans, 1961. *Social Behaviour: Its Elementary Forms,* London: Routledge and Kegan Paul.

J. Horton, 1971. 'The Fetishism of Sociology' in J.D. Colfax and J.L. Roach (eds.), *Radical Sociology,* New York: Basic Books, pp. 171-93.

E.C. Hughes, 1958. *Men and Their Work,* Glencoe: Free Press.

J. Hughes, 1972. 'The Low Paid' in Townsend and Bosanquet 1972, pp. 162-73.

J. Hughes and R. Moore (eds.), 1972. *A Special Case?,* Harmondsworth: Penguin.

E.M. Hugh-Jones (ed.), 1966. *Wage Structure in Theory and Practice,* Amsterdam: North-Holland.

L. Hunter, 1967. 'Income Structure and Mobility', *British Journal of Industrial Relations,* 5, pp. 386-98.

H.H. Hyman, 1942. 'The Psychology of Status', *Archives of Psychology,* 38, No. 269, pp. 1-99.

H.H. Hyman and E. Singer (eds.), 1968. *Readings in Reference Group Theory and Research,* New York: Free Press.

R. Hyman, 1971a. *The Workers' Union,* Oxford: Clarendon Press.

R. Hyman, 1971b. *Marxism and the Sociology of Trade Unionism,* London: Pluto Press.

R. Hyman, 1972a. *Disputes Procedure in Action,* London: Heinemann.

R. Hyman, 1972b. *Strikes,* London: Fontana.

R. Hyman, 1973. 'Industrial Conflict: Trends of the Sixties and Prospects for the Seventies' in R. Miliband and J. Saville (eds.), *Socialist Register 1973,* London: Merlin, pp. 101-53.

R. Hyman, 1974. 'Workers' Control and Revolutionary Theory' in

R. Miliband and J. Saville (eds.), *Socialist Register 1974.*

R. Hyman and R.H. Fryer, 1974. 'Trade Unions: Sociology and Political Economy' in J. McKinlay (ed.), *Processing People: Cases in Organizational Behaviour,* London: Holt-Blond, pp. 150-214.

G.K. Ingham, 1970. *Size of Industrial Organization and Worker Behaviour,* Cambridge: Cambridge University Press.

D. Jackson, H.A. Turner and F. Wilkinson, 1972. *Do Trade Unions Cause Inflation?,* Cambridge: Cambridge University Press.

J.M. Jackson, 1967. 'Wages: Just Reward or Efficient Allocator?', *British Journal of Industrial Relations,* 5, pp. 375-85.

J. Jacobs, 1968. *S.M. Lipset: Social Scientist of the Smooth Society,* Boston: New England Free Press.

E. Jaques, 1956. *Measurement of Responsibility,* London: Heinemann.

E. Jaques, 1958. 'An Objective Approach to Pay Differentials', *New Scientist*, 4, pp. 313-15.

E. Jaques, 1967. *Equitable Payment*, Harmondsworth: Penguin (first published 1961).

E. Jaques, 1969. 'Fair Pay: How to Achieve It', *New Society,* 14, pp. 852-4.

T.J. Johnson, 1972. *Professions and Power,* London: Macmillan.

A. Jones, 1973. *The New Inflation: The Politics of Prices and Incomes,* Harmondsworth: Penguin.

O. Kahn-Freund, 1954. 'Legal Framework' in A. Flanders and H.A. Clegg (eds.), *The System of Industrial Relations in Great Britain,* Oxford: Blackwell, pp. 42-127.

O. Kahn-Freund, 1972. *Labour and the Law,* London: Stevens.

D. Katz, 1954. 'Satisfactions and Deprivations in Industrial Life' in Kornhauser *et al.* 1954, pp. 86-108.

H.H. Kelley, 1952. 'Two Functions of Reference Groups' in G.E. Swanson, T.M. Newcomb and E.L. Hartley (eds.), *Readings in Social Psychology,* New York: Holt, pp. 410-14.

J. Kelly, 1968. *Is Scientific Management Possible?,* London: Faber.

C. Kerr, 1957. 'Wage Relationships: the Comparative Impact of Market and Power Forces' in Dunlop 1957, pp. 173-93.

C. Kerr, 1959. 'The Balkanization of Labor Markets' in E.W. Bakke (ed.), *Labor Mobility and Economic Opportunity,* Cambridge, Mass.: MIT Press.

C. Kerr and A. Siegel, 1954. 'The Interindustry Propensity to Strike' in Kornhauser *et al.* 1954, pp. 189-212.

J.M. Keynes, 1936. *The General Theory of Employment, Interest and Money,* London: Macmillan.

M. Kidron, 1970. *Western Capitalism Since the War,* Harmondsworth: Penguin.

J.C. Kincaid, 1973. *Poverty and Equality in Britain,* Harmondsworth: Penguin.

P. Kinnersly, 1973. *The Hazards of Work,* London: Pluto Press.

L. Klein, 1964. *Multiproducts Ltd,* London: HMSO.

K.G.J.C. Knowles, 1952. *Strikes: A Study in Industrial Conflict,* Oxford: Blackwell.

K.G.J.C. Knowles and D. Robinson, 1962. 'Wage Rounds and Wage Policy', *Bulletin of the Oxford University Institute of Statistics,* 24, pp. 269-329.

A. Kornhauser, R. Dublin and A.M. Ross (eds.), 1954. *Industrial Conflict,* New York: McGraw-Hill.

J.W. Kuhn, 1961. *Bargaining in Grievance Settlement,* New York: Columbia University Press.

T. Lane and K. Roberts, 1971. *Strike at Pilkingtons*, London: Fontana.

J.C. Leggett, 1968. *Class, Race and Labor,* New York: Oxford University Press.

M.W. Leiserson, 1966. 'Wage Decisions and Wage Structure in the United States' in Hugh-Jones 1966, pp. 3-69.

W.M. Leiserson, 1931. 'The Economics of Restriction of Output' in Mathewson 1931, pp. 160-82.

S.W. Lerner and J. Marquand, 1963. 'Regional Variations in Earnings, Demand for Labour and Shop Stewards' Combine Committees', *Manchester School,* 26, pp. 261-96.

S.W. Lerner, J.R. Cable and S. Gupta, 1969. *Workshop Wage Determination*, Oxford: Pergamon.

R.A. Lester, 1946. 'Shortcomings of Marginal Analysis for Wage-Employment Problems', *American Economic Review,* 36, pp. 63-82.

H.M. Levinson, 1966. *Determining Forces in Collective Wage Bargaining,* New York: Wiley.

J.A. Lincoln, 1967. *The Restrictive Society,* London: Allen and Unwin.

C.E. Lindblom, 1948. ' "Bargaining Power" in Price and Wage Determination', *Quarterly Journal of Economics,* 62, pp. 396-417.

S.M. Lipset and M. Trow, 1957. 'Reference Group Theory and Trade Union Wage Policy' in M. Komarovsky (ed.), *Common Frontiers of the Social Sciences,* Glencoe: Free Press, pp. 391-439.

M. Lipton, 1968. *Assessing Economic Performance,* London: Staples.

E.R. Livernash, 1953. 'Job Evaluation' in W.S. Woytinsky (ed.), *Employment and Wages in the United States,* New York: Twentieth Century Fund, pp. 427-34.

E.R. Livernash, 1954. 'Wage Administration and Production Standards' in Kornhauser *et al.* 1954, pp. 330-44.

E.R. Livernash, 1957. 'The Internal Wage Structure' in Taylor and Pierson 1954, pp. 14-72.

Liverpool University, 1954, *The Dock Worker,* Liverpool: Liverpool University Press.

D. Lockwood, 1955. 'Arbitration and Industrial Conflict', *British Journal of Sociology,* 6, pp. 335-47.

D. Lockwood, 1956. 'Some Remarks on "The Social System" ', *British Journal of Sociology,* 7, pp. 134-46.

D. Lockwood, 1958. *The Blackcoated Worker,* London: Allen and Unwin.

D. Lockwood, 1960. 'The "New Working Class" ', *European Journal of Sociology,* 1, pp. 248-59.

D. Lockwood, 1964. 'Social Integration and System Integration' in G.K. Zollschan and W. Hirsch (eds.), *Explorations in Social Change,* London: Routledge and Kegan Paul, pp. 244-57.

D. Lockwood, 1966. 'Sources of Variation in Working Class Images of Society', *Sociological Review,* 14, pp. 249-67.

J. Lovell and B.C. Roberts, 1968. *A Short History of the TUC,* London: Macmillan.

G. Lukacs, 1971. *History and Class Consciousness,* London: Merlin (original publication 1923).

T. Lupton, 1963. *On the Shop Floor,* London: Pergamon.

T. Lupton and R. Hamilton, 1970. 'The Status of the Industrial Worker', *Scottish Journal of Political Economy,* 17, pp. 267-94.

H. Lydall, 1968. *The Structure of Earnings,* Oxford: Oxford University Press.

A.M. McBriar, 1962. *Fabian Socialism and English Politics 1884-1918,* Cambridge: Cambridge University Press.

W.E.J. McCarthy, 1966. *The Role of Shop Stewards in British*

Industrial Relations, London: HMSO.

W.E.J. McCarthy and B.A. Clifford, 1966. 'The Work of Industrial Courts of Inquiry', *British Journal of Industrial Relations,* 4, pp. 39-58.

W.E.J. McCarthy and N.D.Ellis, 1973. *Management by Agreement: An Alternative to the Industrial Relations Act,* London: Hutchinson.

F. Machlup, 1946. 'Marginal Analysis and Empirical Research', *American Economic Review,* 36, pp. 547-54.

A. MacIntyre, 1967. *Secularization and Moral Change,* London: Oxford University Press.

D.I. MacKay, D. Boddy, J. Brack, J.A. Diack and N. Jones, 1971. *Labour Markets under Different Employment Conditions,* London: Allen and Unwin.

C.B. Macpherson, 1962. *The Political Theory of Possessive Individualism,* Oxford: Clarendon Press.

M. Mann, 1970. 'The Social Cohesion of Liberal Democracy', *American Sociological Review,* 35, pp. 423-39.

K. Mannheim, 1936. *Ideology and Utopia,* London: Routledge and Kegan Paul.

H. Marcuse, 1968. *One Dimensional Man,* London: Sphere.

C.J. Margerison, 1969. 'What Do We Mean by Industrial Relations?', *British Journal of Industrial Relations,* 7, pp. 273-86.

R. Marriott, 1957. *Incentive Payment Systems*, London: Staples.

R. Marris, 1964. *The Economic Theory of 'Managerial' Capitalism,* London: Macmillan.

A. Marshall, 1887. 'Preface' to L.L.R.F. Price, *Industrial Peace,* London: Macmillan.

A. Marshall, 1920. *Principles of Economics* (8th edn), London: Macmillan (first published 1890).

R. Martin and R.H. Fryer, 1973. 'The Deferential Worker: Persistence and Disintegration in Paternalist Capitalism' in Bulmer 1973, pp. 326-50.

K. Marx, 1959. *Capital*, Vol. I, London: Lawrence and Wishart (original publication 1867; first English edition 1887).

K. Marx, 1962. *Capital*, Vol. III, London: Lawrence and Wishart (original publication 1893-4; first English edition 1909).

K. Marx, 1963. *Karl Marx: Selected Writings in Sociology and Social Philosophy* (ed. T.B. Bottomore and M. Rubel), Harmondsworth: Penguin.

K. Marx, 1973. *Grundrisse: Foundations of the Critique of Political Economy (Rough Draft),* Harmondsworth: Penguin (written 1857-8; original publication 1953).

K. Marx and F. Engels, 1957. *The Holy Family,* London: Lawrence and Wishart (original publication 1845).

K. Marx and F. Engels, 1958. *Selected Works* (2 vols.), Moscow: Foreign Languages Publishing House.

K. Marx and F. Engels, 1970. *The German Ideology,* London: Lawrence and Wishart (originally written 1846, first published 1932 and first English edition 1938).

A. Maslow, 1943. 'A Theory of Human Motivation', *Psychological Review,* 50, pp. 370-96.

S.B. Mathewson, 1931. *Restriction of Output Among Unorganized Workers,* New York: Viking Press.

M. Meacher, 1972. 'Wealth: Labour's Achilles Heel' in Townsend and Bosanquet 1972, pp. 186-210.

J.E. Meade, 1964. *Efficiency, Equality and the Ownership of Property,* London: Allen and Unwin.

M. Mellish, 1972. *The Docks After Devlin,* London: Heinemann.

A.J. Merrett, 1968. *Executive Remuneration in the United Kingdom,* London: Longmans.

R.K. Merton, 1968. *Social Theory and Social Structure* (3rd edn), New York: Free Press (first published 1949).

R. Miliband, 1964. *Parliamentary Socialism,* London: Merlin.

R. Miliband, 1969. *The State in Capitalist Society,* London: Weidenfeld and Nicolson.

G.T. Milkovich and K. Campbell, 1972. 'A Study of Jaques's Norms of Equitable Payment', *Industrial Relations,* 11, pp. 267-71.

J.S. Mill, 1852. *Principles of Political Economy* (3rd edn), London: Longmans.

D. Miller, 1973. 'Ideology and the Problem of False Consciousness', *Political Studies,* 20, pp. 432-47.

C.W. Mills, 1948. *The New Men of Power,* New York: Harcourt Brace.

C.W. Mills, 1951. *White Collar: the American Middle Classes,* New York: Oxford University Press.

C.W. Mills, 1959. *The Sociological Imagination,* New York: Oxford University Press.

C.W. Mills, 1963. 'Situated Actions and Vocabularies of Motive' in *Power, Politics and People,* New York: Oxford University Press, pp. 439-52.

E.J. Mishan, 1969. *The Costs of Economic Growth,* Harmondsworth: Penguin.

G.D. Mitchell, 1968. *A Dictionary of Sociology,* London: Routledge and Kegan Paul.

P.C. Molhuysen, 1971. 'Wage Decisions of the British National Board for Prices and Incomes, 1965-9', *Journal of Industrial Relations,* 13, pp. 117-29.

G. Myrdal, 1953. *The Political Element in the Development of Economic Thought,* London: Routledge and Kegan Paul.

G. Myrdal, 1958. *Value in Social Theory,* London: Routledge and Kegan Paul.

National Board for Prices and Incomes, 1966. Report 19, *General Report*, London: HMSO, Cmnd. 3087.

National Board for Prices and Incomes, 1967. Report 40, *Second General Report,* London: HMSO, Cmnd. 3394.

National Board for Prices and Incomes, 1968. Report 83, *Job Evaluation,* London: HMSO, Cmnd. 3772.

National Board for Prices and Incomes, 1969. Report 122, *Fourth General Report,* London: HMSO, Cmnd. 4130.

National Board for Prices and Incomes, 1971. Report 169, *General Problems of Low Pay,* London: HMSO, Cmnd. 4648.

National Economic Development Council, 1963. *Conditions Favourable to Faster Growth,* London: HMSO.

E. Nell, 1972. 'Economics: the Revival of Political Economy' in R. Blackburn 1972, pp. 76-95.

E. Nell, 1973. 'The Fall of the House of Efficiency', *Annals,* 409, pp. 102-11.

T. Nichols, 1969. *Ownership, Control and Ideology,* London: Allen and Unwin.

M. Nicolaus, 1972. 'The Professional Organization of Sociology: A View from Below' in R. Blackburn 1972, pp. 45-60.

D.T.B. North, C.J. Woods, R.W. Brewer and W.D. Webb, 1973. *Report on the Study of Some Aspects of National Job Evaluation,* London: Working Together Campaign.

Office of Manpower Economics, 1972. *Equal Pay,* London: HMSO.

S. Ogden, 1971. *Indirect Workers' Wage Agreement at Longbridge, Birmingham,* University of Warwick M.A. Dissertation.

J. O'Neill, 1972. *Sociology as a Skin Trade,* London: Heinemann.

R.L. Opsahl and M.D. Dunnette, 1966. 'The Role of Financial Compensation in Industrial Motivation', *Psychological Bulletin*, 66, pp. 94-118.

T. Paine, 1969. *Rights of Man*, Harmondsworth: Penguin (first published 1791).

F. Parkin, 1971. *Class Inequality and Political Order*, London: MacGibbon and Kee.

T. Parsons, 1937. *The Structure of Social Action*, New York: McGraw-Hill.

T. Parsons, 1951. *The Social System*, London: Routledge and Kegan Paul.

T. Parsons, 1960. *Structure and Process in Modern Societies*, New York: Free Press.

M. Patchen, 1961. *The Choice of Wage Comparisons*, Englewood Cliffs: Prentice-Hall.

T.T. Paterson, 1972. *Job Evaluation: A New Method*, London: Business Books.

Pay Board, 1974. Advisory Report 2, *Relativities*, London: HMSO, Cmnd. 5535.

J. Pen, 1952. 'A General Theory of Bargaining', *American Economic Review*, 42, pp. 24-42.

J. Pen, 1959. *The Wage Rate under Collective Bargaining*, Cambridge, Mass.: Harvard University Press.

J. Pen, 1971. *Income Distribution*, London: Allen Lane.

C. Perrow, 1972. *The Radical Attack on Business*, New York: Harcourt Brace Jovanovich.

E.H. Phelps Brown, 1955. 'Wage Policy and Wage Differences', *Economica*, 22, pp. 349-54.

E.H. Phelps Brown, 1959. *The Growth of British Industrial Relations*, London: Macmillan.

E.H. Phelps Brown, 1962. *The Economics of Labor*, New Haven: Yale University Press.

E.H. Phelps Brown, 1973. 'New Wine in Old Bottles: Reflections on the Changed Working of Collective Bargaining in Great Britain', *British Journal of Industrial Relations*, 11, pp. 329-37.

F.C. Pierson, 1957. 'An Evaluation of Wage Theory' in Taylor and Pierson 1957, pp. 3-31.

A.C. Pigou, 1905. *Principles and Methods of Industrial Peace*, London: Macmillan.

A.C. Pigou, 1920. *The Economics of Welfare* (4th edn 1932), London: Macmillan.

M.J. Piore, 1973. 'Fragments of a "Sociological" Theory of Wages', *American Economic Review,* 43, pp. 377-84.

J. Plamenatz, 1970. *Ideology,* London: Macmillan.

J. Playford, 1971. 'The Myth of Pluralism' in Castles *et al.* 1971, pp. 364-75 (first published *Arena*, 1968).

S. Pollard, 1965. *The Genesis of Modern Management,* London: Arnold.

N.P. Pollis, 1968. 'Reference Group Re-examined', *British Journal of Sociology,* 19, pp. 300-307.

L. Pope, 1942. *Millhands and Preachers,* New Haven: Yale University Press.

R.D. Pritchard, 1969. 'Equity Theory: A Review and Critique' *Organizational Behaviour and Human Performance,* 4, pp. 176-211.

D.D. Raphael, 1970. *Problems of Political Philosophy,* London: Macmillan.

J. Rawls, 1955. 'Two Concepts of Rules', *Philosophical Review,* 64, pp. 3-32.

J. Rawls, 1972. *A Theory of Justice,* Oxford: Clarendon Press.

W.B. Reddaway, 1959. 'Wage Flexibility and the Distribution of Labour', *Lloyds Bank Review,* October 1959.

M.W. Reder, 1952. 'The Theory of Union Wage Policy', *Review of Economics and Statistics,* 34, pp. 34-45.

M.W. Reder, 1958. 'Wage Determination in Theory and Practice' in Chamberlain *et al.* 1958, pp. 64-97.

J. Rex, 1961. *Key Problems of Sociological Theory,* London: Routledge and Kegan Paul.

L.G. Reynolds, 1951. *The Structure of Labor Markets,* New York: Harper.

L.G. Reynolds and J. Shister, 1949. *Job Horizons,* New York: Harper.

L.G. Reynolds and C.H. Taft, 1956. *The Evolution of Wage Structure,* New Haven: Yale University Press.

J.H. Richardson, 1954. *An Introduction to the Study of Industrial Relations,* London: Allen and Unwin.

R. Richardson, 1971. *Fair Pay and Work,* London: Heinemann.

M. Rimmer, 1972. *Race and Industrial Conflict,* London: Heinemann.

B.C. Roberts, 1958. *National Wages Policy in War and Peace,* London: Allen and Unwin.

B.C. Roberts (ed.), 1962. *Industrial Relations: Contemporary Problems and Perspectives*, London: Methuen.

B.C. Roberts, 1966. 'Written Evidence' in Royal Commission on Trade Unions and Employers' Associations, *Minutes of Evidence,* London: HMSO, pp. 1396-1414.

B.C. Roberts (ed.), 1968. *Industrial Relations: Contemporary Issues,* London: Macmillan.

E.J. Robertson, 1970. 'Local Labour Markets and Plant Wage Structures: An Introduction' in Robinson 1970, pp. 15-27.

D. Robinson, 1970. 'External and Internal Labour Markets' and 'Practical Conclusions' in Robinson (ed.) 1970, pp. 28-67 and 261-85.

D. Robinson (ed.), 1970. *Local Labour Markets and Wage Structures,* London: Gower Press.

J. Robinson, 1933. *The Economics of Imperfect Competition,* London: Macmillan.

F.J. Roethlisberger and W.J. Dickson, 1939. *Management and the Worker,* Cambridge, Mass.: Harvard University Press.

A.M. Ross, 1948. *Trade Union Wage Policy,* Berkeley: University of California Press.

G.C. Routh, 1965. *Occupation and Pay in Great Britain 1906-60,* Cambridge: Cambridge University Press.

G.C. Routh, 1973. 'Interpretations of Pay Structure', *International Journal of Social Economics,* 1, pp. 13-39.

J.W.F. Rowe, 1928. *Wages in Practice and Theory,* London: Routledge.

D. Roy, 1952. 'Quota Restriction and Goldbricking in a Machine Shop', *American Journal of Sociology,* 57, pp. 427-42.

D. Roy, 1953. 'Work Satisfaction and Social Reward in Quota Achievement', *American Sociological Review,* 18, pp. 507-14.

D. Roy, 1954. 'Efficiency and "the Fix": Informal Intergroup Relations in a Piecework Machine Shop', *American Journal of Sociology,* 60, pp. 255-66.

D. Roy, 1969. 'Introduction' to new edition of Mathewson 1931, Carbondale: Southern Illinois University Press, xv-lii.

W.G. Runciman, 1966. *Relative Deprivation and Social Justice,* London: Routledge and Kegan Paul.

J.A. Ryan, 1916. *Distributive Justice,* New York: Macmillan.

L.R. Salkever, 1964. *Toward a Wage Structure Theory,* New York: Humanities Press.

L.R. Sayles, 1958. *The Behavior of Industrial Work Groups*, New York: Wiley.

J. Scamp, 1968. Chairman, Court of Inquiry into a Dispute . . . at Pressed Steel Fisher Ltd, Cowley, *Report*, London: HMSO, Cmnd. 3688.

T.C. Schelling, 1956. 'An Essay On Bargaining', *American Economic Review*, 46, 281-306.

D.F. Schloss, 1892. *Methods of Industrial Remuneration*, London: Williams and Norgate.

A. Schutz, 1964. 'Equality and the Meaning Structure of the Social World' in *Collected Papers* (Vol. II, ed. A. Brodersen), The Hague: Nijhoff, pp. 226-73.

T. Scitovsky, 1973. 'Inequalities: Open and Hidden, Measured and Immeasurable', *Annals*, 409, 112-19.

W.H. Scott, J.A. Banks, A.H. Halsey and T. Lupton, 1956. *Technical Change and Industrial Relations*, Liverpool: Liverpool University Press.

W.H. Scott, E. Mumford, I.C. McGivering and J.M. Kirkby, 1963. *Coal and Conflict*, Liverpool: Liverpool University Press.

J. Seidman (ed.), 1970. *Trade Union Government and Collective Bargaining*, New York: Praeger.

P. Selznick, 1969. *Law, Society and Industrial Justice*, New York: Russell Sage Foundation.

N. Senior, 1836. *An Outline of the Science of Political Economy*, London: Clowes.

M. Shanks, 1961. *The Stagnant Society*, Harmondsworth: Penguin.

I.G. Sharp, 1950. *Industrial Conciliation and Arbitration in Great Britain*, London: Allen and Unwin.

E.C. Shepherd, 1923. *The Fixing of Wages in Government Employment*, London: Methuen.

M. Sherif, 1948. *An Outline of Social Psychology*, New York: Harper and Row.

S. Shimmin, 1968. 'A Review of the Literature on Payment by Results' in NBPI, Report No. 65, *Payment by Results (Supplement)*, London: HMSO, Cmnd. 3627-I.

A. Shonfield, 1969. *Modern Capitalism* (2nd edn), London: Oxford University Press.

G. Simmel, 1950. *The Sociology of George Simmel* (ed. K.H. Wolff), Glencoe: Free Press.

G. Simmel, 1955. *Conflict and the Web of Group Affiliations* (ed. K.

H. Wolff and R. Bendix), Glencoe: Free Press (original publication 1908).

H.A. Simon, 1945. *Administrative Behavior*, New York: Free Press.

H.A. Simon, 1957. 'Authority' in C.M. Arensberg (ed.), *Research in Industrial Human Relations,* New York: Harper and Row, pp. 103-15.

K. Sisson, 1975. *Industrial Relations in Fleet Street,* Oxford: Blackwell.

S.H. Slichter, J.J. Healy and E.R. Livernash, 1960. *The Impact of Collective Bargaining on Management,* Washington: Brookings.

N.J. Smelser, 1963. *The Sociology of Economic Life,* Englewood Cliffs: Prentice-Hall.

A. Smith, 1937. *The Wealth of Nations,* New York: Modern Library (first published 1776).

H. Smith, 1962. *The Wage Fixers: A Study of Arbitration in a Free Society,* London: Institute of Economic Affairs.

P. Snowden, 1912. *The Living Wage,* London: Hodder and Stoughton.

W. Stark, 1944. *The History of Economics in its Relation to Social Development,* London: Kegan Paul.

S.A. Stouffer, E.A. Suchman, L.C. DeVinney, S.A. Star and R.M. Williams, 1949. *The American Soldier* (Vol. I), Princeton: Princeton University Press.

A. Strauss, L. Schatzman, D. Ehrlich, R. Bucher and M. Sabshin, 1971. 'The Hospital and its Negotiated Order' in Castles *et al.* 1971, pp. 103-23 (first published 1963 in E. Friedson (ed.), *The Hospital in Modern Society).*

P.P. Streeten, 1958. 'Introduction' in Myrdal 1958, pp. ix-xlvi.

E. Sutcliffe, 1969. 'Factory Money' in R. Fraser (ed.), *Work 2: Twenty Personal Accounts,* Harmondsworth: Penguin, pp. 287-97.

A.J.M. Sykes, 1960. 'Trade Union Workshop Organization in the Printing Industry: The Chapel', *Human Relations,* 13, pp. 49-65.

A.J.M. Sykes, 1967. 'The Cohesion of a Trade Union Workshop Organization', *Sociology*, 1, pp. 141-63.

R.H. Tawney, 1961. *The Acquisitive Society,* London: Fontana (first published 1921).

R.H. Tawney, 1964. *Equality,* London: Allen and Unwin (first published 1931).

F.W. Taylor, 1911. *The Principles of Scientific Management,* New

York: Harper.

G.W. Taylor and F.C. Pierson (eds.), 1957. *New Concepts in Wage Determination,* New York: McGraw-Hill.

L. Taylor and P.W. Walton, 1971. 'Industrial Sabotage: Motives and Meanings' in Cohen 1971, pp. 219-45.

G.F. Thomason, 1968. *Personnel Manager's Guide to Job Evaluation,* London: Institute of Personnel Management.

E.P. Thompson, 1967. 'Time, Work-Discipline and Industrial Capitalism', *Past and Present,* 38, pp. 56-97.

E.P. Thompson, 1968. *The Making of the English Working Class* (2nd edn), Harmondsworth: Penguin.

R.M. Titmuss, 1962. *Income Distribution and Social Change,* London: Allen and Unwin.

N.A. Tolles, 1964. *Origins of Modern Wage Theories,* Englewood Cliffs: Prentice-Hall.

P. Townsend and N. Bosanquet (eds.), 1972. *Labour and Inequality,* London: Fabian Society.

Trades Union Congress, 1966. *Trade Unionism,* London: TUC.

Transport and General Workers' Union, 1970. *The Ford Wage Claim,* London: TGWU.

M. Tumin, 1953. 'Some Principles of Stratification: A Critical Analysis', *American Sociological Review,* 18, pp. 387-93.

A.N. Turner and P. Lawrence, 1966. *Industrial Jobs and the Worker,* Cambridge, Mass.: Harvard University Press.

B.A. Turner, 1971. *Exploring the Industrial Subculture,* London: Macmillan.

H.A. Turner, 1952. 'Trade Unions, Differentials and the Levelling of Wages', *Manchester School,* 20, pp. 227-82.

H.A. Turner, 1957a. *Wage Policy Abroad: And Conclusions for Britain,* London: Fabian Society.

H.A. Turner, 1957b. 'Inflation and Wage Differentials in Great Britain' in Dunlop 1957, pp. 123-35.

H.A. Turner, 1962. *Trade Union Growth, Structure and Policy,* London: Allen and Unwin.

H.A. Turner, 1969. *Is Britain Really Strike-Prone?,* Cambridge: Cambridge University Press.

H.A. Turner, 1970. 'Collective Bargaining and the Eclipse of Incomes Policy: Retrospect, Prospect and Possibilities', *British Journal of Industrial Relations,* 8, pp. 197-212.

H.A. Turner, G. Clack and G. Roberts, 1967. *Labour Relations in*

the Motor Industry, London: Allen and Unwin.
H.A. Turner and D.A.S. Jackson, 1969. 'The Stability of Wage Differences and Productivity-Based Wage Policies: An International Analysis', *British Journal of Industrial Relations*, 7, pp. 1-8.
H.A.Turner and F. Wilkinson, 1971. 'Real Net Incomes and the Wage Explosion', *New Society,* 17, 309-10.
H.A. Turner and H. Zoeteweij, 1966. *Prices, Wages and Incomes Policies in Industrialised Market Economies,* Geneva: International Labour Office.
R.H. Turner, 1956. 'Role-Taking, Role Standpoint and Reference Group Behaviour', *American Journal of Sociology,* 61, pp. 316-28.
R. Turvey, 1971. 'Some Features of Incomes Policy and Comments on the Current Inflation' in H.G. Johnson and A.R. Nobay (eds.), *The Current Inflation,* London: Macmillan, pp. 196-201.
J. Urry and J. Wakeford (eds.), 1973. *Power in Britain,* London: Heinemann.
T. Veblen, 1963. *The Engineers and the Price System,* New York: Harcourt Brace (first published 1921).
W.M. Walker, 1965. *The Cultural Basis of Income Distribution in Industrial Organisations,* University of Birmingham Ph.D. Thesis.
R.E. Walton and R.B. McKersie, 1965. *A Behavioral Theory of Labor Negotiations,* New York: McGraw-Hill.
S. Webb and B. Webb, 1897. *Industrial Democracy*, London: Longmans.
S. Webb and B. Webb, 1920. History of Trade Unionism (2nd edn), London: Longmans.
M. Weber, 1930. *The Protestant Ethic and the Spirit of Capitalism,* London: Allen and Unwin (original publication 1920).
M. Weber, 1947. *The Theory of Social and Economic Organization,* New York: Free Press (original publication 1922).
M. Weber, 1948. *From Max Weber* (ed. H.H. Gerth and C. Wright Mills), London: Routledge and Kegan Paul.
M. Weber, 1968. *Economy and Society,* New York: Bedminster Press (original publication 1925).
D. Wedderburn, 1965. *Redundancy and the Railwaymen,* Cambridge: Cambridge University Press.
D. Wedderburn, 1972. 'Inequality at Work' in Townsend and Bosanquet 1972, pp. 174-85.

D. Wedderburn and R. Crompton, 1972. *Workers' Attitudes and Technology,* Cambridge: Cambridge University Press.

K.W. Wedderburn, 1965, 1971. *The Worker and the Law* (1st and 2nd edns), Harmondsworth: Penguin.

K.E. Weick, 1966. 'The Concept of Equity in the Perception of Pay', *Administrative Science Quarterly,* 11, pp. 414-39.

J.H. Westergaard, 1965. 'The Withering Away of Class: A Contemporary Myth' in Anderson and Blackburn 1965, pp. 77-113.

J.H. Westergaard, 1970. 'The Rediscovery of the Cash Nexus' in R. Miliband and J. Saville (eds.), *Socialist Register 1970,* pp. 111-38.

W.F. Whyte (ed.), 1955. *Money and Motivation,* New York: Harper and Row.

E.L. Wigham, 1972. 'A Royal Commission on Fair Wages?', *CBI Review,* 5, pp. 8-15.

H.L. Wilensky, 1964. 'The Professionalization of Everyone?', *American Journal of Sociology,* 70, pp. 137-58.

G. Williams, 1956. 'The Myth of "Fair" Wages', *Economic Journal,* 66, pp. 621-34.

D.F. Wilson, 1972. *Dockers: the Impact of Industrial Change,* London: Fontana.

S. Wiseman, 1956. 'Wage Criteria for Collective Bargaining', *Industrial and Labor Relations Review,* 9, pp. 252-67.

B. Wootton, 1962. *The Social Foundations of Wage Policy,* London: Allen and Unwin (first published 1955).

G. Wootton, 1966. *Workers, Unions and the State,* London: Routledge and Kegan Paul.

P. Worsley, 1964. 'The Distribution of Power in Industrial Society' in Halmos 1964, pp. 15-34.

J. Young, 1971. *The Drugtakers,* London: MacGibbon and Kee

F. Zeuthen, 1930. *Problems of Monopoly and Economic W*
London: Routledge.

F. Zweig, 1951. *Productivity and Trade Unions,* Oxford